IN PURSUIT OF

ALTERNATIVE

PEACE CAMPAIGNING

A CHRONICLE FROM WREXHAM

Gathered together by

OWEN HARDWICKE

Peace & Justice Centre
35 Kings Mills Road
Wrexham LL13 8NS

Booksellers price £9.50   ISBN 1·84494·024-1

— Private sale £7.50 plus p+p £1·50

In Pursuit of
Alternatives to War

Peace Campaigning in the Eighties
A Chronicle from Wrexham

Gathered together by

Owen Hardwicke

In Pursuit of Alternatives to War
First published in Wales in 2006 by
BRIDGE BOOKS
61 Park Avenue
Wrexham
LL12 7AW

© 2006 Owen Hardwicke

CIP Data for this book is available
from the British Library

ISBN 1-84494-24-1

Printed and bound by
Cromwell Press, Trowbridge

Contents and Rough Index

[C. refers to Chapter number)

4

6

8

10

PREFACE

When I was recording my journey in ministry and priesthood for the book which was published in 2001, entitled *Living Beyond Conformity* I was amazed to find so many letters and documents which I had put on one side, and which enabled me to put together a much more authentic record than if I had relied on my failing memory alone. That wasn't any kind of complete autobiography, even though I traced my intellectual and ecclesiastical movements in a rough chronological order. It stopped the story in 1972 when I returned to Wrexham, after three years away, to start the Lift Project, working with disorganised young adults, and later when I became a lecturer in the North East Wales Institute. The main theme of the book had been a personal understanding of priesthood, and the varied ways in which it could be practised, and by that time I had worked out, at least to my own satisfaction, if not to my bishop's, how to blend my church and my secular 'ministries'. My subsequent activities in the 1980s seemed to raise no new issues on that theme

I had one chapter in the book which took me through my contentious stand as a conscientious objector to military service in the second world war, and my understanding of the value of non-violence. By the end of the 1970s there was a huge revival of the anti-nuclear movements, especially in the Campaign for Nuclear Disarmament, and I decided to get actively involved again. This led, as my story tells here, to a lot of reading as well as organising and actions. Most of it was recorded in the newsletter of the local peace group in Wrexham, and I have uncovered all the issues from 1980 to 1988, as well as the series of broadsheets which I published bi-monthly for several years for anyone who wanted to receive them, under the title of 'Comments and Quotes', until I returned to parish pastoral work in 1989.

So this following 'essay' is partly a personal diary, partly the story of the growth of a local peace group but mainly a commented set of quotations from various books and periodicals which had helped me to weigh up the issues from a moral, political and pragmatic point of view. So many of the issues are still with us as the new century takes us forward that I believe it is useful to see where thinkers have explored things already, in case their wisdom is forgotten. Accordingly I entitle the essay 'In Pursuit of Alternatives to War', but with the sub-title of 'Peace Campaigning in the 1980s — A Chronicle from Wrexham' as I follow through the learning curve of a varied group of activists; with many stories of events on the journey.

I make no apology for this particular mix. I always find it impossible to separate my private thoughts and actions from the public stance of others, and this means that personal anecdotes are as important to me as objective studies. This essay is therefore in my usual un-scholarly style, but it might serve as a resource for any readers to use in developing their own more profound ideas.

OWEN HARDWICKE

'Now then, Mrs Oxley, tell us exactly what it is you don't like about our missiles?'

1. PEACE CAMPAIGNING IN THE 1980s

My time as a lecturer in social work was coming to an end in 1980, not least because I was unhappy about the methods of assessment of the mature students. I had enjoyed my six years of further-education teaching, and learned a great deal from it — about principles and practice, but most of all about humanity. I had never left behind my pacifist convictions, but had allowed my membership of any 'peace group' to become passive; I just read the literature and paid my subscriptions. By 1979 it seemed to me that this was wholly inadequate if my principles meant anything, and I began to take a serious interest again, first of all on the issue of nuclear deterrence. This was becoming the major focus with the intended arrival of the new range of intermediate nuclear weapons — Cruise Missiles and SS20s — on the European scene. In some ways being a staff member in a tertiary college gave me a chance of sharing concerns with a ready audience. Staff and students were likely to be ready to explore and act upon political issues.

In April 1980 I managed to get hold of the famous *War Game* video which was going the rounds. This banned BBC documentary from an earlier period was in some points already out of date; yet it was able to have an impact on people who had not been allowed to face up to the reality of nuclear destruction. It was an easy way of getting people together and to encourage them to get involved in campaigning. The focus in the first instance was to respond to the new World Disarmament Campaign, rather than CND — perhaps because at this stage the latter might have frightened off those who thought CND was altogether too 'leftie' After the showing of the video in Cartrefle College and then in the centre of Wrexham, a first meeting was called for the general public. The following is the press release afterwards.

WREXHAM AGAINST NUCLEAR WAR
Under this title a new campaign was launched at the Wrexham Arts Centre on Monday, May 12th (1980). More than fifty people crowded into a 'committee room' following a not very widely distributed notice. It became clear that desire for action in this field is widespread. The meeting was called not to discuss our first thoughts on nuclear war, but to plan a campaign against it.

Participants included teachers from schools and colleges, ministers of religion, students and a wide variety of people. It was not only a gathering of life-long pacifists, but was for those who are anxious about the state of the world from many points of view — Friends of the Earth and other ecologists, those with strong political views and staunch religious principles, those concerned about the desperate needs of the Third World and about the imprisonment of prisoners of conscience. All were agreed to unite in a focus on Nuclear War, determined that it musty be exposed for what it really is — a threat which is growing, a denial of all moral principle and certainly no solution to any international tension or conflict.

The campaign is to be seen as a local response to the new national World Disarmament Campaign, launched only a month ago in London by Philip Noel-Baker and Fenner Brockway under the chairmanship of the former Lord Chancellor, Gerald Gardiner. The local campaign now has a co-ordinating address at 35 Kings Mills Road, Hightown, Wrexham, where information, posters and literature will soon be available. A co-ordinating clerk, Heather Evans, was appointed to convene the next stages of the campaign.

It is clear from the agenda of the immediate next meeting that we regarded raising public awareness as a major first task. We started to draw attention to the current literature available and began planning a public exhibition for October 24/25. Since that included United Nations Day our first idea was to entitle the event "NATIONS UNITED FOR PEACE AND AGAINST POVERTY", and we sent out invitations to organisations who might like to have a stall — UNA, Welsh Centre for International Affairs, Oxfam, Christian Aid, Cafod, World Development Movement, War on Want, Amnesty International, Quaker Witness for Peace, Pax Christi, Catholic Commission for International Justice and Peace. We also started to make formal contacts with religious groups — such as Cytun, and political groups like those organising support for the Labour Rally for Peace in London We offered action items for the coming months in which people could start to register their convictions in a public way: e.g. a sponsored walk for peace, sponsored fast for 35th anniversary of Hiroshima Day. Then came ideas for Armistice Day with possible messages like *'WAR IS NOT GLORIOUS: NUCLEAR WAR IS MADNESS'* In some ways the most useful means of contact was by issuing a bulletin; and it is from these bulletins that I now gather facts about the developing campaign.

Revd Pryderi Llwyd Jones (then of Capel y Groes; now of Aberystwyth) led a 12-language placard presence outside the main field at the Llangollen International Eisteddfod. Again Pryderi with Revd Alun Suter, (now vicar of Rossett) and Deacon Linda-Mary Evans (now vicar of Llangynog & Pennant Melangell) and myself entered the 48 hour fast proposed by Pax Christi and with others staffed a table in the street near W H Smiths with propaganda material. A hand-out we had ready said: 'At 8.30 am on 6th August 1945, 140,000 men, women and children were annihilated at Hiroshima. The horrors did not end there. Even in 1978, 2000 people died from the long-delayed effects of the bomb;

thousands are still diseased as a result. To commemorate that dreadful day Pax Christi (an international Peace Movement), asks some people to undertake a 48 hour fast from all solid foods. If you sponsor someone at 1p per hour, the money will be used in support of the United Nations work for peace and disarmament through Pax Christi. Please join in special prayers of sorrow and repentance for the death and disease imposed on so many non-combatant people by a western nation.'

Every 15 minutes we had a moment of silence and a short prayer. Some 700 leaflets were handed out. A fair number stopped to sign the petition from CND for a Nuclear Free Europe. Our bulletin reported that others stayed to discuss and argue with us. 'It was a wet day and half-day closing; not the best of choices. As someone said: 'Why on earth did they have to drop the bomb on a Wednesday ?'' We agreed that next year we should try other demonstrations, between 6th and 9th August. We noted that Malpas now had a peace group, and Chester planned a new group to start in September.; and we had contact with other groups shaping up in Llangefni, Beaumaris and Bangor.

We had a lot of co-operation from the local press. We had already discovered a clash with the views of the local member of parliament from the Labour Party, Tom Ellis. I had had earlier contact with him on other matters in my parish days; I liked and respected him, and was shattered by his opposition to CND. A four-page feature was prepared with the views of four north Wales MPs and the views of Alan Suter and myself. Our local bulletin printed my contribution in advance, but I am unsure now whether the *Evening Leader* actually used it.

Our planning for the October Exhibition continued. By now we had changed the title to 'SURVIVORS WORLD' and had started to devise competitive items for the occasion especially through the schools, asking the juniors for a Poster for Peace, and seniors a Song for Peace.

It really was a mammoth undertaking, but, as we sought people to take on various items it hugely increased involvement for our local group first of all. All the time we urged people to join the national and international organisations already in existence, so that they would be better informed and committed. We had no intention of taking everything on board within our own local campaigning group.

We also noted that a major anti-nuclear rally would take place in London the day after our exhibition, We were determined to be represented there also. This turned out to be a major event with some 10,000 taking part; so our local two-day event linked well with this for publicity. The Mayor and Mayoress came to the exhibition which, our report says, 'was master-minded for design and presentation by Fred Starkey of Mold, without whom our eventual coming-together would have been chaotic and lacking in any style'. We also published a booklet with text and cartoons to be taken away; supporters spent hours stapling and folding the pages. We continued to sell 2,500 of these after the event, and our aim was to engage with the sort of objections which ordinary people raised to our efforts to challenge the standard justification for nuclear deterrence. Looking back on the text, it is interesting to recognise how much popular understanding had to change. People need less persuasion in the post cold war days perhaps; yet it is still worth repeating the comments we published.

2. THE BASIC ARGUMENTS

We started with an expanded explanation of our title 'Survivors' World'.

Who will survive for long, unless we take action to ensure it? Poverty, disease, malnutrition kill millions of people every year. Yet some parts of the world get richer and more affluent. The Super-powers continue to spend millions on armaments, and run an organised trade in weapons to the rest of the world. Who cares? Do you? Too little money is set aside to aid the Third World. The British contribution went down, not up, recently. British expenditure on arms increases every year. The official title is for 'defence' because of possible political threats. Meantime the actual scandal of death from disease and malnutrition continues, and the danger of war increases.

In 1979 fifteen million children died of starvation. In 1979 Britain spent £8,500 million on armaments: that's more than £500 for each of the children who died.

People often say:'There won't be another war. It would be too awful'. Yes; it would be too awful; but the West and the East are stockpiling and researching more and more hideous weapons. What for, if people don't really want war?

'Well; at least the threat of nuclear bombs has kept a world war off for 30 years' Yes; maybe the fear has kept world war away — so far. But this is not détente; nor is it peace. At best it is murderous stalemate; and in fact it isn't static. Thirty years ago we had enough weapons in existence to destroy all the world's major cities — it only takes 200 devices. Now we have 50,000 of them; and each year new 'modernisations' of them are introduced. Where will it stop?

'But we can't trust the Soviet Union. If we disarmed in the West, they wouldn't follow suit; or perhaps they'd only pretend to do so.' Everyone seems to presume the USSR is an enemy. It wasn't long ago she was our ally. What has changed? Now we all know the

Soviet government has betrayed its publicly avowed principles many times; even the Helsinki agreement is contravened. Soviet dissidents struggle to change this from within. We undermine the efforts of these brave men and women if we increase the build-up of armaments in the West. Meantime don't let us pretend that the West is not guilty of deception, oppression and even aggression. Look at the Vietnam war. What of the CIA's part in the overthrow of Allende's Chile? Aren't we fools and liars to believe the British have been innocent? Of course disarmament is a risk; but it couldn't be more risky than a world armed to the teeth.

'But we know the Soviets are pointing weapons at our cities even now. They could destroy us at any moment.' And we are pointing our Polaris missiles at their cities even now. The government is now planning to spend another £500 million for even more sophisticated (i.e. murderous) weapons, called Trident, to be aimed at the Soviets — that is, unless we stop it. Let's not forget that the Soviet Union is ringed round by her enemies. Of course she's afraid. Fear and distrust breed panic. And remember the only people ever to have used nuclear weapons upon a civilian population have been those of the West on Hiroshima and Nagasaki. Even a mistake in the USA computer could bring devastation on the Soviet Union. Let's stop acting like kids saying, 'You first; I'm not going to disarm till you do' Let's grow up and say 'I don't even want to threaten you, let alone destroy you.'

'Why doesn't the United Nations Organisation do something about it — to prevent the nations going to war?' All the UN signatories, including the UK, the USA and the USSR have already had a major Special Session on Disarmament in 1978. They pledged themselves to halt the arms race and then to disarm. The event was almost wholly unreported in our press; and the politicians go on arming. We constantly betray the United Nations. If the people took a bit more interest, we might check this betrayal. That's what the United Nations Association is for. The next Special Session on Disarmament is to be in 1982. We must see to it that people know about it and support it. Governments in the end can be made to do what the people want, if enough of them are active and speak their minds.

'It surely isn't that our government wants war. Wars are just inevitable in our sort of world.' That is a despairing lie. There cannot be wars if we are unwilling to support them. It is our money in taxes which the government uses to prepare the war machinery. We must not be so submissive in accepting the euphemism of 'defence'. Peace-makers unfortunately do not have the press at their disposal. There are massive vested interests against disarmament. Sean McBride, the Nobel Peace Prize winner in 1974 declared: 'The issue of peace or war, or the armaments race versus disarmament are never put to the people. the people are never given the opportunity of either knowing the facts or deciding the issues. Even parliaments are often bypassed on such issues or only partially consulted. The real decisions relating to armaments are taken behind closed doors by the Joint Chiefs of Staff or the General staff of the Defence Forces ... It would be foolish to under-rate the massive influence of the organised lobbies of military-industrial complexes in the USA and western Europe. They constitute an unseen and an unmentioned force operating silently in the corridors of NATO and of most western governments. This constitutes a huge vested interest which works silently against general and complete disarmament ... The time has come for 'We, the People' to assert ourselves and to demand the outlawing of all nuclear weapons and the achievement of general and complete disarmament. It is essential that the ordinary people of the world should have a say about their own survival. The non-governmental section is just as qualified as the 'experts' who have a vested interest in armament and war.' Mr Callaghan and Dr Owen and two others of the Labour Cabinet set off the expenditure for the renewal of Polaris, keeping it a secret from the rest of the Cabinet, let alone the House of Commons. The current Defence Minister has simply informed the House that NATO will deploy Cruise missiles in England, manned and controlled entirely by Americans, each one with the destructive power of one Hiroshima bomb, in 1982/3. Our parliamentary representatives were not asked; they were simply told. When the latest £500 million was voted for the new Trident missiles to replace Polaris in the next few years, the members of Parliament present in the House were 5 Conservatives, 1 Ulster Unionist; 4 Labour members and Liberals. Is that what we call democracy? You are not told these things in Britain.

You have to find them out for yourselves. Totalitarian states are tyrannies with little pretence to freedom of information. We are simply not told the whole truth. The media do not often call the establishment in question.

'If war can't be prevented, at least some of us might survive; so we'd better work hard at Civil Defence.' War can be prevented if we refuse to support the preparations, and expose the dishonesties already rampant. But survival? If one ten megaton bomb alone dropped on Lime Street station in Liverpool, and you happened to be looking in that direction in Lampeter, Llandeilo, Brecon and Hereford, your eyesight would be permanently damaged. Windows would be out in Aberystwyth, Ludlow and Birmingham. In Holywell, Connah's Quay, Chester and Wrexham, most houses would be on fire, and virtually all people outside fatally burned by the heat-flash. Within a 24 miles circle the whole area would be shattered to pieces. Earl Mountbatten said: 'In the event of a nuclear war, there will be no survivors. All will be obliterated. I repeat as a military man, I can see no use for any nuclear weapons which would not end in escalation with consequences no-one can conceive.'

'It may be immoral to use nuclear weapons, but can we be sure it is wrong to possess them for security — to make others afraid to attack us?' Earl Mountbatten also said: 'As a military man who has given half a century of active service, I say in all sincerity that the nuclear arms race has no military purpose. Wars cannot be fought with nuclear weapons. Their existence only adds to our perils because of the illusions they have generated.' What it is wrong to do, it is also wrong to threaten to do. There can be no pretence or bluff.

Our text ended up with strong moral statements against nuclear armaments from the Methodist Conference, and the Lambeth Conference of 1978, from the Baptist Union Assembly and the British Council of Churches of 1979 as well as quoting the Vatican Council document with its emphatic statement: 'Any act of war which aims indiscriminately at the destruction of entire cities or wide areas with their inhabitants is a crime against God and man, to be firmly and unhesitatingly condemned.'

All this may seem rather elementary and old-hat now, but since the nuclear protests seemed to fade away from people's minds, it is worthwhile re-visiting these fundamental points. Our event, together with the booklet, made quite a significant mark locally; and we didn't rest content afterwards. The campaigners had a thorough 'post mortem' session to make sure the pluses and minuses of our great efforts were taken properly into account for the future. It was in November that we decided after a lively discussion, that we would gradually change our name to 'WREXHAM FOR NUCLEAR DISARMAMENT'. I suppose this was in recognition that it was CND that carried the main focus of our interest; and a national structure of CND Cymru was now being formed; but we had by no means lost touch with the special project of Noel-Baker and Fenner Brockway's World Disarmament Campaign for a signed document for the United Nations by 1982. This brought us into contact with people like Brigadier Harbottle (joint founder of Generals for Peace &

Disarmament) and Professor James O'Connell of the Bradford School of Peace Studies, and I found myself taking part in a debate with them for a Sixth Form Conference in Mold.

The bulletins record contacts with more and

more new peace groups in Colwyn Bay, Ruthin, Holywell and Oswestry. My travelling began, as I was sent to Amsterdam to take Bruce Kent's place for an International Forum. Here I was able to sense the rising tide of European concern, and some emphasis that we were not only campaigning against something, but for something. A Dutch professor urged us to think of programmes to build trust and confidence to replace the measures of military 'security' which were so fragile and counter-productive. We met up with East German people who spoke of Education for Peace initiatives. Surprisingly also a captain from the Dutch Air Force affirmed the moral responsibility of armed forces in the light of the principles enunciated at Nuremberg and Tokyo. 'It was no excuse for crimes against humanity and peace to say they were committed under orders.' He outlined the principles of international military conventions through the last century up to and including the United Nations' declarations. 'On this basis, the use of nuclear weapons was clearly a crime against peace and against humanity by virtue of their indiscriminate effects.' I noted that he continued to hold this vigorous moral stand while his superiors and the government tried to get him out of the air force

I had never been part of a political movement on this scale before, and it was energising to have an experience wider than Wrexham. I was also beginning to read more widely, and building up a library of relevant books. I started to pepper the local bulletins with quotations that served to encourage us. From an important film that was going around I culled several sentences from the mouth of former President Eisenhower — not exactly a 'peace man'. I still refer to it twenty years later:

> I like to believe that the people in the long run are going to do more to promote peace than our governments. Indeed, I think that people want peace so much that one of these days governments had better get out of the way and let them have it.

I'm glad to remember that we were a cheerful lot beneath our desperately serious concerns. There was a lot of laughter and sharing of comic situations; and the bulletins contained some bright poems and songs. This was one that came from Rip Bulkeley of Oxford and was fitted to the tune of *Daisy, Daisy* ...:

> Trident, Trident; what an insane idea
> Thousands homeless, all for the cost of fear.
> We can't afford medication, or proper education,
> But we must pay a million a day so that Britain can disappear.
>
> Trident, Trident, Maggie has gone too far
> A nuclear tyrant's as bad as a commissar
> Before she starts attacking, we'll have to send her packing,
> And pull the chain on all who gain from the criminal arms bazaar!

3. WIDENING OUR UNDERSTANDING AND OUR LINKS

As the year turned into 1981 we were developing 'awareness raising' into more adequate self-education. We set up two 'teach-ins', firstly on 'Nuclear Weapons and the Arms Race', the second one on 'Facing and Using the Press, Radio and TV'. We welcomed the Quaker Peace Caravan to give us a special session on Practical Peacemaking. It was at this time that my house at 35 Kings Mills Road, which had already acted as a base for the Lift Project, and the co-ordinating address for WND was now labelled Peace Studies Centre. I had made over the property to a new Trust (Wrexham Concern Trust) and soon we acquired Charity status and I had built up a collection of books and pamphlets which were of use to the groups that met here.

It seemed a sensible use for a sizeable property which otherwise provided accommodation for one or two people I came across when wearing other hats.

We kept in touch with, and sometimes joined, the events and activities outside our own; I had now become the Convenor for the county of Clwyd for CND Cymru. Some of us went with Merseyside Peace Festival people on a march to Burtonwood, Cheshire's US Air Force base; others with Oswestry people to Criggion, the Shropshire communications centre for nuclear submarines. In February we were delighted that Jill McMinn from our group had been chosen as one of four 'Mothers for Peace' to travel to the Soviet Union. Much time and effort was given to ensure this had good press and other public coverage. Plainly it was a symbolic event. So we published the message that these mothers would take. It read:

> We British mothers do not wish to harm your children, nor do we believe you wish to harm ours. The link between us is the love of our children and the desire to give them a happy childhood and secure future. This can only be achieved if disarmament — first nuclear, then general — takes place. We must break down the barrier of fear between us,

which is one of the factors preventing disarmament, and work together to persuade our governments to halt the arms race and then to disarm. We thank you for your peace work to date and wish you well. Mothers of Britain.

At Easter a major town event was organised with a silent vigil and 'sit-down' round a specially designed construct by Fred Starkey which was towered by a cross in coloured glass. And again the passers-by were encouraged to sign the petition which was due to go to New York in 1982. The goal was to have a hundred million signatures world-wide.

Our bulletin noted the frequent belligerent tone of national anthems, including the third verse of *God save the Queen* (O Lord our God arise, Scatter her enemies …) and some attempts at alternatives e.g. 'Not on this land alone, But be God's mercies shown from shore to shore'. We were perhaps rather better at parodies. We heard that Professor Michael Pentz, Dean of Science in the Open University had prepared a lecture for TV presentation under the title of 'The Final Abyss'. The BBC Director General, discovering it was to be about nuclear disarmament, cancelled it as inappropriate and unsuitable. Pressure of public opinion made him reverse this decision and the lecture was duly presented. The *New Statesman* then gave us this item:

> I am the very model of a safe Director General
> The water coursing through my veins is very largely mineral
> The way my powers are exercised, though more or less inscrutable,
> Denotes an awful fear of things I deem to be unsuitable.
>
> In controversial matters I display a certain latitude,
> Except where the Establishment requires a kneeling attitude.
> And while allowing programmes which are slightly on the bluey-side
> I cannot think it wise to question universal suicide.
>
> I draw the line at dissidents in matters academical
> Believing it disturbing to indulge in the polemical.
> And if, instead of blessing war, a scientist should curse it, he
> Will find the door is bolted at the Open University.

(Before too long we managed to get Professor Pentz to address one of our public meetings.)

Rather more seriously, our bulletin contained other quotations which were more sinister. Here is one I published in March 1981. It came from Lord Zuckerman, the former chief atomic advisor to HM Government:

> … military chiefs who by convention are the official advisers in national security, merely serve as a channel through which the men in the laboratories transmit their views.

For it is the man in the laboratory — not the soldier sailor or airman — who at the start proposes that for this or that arcane reason it would be useful to improve an old, or devise a new, nuclear warhead; and if a new warhead, then a new missile; and given a new missile a new system within which it has to fit…. The men in the nuclear weapons laboratories of both sides have succeeded in creating a world with an irrational foundation, on which a new set of political realities is in turn to be built.'

I remarked 'So it seems that it is the tail that wags the dog some of the time; these men, politicians, scientists, need rescuing from the spiral they have got us all into. 'Leave it to the governments and the experts' is a prescription for disaster. We, the people, men, women and children, should be the real 'experts' on survival.

We made some well considered efforts to reach different 'constituents' to try to make sure they were taking into account the important issues of nuclear disarmament — Cytun (the local Council of Churches), councillors, trade unions, and we found groups shaping up such as Wrexham Youth Action for Peace. Our membership numbers had grown, and the campaigners' meeting in April 1981 was already larger than was comfortable at the Peace Studies Centre — publicity was improving, especially at the send off for Jill for the Moscow visit. The mayor and the station-master attended formally, and the Bryn Offa School band and choir sang and played music for peace. Ten days later Jill was back facing BBC, HTV and local press reporters, even before she had had time to tell us peaceniks all about it.

4. A PLURALIST MOVEMENT

One fact and consequent anxiety arose as CND grew nationally. Our bulletin for May 1981 said:

We regret to have to report that in some parts of the country there is a definite programme to take over CND by political movements which have every right to exist, but not to programme the peace movement under one political banner. It is an unfortunate fact that there is something of a polarisation against one political party because of its lack of concern for nuclear disarmament; but it does not follow that any political ideology should take over the peace movement which is anxious to hold together a wide spectrum of political, religious and humanist concerns. We have thankfully a marvellous coming together of people from most political viewpoints united against nuclear arms race and war. Our issues are not 'Troops out', 'H Block reform', or anything else, even when our members may also favour these causes.

Very often some of the noisiest participants at rallies have been those pushing the sale of *Socialist Worker*, as though the red revolution was still the only way to get rid of nuclear weapons. This can sometimes be a delicate matter to deal with. I recall a major CND rally through the streets of Cardiff. When the procession reached St Mary Street on the way towards Cardiff Castle, a sizeable group of anarchists, mostly in black clothes with black banners were fiercely shouting 'Smash the State'. A number of us simply declined to keep the procession going until somehow we were dis-associated from this singularly un-peaceful cry. At a more recent (July 2002) gathering in Chester Friends Meeting House over the likely US invasion of Iraq at least two articulate speakers from the floor spoke about the rallying of the working-classes, and urged the sale of *Socialist Worker*. It was of course not surprising that such movements might well find new members from among those who are publicly challenging current political standpoints. They should be welcome to have a 'stall' on public occasions. But we need to clarify to them, and especially to attending reporters, that theirs is only one approach to the wider issues of peace and disarmament. A not dissimilar situation seems to have arisen with CND in 2003.

Quoting President Eisenhower again, the bulletin said: 'Some day, the demand for disarmament by hundreds of millions will be so universal and so insistent that no person, no nation, can withstand it.' That surely meant that we had to build a campaign together that united people of widely different philosophies and viewpoints. We were finding that general support was widespread, but it was harder to make sure that the message was getting to them beyond the limited number of campaign activists. After an initial agreement with our aims, it was too easy to imagine that nothing was changing, and very little going on, unless you were at the heart of things. In our monthly bulletin we noted '*On at least eighteen days in the last month there have been events, or activities with one, several or lots of campaigners at work. We have helped groups to start in Corwen, Ruabon and Acrefair*' Jill had been giving talks in several places, and I had been leading discussions in Wilmslow, Ludlow and Birkenhead.'*But*, we added, *we really have a long way to go before enough people will take action to change the policies of governments and nations.*'

Some of us travelled to Brawdy in west Wales for a demonstration outside the US submarine tracking base, where we handed in a petition which read; '*Now that Dyfed has declared itself a Nuclear Free zone, we, the undersigned, demand that the US Naval base at Brawdy, a primary nuclear target, be closed.*'

Up north, when we discovered that under-16s were not allowed to sign the World Disarmament Campaign's petition for New York, the local Youth Action group produced their own. We kept encouraging people to join the national movements of their choice — CND itself, the Fellowship of Reconciliation, Pax Christi, Peace Pledge Union — so that their newsletters, could inform people more thoroughly. Meantime virtually all this literature, and loads of relevant books were coming into our base in Hightown, and was justifying its newer title of the Peace Studies Centre.

When editing our monthly bulletin I drew on material from various sources. For instance John Harriott, a former Jesuit priest, writing in the Tablet had this to say:

HOW DID WE EVER GET INVOLVED IN ANYTHING AS STUPID AS OVERKILL?

UNDERTHINK—

Let us suppose that the heads of states announced they would be standing down all their armed forces except a handful of units for internal security, sending their military equipment to the breaker's yard and ceasing all future arms production. My guess is that before they had ceased to broadcast, a large number of anguished and desperate gentlemen would be banging on their doors telling them to hold their horses. Presidents of industrial corporations which depend on defence contracts, heads of research establishments geared to development of new weapons, politicians and union officials protesting about the loss of thousands of jobs, economists warning that the world economy would disintegrate. All of them claiming that it could not, must not, be done. Such a thought is not entirely fanciful. Last year (1980) the world's military expenditure rose to more than £250,000 million. Quite apart from the threat to world peace which such a massive tonnage of weaponry represents, it lends credence to the belief that weapons manufacture is not self perpetuating. There is so much money to be made from the business, so much scientific activity attached to it, so many people depend on it for their livelihood, so many remoter industries are drawn by the engine that literally millions of human beings have a stake in keeping it going......When on the opposite side we hear of a universal desire for disarmament and peace, it is disquieting to think that the last thing millions of people would want is peace.

He was emphasising an item that should rank high on our agenda twenty years on. As well as this it seemed important to try to lessen the fear and suspicion of our official 'enemies'. This meant highlighting items that might not get wide coverage elsewhere. The bogey was still of course the militaristic Soviet Union, over against which the deterrence policy was aimed. But well before the break-through of the Gorbachev era we noted President Brezhnev — not usually listed among the peace-makers, saying at the Communist Party Congress in February 1981 —

> Today the state of world affairs requires new additional efforts to remove the threat of war, and buttress international security…. In recent years, as you know, flashpoints of military conflict, often threatening to grow into a major conflagration, flared up now in one and now in another region of the world. Experience has shown it is not easy to extinguish them. It would be far better to take preventive measures to forestall their emergence.'

Then, after supporting some of the confidence-building measures already suggested in Europe, he added:

> The USSR is prepared to negotiate on limitation of weapons of all types. At one time we offered to ban the development of the naval Trident missile system in the US and of a corresponding system in our country. The proposal was not accepted. As a result the US has built the new Ohio submarine armed with trident missiles, while analogous system, the Typhoon, was built in our country. So who has stood to gain? We are prepared to come to terms on limiting the deployment of the new submarines … We could also agree to banning modernisation of existing and development of new ballistic missiles for these submarines.'

He went on to suggest the setting up of a competent international committee to demonstrate the vital necessity of preventing nuclear catastrophe. An interesting quotation from such a source was this:'Not war preparations which doom people to a senseless squandering of their material and spiritual wealth, but the consolidation of peace - that is the clue to the future'.

5. PROPAGANDA FOR PEACE

Looking for good opportunities to spread the message, we naturally looked to the International Eisteddfod at Llangollen in July. Here was an annual event founded to soften the wounds of the World War, which had successfully brought together musicians and dancers every year since 1945. Some fifty different nationalities took part. When a German choir first came in 1948, they arrived in great trepidation, but were so warmly received that they openly cried after their performance.

Our introductory leaflet to our own members now stressed, 'These are not 'protest' events, but are meant to integrate with the Eisteddfod theme of Peace and Friendship, and remind people of its *raison d'etre.*' A Peace Dance was devised, which took place on the campus itself, and we held a torchlight canal-side procession with songs for peace which drew some 300 people, but did not, as we later reported, make sufficient contact with the overseas participants of the Eisteddfod itself. The peace dance was repeated a few days later, when a small group of dancers, with music provided by Chris Potter (now an Anglican priest and Dean of St Asaph cathedral) moved through the town with some of the onlookers joining in.

We immediately wondered what we should organise for next year, perhaps linking with The United Nations Association, International Fellowship of Reconciliation, International Pax Christi for a tent on the campus. Some of us have been asking this again twenty years later.

Locally we supported a meeting led by Stanley Keeble for the Peace Tax campaign, and our bulletin quoted an American Catholic Archbishop, Raymond Hunthausen of Seattle, addressing a Lutheran Convention: 'I am told by some that unilateral disarmament in the face of atheistic communism is insane. I find myself observing that nuclear armament by anyone is itself atheistic and anything but sane.' He went on to suggest that Christians in the US should refuse to pay half of their federal income tax as a non-violent protest against 'nuclear murder and suicide', saying 'it is time for Christians to return to the Gospel with open hearts and to learn again what it is to have faith'

That same month, the *New Statesman* offered us another hymn parody:

The Army's one foundation	Though we salute the Master
Is Jesus Christ our Lord	We call the Prince of Peace
We are his true creation	Our methods work much faster
By missile and the sword	To speed the soul's release
The Army's heart rejoices	His saints are marching slowly
That He is on our side	Towards the promised land
Yea, even when he voices	Though God forbid the lowly
His doubts at genocide	Should gain the upper hand.

His voice was never strident
His manner ever meek
He would have wept at Trident
And turned the other cheek.
Still in His name we foster
The spirit of the corps
And breathe a pater noster
As we prepare for war.

In our July bulletin we had suggestions being shared about how to commemorate Hiroshima and Nagasaki days (Aug.6th–9th) We wondered if people would be willing to wear black armbands for the four days. It was of course left to individuals to do what they thought suitable. I am reminded by a photo in the *Wrexham Evening Leader* of August 9th that I apparently stood in a solo silent vigil in Lord Street. I hardly recall this now; except that being still for a couple of hours was quite valuable in itself, and there were some friendly and jocular comments in my ear from some of the lads who used to be in my Youth Club in Ruabon twelve years ago. Others had done street leafleting. Over three days we gave out 1500 leaflets to explain the meaning of our commemoration. Those involved included last year's mayor, another ex-mayor and a county councillor.

President Reagan, 'with characteristic insensitivity, chose the anniversary to announce the go-ahead for the Neutron Bomb' We quoted Professor Eric Burhop who said: 'The development of such a weapon, so eminently suited for aggression by order first of President Carter....cannot fail to raise doubts everywhere about the real aims of the NATO alliance.' It was all part of a developing idea of limited nuclear war, and the Professor gave gruesome details of the radiation effects on human beings taken from the US Atomic Energy Commission, ending with 'The fortunate ones may die within two to four weeks. Those one or two kilometres away at the time of the explosion may linger on for years with distressing conditions of this kind'.

August 27th saw the start of the women's walk from Cardiff to Greenham Common. We were proud that our Janet Tyrrell and some of her family were taking part. In the event this turned into one of the most significant items in peace campaigning. At Greenham the women demanded an interview with government ministers about the arrival of the intermediate weapons of mass destruction — Cruise missiles. When this was refused they camped there, and stayed for years.

Peace movement supporters were already charged with being crypto-communists. The trouble with our findings was that we were in danger of becoming fiercely anti-American, so we made a note of the danger here. I reported that in conversation with Professor Donald Nicholl, recently returned from several years in California, he said it was unjust 'if we did not make people aware of the lively, practical and experienced anti-war activities of many in the USA. He urged us to make contact, and to benefit from the hard-won knowledge about the practice of non-violent resistance which has been gained there.' That remains the case today; so some of us have been eager to spread the news often poorly reported in our press, of the splendid gestures of so many Americans after the tragedy and horror of September 11th, 2001, especially in their compassion for the Afghan victims of American bombing.

6. VETERANS AND HISTORY

As I have explained, the Wrexham group began in support of the World Disarmament Campaign to take thousands, perhaps millions, of signatures to New York for the 1982 Special Session of the United Nations on Disarmament. I reported to our group in August : 'As the representative of British Pax Christi I attended the Executive Committee of WDC in the House of Lords two weeks ago. There were ten of us in one of the elegant committee rooms, with Lord Fenner Brockway chairing the meeting with extraordinary acumen. In front of him sat Lord Philip Noel-Baker, the second nonagenarian founder of WDC, then Lord Hugh Jenkins, Brigadier Harbottle, his wife Eirwen, and four others.' This was the start of several occasions working alongside these wonderful and distinguished people. I recall one meeting in Noel-Baker's flat near Sloane Square, which was a charmingly informal setting for serious discussions. As I have yet to tell, I travelled with Brockway to the Soviet Union within a few months; and I drew on the fascinating writing of Noel-Baker about the first World Disarmament Conference of 1932/3, when he was personal assistant to the President of the Conference. I thought it was worthwhile to include the following long quotation from his book about all this, because in large measure the situation had not really changed.

> There will be many readers who feel as I did on November 30th 1918…They will say 'Everybody wants disarmament, lasting peace, the rule of law. But alas experience has shown in all these Conferences and Commissions that….a Disarmament Treaty is technically impossible to make; and without disarmament, the rest has failed.' With respect that is the exact opposite of the truth. The Conferences and Commissions have proved that all the technical problems of disarmament have been solved; that the further disarmament is taken, the more swiftly and completely would the difficulties disappear. The only problem that remains unsolved is that of creating the popular support that will enable, or compel, the statesmen to see it through. The Conferences and Commissions have proved something else; that there are men, very powerful men in the delegations and in their governments at home, who do not want disarmament and the rule of law; men who hate and fear them and who fight against them with tenacity and skill ….
>
> I was personally involved in the struggle; I know the men and what they did. In that struggle for three-quarters of a century, the internationalists have won all the arguments, but the bureaucrats and militarists have won all the material victories that count. They sterilised the first and second Hague Conferences in 1899 and 1907 …They finally destroyed the Hague Conference movement altogether … They destroyed the League of nations Conference on Disarmament in 1932/3 … In spite of its remarkable success, they destroyed the League of Nations … They have destroyed the binding force of the UN Charter Law; they have taken us far back along the road to the international anarchy of pre-League days. The motives of these bureaucrats and militarists were 'honourable' and according to their lights patriotic. But their guilt before history, and before past, present and future generations, is appaling.

It was Sir Winston Churchill who said that the second World War should be called the 'unnecessary war'; that it 'could easily have been prevented if the League of Nations had been used with courage and loyalty by the associated nations'. In 1978 the true realists are still the men who stand for the United Nations, world disarmament and the rule of law. Only their policy can avert the cataclysm. More than ever before, the bureaucrats and militarists are in 1978 the prophets of illusion and of doom. Yet today they seem to be in charge of policy, more perhaps than ever before.

This was pretty withering stuff, but his story of 1932/3 fills out his charges with evidence. (I take this up in a later section of this chronicle).

Surprisingly enough even Peregrine Worsthorne in the *Sunday Telegraph* was saying:

> Western politicians still seem to suppose that adherents of nuclear pacifism are all a bit cranky as were pacifists of old. But the truth is that it is no longer cranky to be a pacifist. Indeed one might say that one has to be a bit cranky to be anything else. To envisage blowing up the world really is a bit abnormal.

I recorded that campaigners had done another ward with door-to-door calls for the WDC petition. Jill had given talks in St.Asaph, Llay and Manchester; while I had been talking in Oxford, Lampeter and Newtown. By September 12th there was enough strength across Wales for there to be the inaugural conference of CND Cymru as a distinct part of the British campaign. Three days later representatives of all peace groups in the county of Clwyd started to shape this sub-division. By now I was a part-time secretary of CND Cymru, which I tried to combine with visits to London to help co-ordinate disarmament work for Pax Christi UK; so our horizons were constantly widening.

Drawing on the FOR quarterly journal our bulletin quoted General Douglas MacArthur who said on 2nd September 1945 'Military alliances, balances of power, League of Nations, all in turn failed, leaving the only path to be by way of the crucible of war. The utter destructiveness of war now blocks out this alternative. We have had our last chance. If we will not devise some greater and more equitable system, armageddon will be at our door'.

Then a former RAF pilot, Bernard Benson, offered three propositions: '(a) Beyond their differences of opinion and ideology, four billion human beings have one thing in common: they do not want to be killed. (b) The decision whether to produce armaments or to disarm is in the hands of fewer than 200 people (c) We are all limited to a network of communications that can be used to radiate peace. Conclusion. Peace Is Possible, if those who do not want to be killed will gather together.'

7. MASSIVE RALLYING

By October 1981 the groundswell of the international peace movements was growing. Our bulletin reports what several important figures were saying. The National Peace Council, based in London reported on the staunch remarks of Japanese people at the World Conference against Atomic and Hydrogen bombs, held in Tokyo. They were determined that the next nine months before the UN's Second Special Disarmament would be spent gathering even more determined voices for peace. 'We shall resolutely reject the menace of the nuclear arms race which may turn this earth into a planet of death.'

The International Peace Bureau kept its eye on the Geneva Committee on Disarmament which was supposed to be making forward steps since the First Special Session in 1978. Instead of being a negotiating body, it had drifted into being another deliberative forum.

We took some heart from the action of Bishop Matthiesen of Amarillo who advised workers at a US weapons' assembly plant in his diocese to give up their jobs rather than participate in the production of the neutron bomb. Twelve other Texan bishops signed a statement supporting his stand. The organisation of International Physicians Against Nuclear War was growing apace, and at the Royal Society of Medicine in London were preparing their next international congress. Here Russian, American and European doctors declared with one voice that the most serious disease facing humankind was the prospect of nuclear war. The West German Rally for disarmament had 250,000 taking part. That made us all the more eager to make the second major London rally on October 24th a really vast one; we planned to fill two coaches, and another two would go from Cartrefle and Aston Colleges. We had decided on a whole week of a Peace Festival. Organising this with so many varied items really absorbed our energies. The special poster showed how far we were ready to stretch ourselves.

British Catholic bishops were rarely willing to get involved in the issues — a terrible disappointment to many of us. However Bishop Christopher Butler attended the WDC Vigil in Westminster and said:

> The central issue seems to me to be something like this. Would it be morally permissible to kill and mutilate millions of civilians to prevent, or avenge, the killing of millions of our own civilians in the West? Has the dictum that the end justifies the means got no limits to its validity? If we hold, as I think we must, that the killing of massive numbers of civilians in retaliation for the killing of similar numbers of our own civilians would be doubly sinful — as being the killing of the innocent and also as an act of revenge, then the maintenance of the nuclear deterrence policy inevitably corrupts the consciences of those engaged in the development, manufacture and deployment of the nuclear weapons and the conscience of those who are trained to release these weapons,

to 'press the button' on orders received from above, or without such orders actually received.

Despite the moral clarity of these remarks, there was no sign of support from other bishops.

The great London Rally on October 24th turned out to be an enormous success as far as numbers go; the whole atmosphere was euphoric; we really began to think we were going to change things. There was a wonderful carnival spirit, and our November bulletin carried a lovely diary-piece from Dennis Carter. He referred to the great 'shouts' which went like this:

'One, two, three, four. We don't want a nuclear war. Five, six, seven, eight. We don't want to radiate.' Dennis said:

> My voice, after shouting this for the hundredth time is like a teenage boy's — all squeaks, and bleats and ah-ee-ah-ee-ahs. A plane tree leaf drifts down and taps my friend on the arm with its natural dying finger from the thinning tree. Placards and badges and stickers and banners make their own foliage. So much invention and skill and passion for the cause of life for a thousand million lifetimes have been stitched and sprayed and painted and glued and stapled by so many caring fingers. It makes you cry to think of it. Cry in anger at Goneril and Reagan. Cry for joy. Weep in silence through the feeling of solidarity you get with all these beautiful people. And they picnicked too in the park. Families and friends, lovers and strangers picnicked among the protest banners. There was joy and love. There was no scuffle, no push, no shove. Not even a scowl was seen on any faces. And those faces had been awake since 5.00 a.m. at least. It was all give and take with a touch of gentleness …
>
> When my grandchildren say 'What did you do to stop the bomb, gramps?' at least I can say that I picnicked in the park on Saturday October 24th 1981 with my wife and newly found friends in peace and for peace.

By the time we'd got over our immediate tiredness from the Rally, and even more from the variety of events in our Festival for Peace, we realised that a new phase was beginning. The November bulletin said: 'We pride ourselves in not having created a 'committee' after 18 months; but the tasks are growing in number and there is, happily, a willingness to take them on.' We now had a Membership Secretary, Treasurer, Speakers Secretary; A Women for Life Group, Someone for Filing, another for Welsh Translations, and contacts for Cymdeithas y Cymod, Quaker Peace & Service, Pax Christi, someone for the WDC Petition, another for Peace goods, badges etc. and theoretically I was still the 'co-ordinator' and editor of the bulletin. By December we reported that it was hard to keep up the momentum. 'Maybe we are trying to handle too much at one time? Maybe we now need to have a more formal structure? Certain it is that my own frequent absences (45 meetings in 3 months including last week's five day absence in Antwerp and London for Pax Christi and WDC meetings,) does not make for efficiency.' So we had a special meeting on December 30th to share a mince pie and have a think together. This led to the recognition that we had a range of eleven projects, tasks, activities which needed sub-groups to be responsible for, if we were to progress

8. TO THE SOVIET UNION WITH LOVE

We were however able to announce that 'Following the visit of a Soviet Peace Committee delegation to Britain in April/May, the Northern Friends Peace Board has co-ordinated arrangements for a delegation of twenty to visit the Soviet Union Jan 5-15th 1982.... I shall be going for the National Peace Council, Lord Fenner Brockway for WDC, Bill Hetherington for PPU, Dr Michael Dando for Bradford School of Peace Studies, Ron Huzzard for QPS, Councillor Ruby for Manchester City Council, John Gleisner for the Medical Campaign against Nuclear War, Lee Chadwick for Manchester against Missiles' and I gave the whole list.

Looking back now I see how significant this event was for me personally, as well as for the peace movement generally as we were exploring the possibilities for non-governmental people to confront those with power.

Nationally this event had been well handled for publicity, including a London Press Conference immediately on our return, so we did what we could to ensure coverage locally. BBC Radio Clwyd recorded a piece for inclusion just before we set off; the *Wrexham Leader* had an article ready for January 8th. I was able to say that I would carry 'a very gracious message from the Mayor of Wrexham to the Chairman of Moscow's Council, and another greeting from the Bishop of Menevia to the Patriarch of Moscow.' Our hope was to be able to break up into smaller interest groups:; teachers to teachers, doctors to doctors, likewise with social workers and scientists; and I hoped to make contact with Orthodox priests, and thought that might be facilitated by the fact that we would be there for the Orthodox 'Christmas' on January 6th.

The whole event turned out to be a mind-blowing experience for me. As the plane touched down in Moscow it was already late evening, and about 30 degrees below freezing. No need for water-resisting boots or shoes; everything was so crisp and hard. We got through customs without too much fuss, and reached our hotel soon enough. I shared a two bedded little suite with Fenner Brockway. At 93 years of age he was a most considerate companion, and went straight off to bed when we got there, and appeared to be fast asleep when I finished writing up my diary in our sitting room. However as I slipped into my bed, he chirped up suddenly 'Goodnight Owen'.

What is it boy?　*Please sir are the Russians people?*

As I awoke fairly early and completed my shaving etc. the next morning, he was silent enough till asking 'What's the time? Only 7.15? Another half hour then.' And back to sleep!

We were royally treated by the Soviet Peace Committee, and taken all over the great city, led by our interpreter, who was also our 'minder'. We had no illusions about the care with which we would be watched. Hotel officials, floor concierges were all obliged under their system to be 'security' people as well. This was not particularly oppressive, but it limited our chances of talking to 'ordinary' people. The delegation visits to various institutions were necessarily formal, but now and again, over refreshments we could occasionally speak to someone on their own. This was especially true of our visit to the Kremlin, when we were met by the Chairman of the House of Nationalities — one of their 'parliamentary' structures. We were told to expect about 40 minutes for this reception; in fact it lasted several hours. To begin with, sitting in a line on one side of a long table opposite twenty Soviet representatives we introduced ourselves in turn, and then exchanged formal messages. The purpose of our delegation was simply to make personal contacts, and to try to understand the perspective of Russian people on the threatening stance of nuclear deterrence, and the notion of Mutual Assured Destruction. However when we did break up for coffee, and selecting some individuals who were not near the centre of their hierarchical group, several of us had really interesting chats. We were able to challenge what seemed to us the severe limitations on human freedoms, and to hear their explanations, even if not excuses. One of them even agreed that while civil rights were sometimes curtailed, they wondered about our British social rights, with over 2 million unemployed and many people homeless — which was not replicated in the Soviet Union. Even the formal group had not apparently resented our questioning the treatment which had been given to a few named Russian peace activists. When in another five years Gorbachev was showing a different side to Russian diplomacy, somehow I felt that he wasn't the only one. We had met some real human beings at quite high levels in the course of our stay.

Wherever we went, dear old Fenner Brockway seemed to have had some contact in the past. For example in Kropotkin Square he said 'Of course I knew him' (He meant Prince Kropotkin), and this became a frequent phrase as we moved around the historical points of the city with its unfolding history. It was the same in Leningrad, where I was determined to move around a bit on my own if possible. As our leader/interpreter took the delegation out one morning, I developed a diplomatic headache till they had gone; then I set out myself. I walked through the city to the riverside, totally frozen over, of course, and tried to take a photo of the battleship moored at one side. With gloves on this was difficult, so I removed one, and found the hand sweat freezing a finger to the metal; not comfortable. I got a bit lost walking back, and, fearful I might be late for an arranged hotel meeting, I jumped on a tram going I hoped in the right direction; but the windows were frozen over and when I felt us take a sharp right turn, I decided it would be wiser to proceed on foot. Stopping passers-by to ask directions wasn't very fruitful — perhaps because it was too cold to stop; perhaps because citizens were not encouraged to be seen talking to foreign visitors. Wandering around on my own I might get lost, but I never felt unsafe. I wouldn't do that so calmly in Russia today; and certainly not in New York!

I shared a couchette with Fenner for the over-night train journey to Leningrad; and this was the occasion of one of the most fascinating conversations I have ever had. He told me of his friendship with Bernard Shaw, who treated him like a son; of people like Ethel Mannin, and in more recent times of his work to help change the violence of some IRA prisoners in London to the ways of peace. When someone brought him a glass of whiskey he gladly took it, and said to me surprisingly: 'You know, Owen, I never touched this stuff till I met Gandhi'. Apparently he met up with him in India, when Fenner had been taken to hospital for sudden sickness.

'You know I'm an agnostic', he said, 'but I'll tell you that Gandhi was special. He came to my bedside where I had spent some restless hours. He took my hand, and something seemed to flow from him into me, and I became totally calm. I don't know how you explain that.'

We then flew three hours south to Uzbekistan, and were impressed with the development that had clearly taken place since it was incorporated in the Soviet Union. It was of course a 'colony' but educational and health programmes had unquestionably developed the state. We were shown round Tashkent, the capital, and visited Samarkand and its beautiful mosques. We had a significant interview with the Grand Mufti for Soviet Central Asia. A blind 82 year old, he was willing to be asked questions about religious freedom. It was a bit of an ordeal, because he appeared to speak in Arabic, then translated into Uzbek, and then into Russian before we reached the English version. Conversation was understandably slow! On one occasion the translation eventually came like this : 'And so I say to you that Allah — blessed be his holy name ...' Then in a loud whisper one of our playful delegates said, taking on Fenner's frequent tone of voice, 'I knew him'!

In Moscow I had managed to get to the patriarchal cathedral for the great Christmas feast. I am reasonably conversant with the Byzantine rite, and knew I was in for a long 2-3 hour stand. What impressed me was the huge numbers of worshippers, including a range of ages; it was <u>not</u> a case of only old babushkas. It was a glorious and colourful liturgy. Some days later a few of us went to the Baptist church where there seemed to be over twenty leading ministers. Another crowded church, singing several carols we recognised, led by a youth choir. What we discovered was that people were not forbidden to celebrate their faith nowadays, but, if you wanted to get on in society you had better not be known to be a believer. That was one thing that Orthodox Archbishop Bartolomem said to me in Tashkent: 'It costs something to be a believer in the Soviet Union'. It doesn't cost us anything in Britain, I thought, because we don't rock the boat much, even when it needs a good shake-up.

I cannot say that I was altogether impressed by the smoothness of Archbishop Pitirim, who was responsible for all publications for the Orthodox Church, to show us around. His premises were lavish, and there wasn't any crack in his presentation, such that we could ask pointed questions. Oddly enough it was when we were assured that everything in the garden was lovely in the Soviet Union that we remained sceptical. Occasionally it was the Russian quietly remarked jokes that we found helpful. On one occasion one of our contacts said: 'The real difference between Soviet propaganda, and your British propaganda is that you believe yours.' *Touché*!

Altogether I took heart from this visit. Russians were not unapproachable — even quite senior officials — if spoken to in the right spirit. But of course the right-wing press in Britain were not going to let that out. The Daily Mail described our delegation as 'dupes of the Soviet Union' when we got back. But others were ready to hear what we had experienced. I note that I was called on to speak at the new Mold Peace Group, also in Neath and Carmarthen, Manchester and Colwyn Bay. Incidentally for several months after my return from Russia, we had reason to believe that my phone was tapped. Obviously I cannot say here how this was confirmed to me, but in the meantime it was no great worry; I had no secrets to reveal or cover up; sometimes I ended a conversation with a jocular 'Goodnight to all my listeners'.

9. MORE EDUCATION

Members of our group had meantime taken part in several educational events, Fred Starkey and Chris Spragg had attended a training course in Bristol on non-violent direct action. Others had participated in a series of WEA lectures, and our March 1982 bulletin was full of wise advice from Fred about the conduct of particular projects. 'If actions are to be genuinely non-violent', he said, 'we need more than enthusiasm, good intentions and comradeship, necessary though these are.' He argued impressively for reliability, responsibility, efficiency, and legality. 'We do not have the right to break any law which is not morally unjust', adding, 'I follow Gandhi in this' On openness' he said, 'We abhor secrecy in government and other institutions. We should inform persons who need to know, including the police, in good time. Openness is the badge of our integrity.'

"Nuclear war is a destructive thing but still in large part a physics problem... It is possible to survive and prevail over the enemy."
(Charles Kupperman, Executive Director, General Advisory Committee to US Arms Control and Disarmament Agency, 28 September 1981)

We included a piece written by a well-known US peace campaigner, James Douglass, who, at a later stage, visited our Centre. It is no less relevant today.

'CAN WE UNDERSTAND THE POWER OF OUR WEAPONS ?'

'What is Trident? TRIDENT is a nuclear submarine being built now, which is able to destroy 408 cities or areas at one time, each with a blast five times more powerful than the Hiroshima bomb.

TRIDENT is 2,040 Hiroshimas. One Trident submarine can destroy any country on earth. A fleet of Trident submarines (30 are planned in USA) can end life on earth How can anyone understand that?

Begin with a meditation. To understand Trident, say the word 'Hiroshima', Reflect on its meaning for one second. Say and understand 'Hiroshima' again, and again, and again — 2040 times. Assuming you are able to understand 'Hiroshima' in one second, you will be able to understand Trident in 34 minutes. That is one Trident submarine.

To understand the destructive power of the whole Trident fleet, it would take you 17 hours, devoting one second to each 'Hiroshima'.

Your meditation is impossible. To understand 'Hiroshima' alone would take a lifetime.

The Cold War was declared to be over some time ago. Trident submarines are still, twenty years later, cruising round our world from British bases. If you have these weapons, you have to have enemies. If we don't invent them, others, especially US administrations will surely find them. Our April bulletin quoted

Captain Liddell Hart: 'The study of war has taught me that almost every war was avoidable, and that the outbreak was most often produced by statesmen losing their heads or their patience, and putting their opponent in a position where he could not withdraw without serious loss of face.' Attributed to him also is the remark: 'The only thing we learn from history is that we never learn from history.'

The bulletin also quoted an un-named First World War statesman:

'Fear begets suspicion and distrust and evil imaginings of all sorts till each government feels it would be criminal and a betrayal of his country not to take every precaution ... while every government regards the precautions of every other government as evidence of hostile intent.'

That remark was one of the considerations we had in our delegation to the USSR. There were, according to Britain, vast civil defence precautions being taken over there, which were seen as evidence of their aggressive intent to open up nuclear war with the West. So everywhere we went we asked about these preparations, and we were met with incomprehension or laughter. Back in Moscow in conversation with Mr Kuznezov, the editor of a subsidiary paper to *Pravda*, he only told us one of the local jokes: 'What do we do if the crisis builds up, and the siren sounds? Answer: Cover yourself with a white sheet, and move towards the cemetery very slowly. Why slowly? Well, you don't want to cause a panic, do you?'

In April we reported that several members of our peace group had been researching on 'Emergency Planning' locally. An Observer Corps officer gave them time to ask many searching questions, and on another occasion the Emergency Planning Officer showed us the underground bunker which could accommodate 50-plus staff. We were grateful even for this limited openness. At this time we heard of the activity of Mid-Glamorgan activists who had actually occupied the County War Bunker to expose the reality of civil defence plans, and to further the Council's official nuclear free zone policy.

The same bulletin contained a lively report from Janet Tyrrell, who had remained with the Greenham women. In another month we were reporting the High Court action being taken against the women, and the possible attempt to evict them altogether. Several of our members went to Greenham to associate themselves with the women's brave action.

10. NUCLEAR FREE WALES

February 23rd 1982 was the day of Clwyd County Council's Declaration as a nuclear free zone. It was passed by 41 to 15 in favour, and Clwyd became the eighth and last county in Wales to make this declaration.

WALES SPREADS ITS NUCLEAR MESSAGE

Within hours of the county council's announcement that Clwyd is to be a nuclear free zone yesterday, a sign declaring Nuclear Free Wales was erected on the A5 at the border with Shropshire near Chirk.

CND Cymru, who posted the bi-lingual sign, hurriedly despatched letters to each of the eight county chiefs executives in Wales after the meeting.

The organisation wants the letter passing on to all councillors.

CND Cymru secretary and a leading disarmament campaigner in Wrexham, Father Owen Hardwicke, points out in the letter that Wales has now given a lead to the whole of Europe by becoming the first country to be a nuclear weapon-free zone.

He calls on all councils to work together and make available to the public the maximum information on civil defence, in particular Home Office circulars.

Spell out

Father Hardwicke said: "These circulars spell out the horrifying details of how central Government expects a nuclear attack to devastate the community."

The organisation believes that by learning of the plans, people will realise the futility of Government policy on civil defence.

"And the more they will declare that the only true civil defence is an end to the arms race," he said.

Evening Leader, Wednesday.
1982 24 February

THE CLWYD DECLARATION

'The decision made today by the Clwyd County Council to declare its county a nuclear-free zone is of special significance to the whole of Wales. During the past years similar decisions have been made by one Welsh County after another, beginning with Dyfed and culminating this very day with Clwyd.

The consensus of opinion of the Welsh people in this matter has long been evident. Local anti-nuclear groups which sprang up voluntarily have been able to co-ordinate their activities so that Wales as an entity be made a nuclear-free zone, and surveys and petitions have shown the overwhelming support for their campaign by a populace which is deeply concerned by nuclear escalation and which wants the right to have its say in the future of humanity.

Because of today's decision we are now in a position to proclaim to the world that the whole of Wales, through its democratically elected representatives, has declared itself a nuclear-free zone. By this action Wales has given a moral lead to the other countries of Europe and the world.

In passing onto them our message of hope and inspiration, we call upon the other nations of Europe to make known their deep concern for the future of civilisation. We call upon them to commit themselves to the cause of redeeming Europe from total destruction by taking the initial step of declaring their homelands nuclear-free zones.'

Signed (among others) by Gwynfor Evans: Henry Roberts (Chair Gwynedd County Council); R.S.Thomas, Dafydd Ellis Thomas, John Landon, Ennys Kelly, E.Griffiths (Chairman Gwent Council) W. R. Phillips (Powys County Council) R. G. Harris (Dyfed County Council) Robert Morgan (Leader South Glamorgan County Council) Morgan Chambers (Mid-Glamorgan Count Council) Martyn Jones (Clwyd County Council) Owen Hardwicke (CND Cymru & Pax Christi).

A relay of young people immediately carried a flaming torch to the border of Wales near Sealand, with a notice to be appended to the Welcome to Wales notice, saying 'You are now entering a nuclear free country' Similar notices went up near Lavister and Chirk. It was the several untidy qualities of these actions that led Fred Starkey to issue his sound warnings.

In May we had to take into account the Falklands/Malvinas war. There was risk of a split within the peace movement, because this was not immediately a nuclear issue. The members were certainly not all pacifists as I was. Everyone disliked the jingoistic spirit that the popular press was stirring up, and we certainly felt it was legitimate to remind people that Britain was selling arms to Argentina up to a few weeks before the outbreak of hostilities. The Campaign against the Arms Trade gave a complete list of the deals and dates of the agreements.

Anyway at our next Campaigners' meeting on 12th May we decided to send a message to John Nott, the Secretary of State for Defence with the names of 35 people. We didn't think it fair to presume the whole Group of Wrexham for Nuclear Disarmament would concur. We said:

> We, some citizens of Wrexham and District, meeting together for other matters, agreed to send you the following statement. While we whole-heartedly condemn the breach of international law by the Argentine government in its invasion of the Falkland Islands, we are profoundly disturbed at the military action being taken by the British forces without the sanction of the United Nations. In our view the risks of a futile loss of life in the Task Force, and of a possible drift into world war, are not commensurate with the righting of a wrong which ultimately will have to be guaranteed by peaceful negotiation. We are also anxious that the government has refused to assure the public that no nuclear weapons are being deployed. The crisis certainly shows the absurdity of a defence policy based on the deployment of nuclear weapons' systems.

The message was formally acknowledged by the Ministry of Defence.

11. UNITED NATIONS SPECIAL SESSION

By now we had gathered 11,000 signatures for the petition to the UN, ready for June, and my own time was focussed on getting ready to join the British delegation to the Second Special Assembly on Disarmament. The energy of the rest of the Wrexham group was fervent and constructive. The next three mid-month meetings (which we used for 'educational' purposes in contrast to the end of month campaigning meetings) were to be led by Sue Stanford and Hilary Appleton on the problematic Nuclear Power/ Nuclear Weapons links. Jill had rallied helpers for the visit of Russian and American Mothers for Peace, and was able to say this was a successful venture to have followed her journeyings.

Our bulletin for June 17th was prepared in the euphoria I had experienced by the end of the UN Special Session. At a major London Rally on June 6th, before setting off with the British Delegation, we heard of the Declaration issued by the European Peace Movements which was to go forward. It was a powerful inspiration and is worth quoting in full.

Considering that we in this living generation hold in trust the survival of our civilisation, the prospects of future generations and the fate of the earth itself: we accept our trusteeship. We dedicate our lives to the cause of peace. We reject altogether the use or preparation of nuclear weapons or of any weapons of mass destruction. We reject also the arguments of 'deterrence' or of 'balance' which justify these weapons and delay disarmament.

We have lost count of the weapons poised above our heads, and we have lost interest in counting. We refuse them. We call upon our friends throughout the world,, in East or West, to refuse them also. We call upon governments to refuse them by actions. Let any nation initiate this action by a full or partial refusal of any nuclear weapons system, or by refusing the deployment of any system upon its territory; and then let us muster world-wide support. Let refusals proliferate!

We refuse also every measure which seeks to marshal humankind into two oppressive blocs. We refuse Cold War and we disown allegiance to its ideologies and to its opposed security systems. We affirm our citizenship of a healed world.

Let us place our loyalty above loyalty to the armourers. Do not allow anyone to divide us. We are already in our movements creating a new kind of politics, an international fellowship of

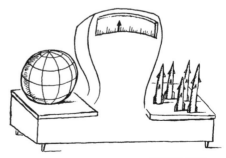

Paul Valerry, West Germany

resistance and friendship which refuses advantage to either 'side', because it refuses to acknowledge any 'side' except that of our common future — a future which will never come unless we in this living generation honour our trust.

We managed to have several days in New York before the opening of the Special Session when we did some important lobbying of the official delegates. I managed to get a ticket to the gallery for a meeting of the Security Council when the Falklands war was debated. We heard Spain (a NATO ally of Britain) and Panama put up a joint emergency resolution calling for a cease-fire; and watched the UK ambassador veto the vote, and then listened to Panama's denunciation of this veto. We registered the fact that the 'permanent members' of the Council could frustrate the effectiveness of the United Nations. Francis Pym was later to show distress at the failure of Israel to observe the cease-fire demanded by the Council; it had now a hollow ring.

We took new heart from the opening words of the President of the Special Session on Disarmament Ismat Kissani. He gave a wonderfully truthful appraisal on what had <u>not</u> been happening since the first Special Session.

> Four years ago, he said, the UN convened the first Special Session on Disarmament. Many of you were in this hall when that session adopted a final document which was hailed by many as a break-through in the frustrating search for a workable formula to halt the arms race What has happened in the intervening years? What measures have been taken that have resulted in reduction in armaments? In short what have the governments of the world done to respond to the fervent demand of the people of the world that this insane arms race be stopped? You and I both know the answer, but I want to state it loudly and clearly for the world to hear: Nothing. Not a single weapon has been destroyed over the past four years as a result of a disarmament agreement. Nothing of significance has been done to reduce the imminent threat of self-extinction that makes the present so dangerous and the future so uncertain. It is a sorry record of failure.

He went on to say that in some circles there was an increasing tendency to accept the idea of 'limited' nuclear war as winnable. 'This is not merely analytically foolish; it is dangerous ... It is clear that to seek national security in more arms, in more destructive power, is doomed to fail. You cannot destroy the enemy, or the earth, more than once. I firmly believe that we must step back from the conventional wisdom of constantly seeking to be stronger than the perceived adversary.'

He then affirmed several reasons for optimism all the same. The second one, which he described as 'the most encouraging development in the disarmament picture since 1978 is the growing and increasingly organised and assertive public movement against the arms race. This ground-swell of public opinion is world-wide and cuts across the entire political spectrum. It is to me particularly significant that in many countries, religious leaders are in the fore-front of this movement ... We are witnessing the truly democratic process of public opinion moving governments to adopt more rational approaches and take more seriously the decisions they agree to at the international level. I am pleased to note the broad and impressive representation and activities of non-governmental organisations at this session, both in this hall and outside. That alone is an indication of public interest and concern. I would like to welcome them and tell them that their participation is most important; on behalf of the Assembly I want to thank them for their continuing efforts in the cause of peace. We still have a chance. We still have time: but not much. The odds are lengthening against humanity. It is time to put an end to the arms race and begin the peace race.'

New York was alive with peace activists. Bus-drivers, taxi-drivers and shop-window notices were all wishing us well. The American peace movements were enormous. The great march and rally in Central Park was over a million strong; it took seven hours to get there through the streets, with banners and flags, and much music. The police remarked that they hadn't seen anything like this since the call for an end to the Vietnam war — and that was successful. All the fringe political, religious and other movements were there, but no trouble at all; it was a real carnival.It was wonderful to see the Palestine Liberation Organisation marching with another banner in their midst 'Jews in Solidarity with Palestinians' There were columns of friars, and apostolic sisters under banners 'Dominicans for Peace', 'Franciscans for Peace' 'Little Sisters for Peace' singing and chanting as they walked. My report went on:

Can you envisage a vast eucharistic assembly in St.John's Episcopal cathedral with the Dean and one or two women priests presiding, with Martin Luther King's widow, Coretta, preaching, and standing by the altar swathed in incense smoke, with a powerful jazz group weaving amazing music round the Gregorian chant — all in a vast prayer for peace?

There were international lawyers in a three-day symposium, passing firm declarations on the illegality and immorality of nuclear weapons. Parliamentarians for World Peace formed another group — I sat behind a north Wales MP, and a Welsh Euro MP during one session. One was able to chat with Sean McBride, the Nobel Prize winner and other figures from the international scene '

Back on the diplomatic scene, it was not so cheerful. Yet our ambassador, David Summerhayes, could hardly have been more open to meeting us. Altogether there were five occasions when he was in direct consultation, when we expressed our gross dissatisfaction with the UK government's proposals. He impressed on us that he was only a government spokesman, but it is fair to say that he was impressed with the fact that we represented a knowledgeable and committed section of the population, and were not happy to accept mere lip-service to our presence. We can expect nothing very helpful from the UK in the Assembly at this stage; but, as with parliament, some of the real work is done not in the full Assembly, but in the working groups. These have already started their work, and we sense that the tidal wave of world opinion could drive these into positive directions.

'We have all returned from New York with the feeling that we have power, real power if only we stick together and keep vociferous. Increasingly the politicians are having to acknowledge that the United Nations is not primarily for governments but for 'We, the Peoples …' as the Charter says.

I interpose here an anecdote from my own experiences in New York. I was delighted at the way in which with a little initiative (or do I mean cheek?) one could move around interesting events and places. I happened to be in the Church Centre, opposite the UN buildings when a message came for Anthony Coles, the administrator of the British delegation's visit, from the British embassy who needed to have a list of those who would attend at the first interview with the ambassador the following day. Anthony wasn't around, so I volunteered to take the list to the embassy at once. I was really only expected to hand in the list, but I passed in my little business card, and was asked to wait a moment. Then in ten minutes the ambassador invited me in to his office and I had 20 minutes of amiable chat about our delegation with him. So when the delegation visit took place I was already known there, and I chatted further with a charming lady who was third secretary. She was keen to know about the Moscow visit and I retailed our experience of the large formal meeting, which really only came to life, and to some degree of honesty when one chatted informally with, not the chairman, but perhaps the third secretary!

(In another year or so, I was asked to debate 'the nuclear issue' at the Anglican Synod of Derby. I found that my opponent, in favour of nuclear deterrence, was to be David Summerhayes, who had now left the UN post. I had in the meantime discovered that he had been a contemporary of mine at Marlborough, indeed in the adjoining 'house'. I'm not sure whether this resulted in a more tender debate).

One great event was the reception given by the UN Secretary General, Perez de Cuellar, for the world-wide Petitions. Over two and a quarter million signatures had been gathered by the World Disarmament Campaign to which we had contributed. The world-wide total which Fenner Brockway and Noel-Baker handed over was about ninety million.

12. REPORTING IN OUR BULLETIN

When we had returned from the Special Session, it seemed important to keep everyone informed of its progress which continued till mid-July. So I started a special bulletin which had two editions. I had to record that very little of substance seemed to have come from the session. I noted: 'As usual there were a lot of procedural difficulties: all about the 'balance' of membership of the

Drafting groups, the lobbying for chairpersons. We were into the third week before some things began to move ahead at all. A Soviet delegate (Shustov) said: 'You know how the UN machinery starts to work; slowly, and then in the last week everybody is in a rush, and tries to finish in three days what could be done in three weeks' They did at least establish three working

"But sir — you asked to see our war toys."

groups i. to prepare a Comprehensive Programme of Disarmament. ii. to review the implementation of Special Session I. and iii. to plan the second Disarmament Decade and measures to mobilise public opinion.

The bulletin also said: 'Reagan spent time attacking the USSR for its 'imperialistic adventures' and 'the most massive build-up of military power in history' — without of course referring to his own proposed vast military budget increase. Then the USSR with almost customary ineptitude set off some nuclear tests back home, which caused Secretary Haig to attack verbally again. Gromyko responded by asserting that no agreement had been violated (as if that were the only criterion for prudent action) and said these tests would be continued until Moscow and Washington reached agreement on controlling and reducing nuclear arsenals. He attacked the USA's attempt to block the European pipe-line negotiations and added that the Soviet Union wants to live in peace with the USA, and that "not a hair"of an American head would be touched if an arms agreement can be reached on the basis of equality and equal security.'

Meanwhile others were keeping up the momentum: CND had its festival at Glastonbury; there was a Wales Against the Bomb Conference in Cardiff. A new peace group was formed in Llandudno. Our own Wrexham-based group had an Action Study Day for Non-violent Direct Action organised by Rob Watling and Christopher Spragg; and the regular end-of-month Campaigners Meeting. I recorded that a successful event had been held at the Arts Centre when over 50 people debated the nuclear power issue led by Vernon Hale, speaking against, and a Mr Maxwell, of the Central Electricity Generating Board speaking for. It was noted that the event had 'stimulated people to think more thoroughly about the issue.'

The bulletin also quoted the uplifting words of Pope John-Paul II, who had made his UK visit even as the Falkland/Malvinas war broke out. He said:

What is this peace symbolised by the new cathedral of Coventry? Peace is not just the absence of war. It involves mutual respect and confidence between people and nations. It involves collaboration and binding agreements. Like a cathedral peace has to be constructed patiently and with unshakeable faith.

Today the scale and horror of modern warfare –whether nuclear or not — makes it totally unacceptable as a means of settling differences between nations. War should belong to the tragic past, to history; it should find no place in humanity's agenda for the future.

Let us pray earnestly for the Special Session of the UN on Disarmament. Christians join with others in urging leaders of the world to abandon confrontation, and to turn their backs on policies which require the nations to spend vast sums of money for weapons of mass destruction.

Yet the cathedral of peace is built of many small stones. Each person has to become a stone in that beautiful edifice. All people must deliberately commit themselves to the pursuit of peace. Mistrust and divisions between nations begin in the heart of individuals. Work for peace starts when we listen to the call of Christ, 'Repent and believe in the Gospel'. We must turn from domination to service; we must turn from violence to peace.

The 'Palme Report' named after Olof Palme, who had chaired the Independent Commission on Common Security, had been published a week before the Special Session, but certainly no copy had arrived at the UK Mission to the UN by June 3rd, when we arrived in New York. His whole thesis was that basing security on deterrence leads to disaster. We have to find a way ahead where the adversaries work together to find a basis for Common Security. He followed this general statement up with detailed proposals.

The Non-governmental Organisations had their first major day on June 24th. The International Physicians for the Prevention of Nuclear War re-asserted; 'There is no credible medical response to massive nuclear war. Burn or freeze? Which is it?' Joan Ruddock spoke for CND and was one of those most warmly applauded. She called for a specific declaration that the use of nuclear weapons was a crime against humanity. Dom Helder Camara spoke for International Pax Christi in his usual charismatic style: 'The West must acknowledge the materialistic foundations of capitalism and stop posing as the Defender of Christian civilisation; while the East must acknowledge its own imperialism and the suppression of liberty, especially religious liberty and the rights of workers'. He also called for the abandonment of the scandalously undemocratic right to the veto by the super-powers, and for a new role of the armies of the world. Philip Noel-Baker spoke for the Schweitzer Association.

In a subsequent interview he reminded people of his life-long theme, that the major impediment to progress is

the influence of the militarists and officials of whom there are some in virtually every government, who believe that war is sure to come again and that 'disarmament is bunk'.

These people have to be exposed. We must 'talk about the opponents of disarmament, some of whom have a vested money interest. The arms manufacturers are very influential, particularly with the press ... The masses of non-political citizens are beginning to wake up to the dangers of the arms race. They failed completely to comprehend it before 1914. They understood it better but were defeated by the militarists before 1939. Today they are getting a glimpse of what the militarists are up to, and of what will happen if they get their third world war. In that sense the basis of the peace movement is far broader than it has ever been before.

Professor Frank Barnaby, the former Director of the Stockholm International Peace Institute said, at about this time: 'The peace movement will succeed in persuading political leaders to negotiate nuclear disarmament only if it can maintain considerable political pressure for a significant time. The nuclear arms race will not be stopped, let alone reversed, unless public pressure exceeds the enormous pressure exerted by the military-industrial-academic-bureaucratic complex. This greater pressure has to be maintained long enough to be effective in elections. Many more millions of people must be convinced of the dangers we face.'

13. PERSEVERING PRESSURE

That was still the spirit of most of us, though continual campaigning was tiring. I quoted a calmer voice in the next bulletin. That was E. F. Schumacher in a wider context: 'I certainly never feel discouraged. I can't myself raise the winds that might blow us, or this ship, into a better world. But I can at least put up the sail so that, when the wind comes, I can catch it.'

A rather more urgent plea was being circulated through the local groups from Dan Plesch of Bristol (later to become an influential researcher) who said:

What I have to say is unglamorous and not very palatable. As individuals we must be prepared to push ourselves beyond what we feel able to do .... If we want to stay alive it will take more wit and wisdom than we are at present giving. If we 'cop out' and plead other commitments — be they Labour party, or a social life, then we are conning ourselves and everyone else....Are our problems greater than those of the people of Zimbabwe or Nicaragua or all those other paces we have worn badges for? I think not .... The task: building a permanent force in society — a deterrent to war in the 21st century. In the short term our targets are Cruise and Trident. If we put our energies into it, it should be possible to pile on so much pressure to members of parliament that we can get these decisions reversed. Don't forget; we stopped Hard Rock.

'Hard Rock'. That was the planned government exercise to practice 'civil defence'. There was a growing official line that Civil Defence would make a significant difference to casualty figures. Many people were being led to think this was a humanitarian exercise to protect the public. Our belief was that this was basically false, and liable to lull people into thinking that nuclear war is somehow survivable. When many Councils across Britain decided not to take part, the exercise was postponed, and later cancelled. That was seen as a real CND victory. But we still needed to know what war plans our county authorities were devising. Peter and Hilary Appleton were commissioned to prepare a leaflet on the issue for use at major events in the future.

In our August bulletin I gave an encouraging quotation:

> We believe it is high time for the public at large not only to put peace and disarmament proposals before the decision-making politicians, but to solve their problems with them … It is high time for the politicians to include the enormous creative potential of the general public in the search for disarmament and peace.

Any guesses, I asked, for the origin of that fine assertion? It so exactly accords with the feelings of the non-governmental organisations who were present at the UN Special Session — but it came from the Soviet Group for the Establishment of Trust between the Peoples and Governments of the USSR and the USA. I had then to report that this small group had just been suppressed in spite of its clear intention not to be 'anti-Soviet' but just independent. I little thought, as I encouraged people to write in protest to the Soviet embassy, that I would be meeting some of this group in a couple of years hence.

Our efforts were always even-handed in protest against governments, but as the peace movement was growing there was an increasing witch-hunt. Bruce Kent took up the cudgels for CND at this time offering £100 reward for anyone providing evidence that CND was Soviet funded or manipulated. Meantime we welcomed Communist party members in the peace movement; we wanted to bear witness to the 'mature and broad-based support of many known Communist members'. An additional interest fact was that our Wrexham group had three members who would stand as parliamentary candidates for Labour at the next election — Joe Wilson (who later became an MEP) Jim Colbert and Dennis Carter.

The August bulletin also recorded the following: 'A temporarily homeless young man was given a couch for the night at the Peace Studies Centre, (i.e. my home) He was encouraged to browse among the books and pamphlets. When he had gone the next day, the following verse was lying on the table:

Hiroshima, an event of the past
The grief, the suffering, the strife
It's had no effect on most of us
It hasn't changed our life.
Are we so blind that we can't see,
Or don't we want to know,
That surely one day will be dealt to us
A cruel and crushing blow?
Fire, blindness, sickness, death
Are on their way to us
Unless we rise against it,
Unless we make a fuss.
Help all the groups and centres
Throughout their great campaign
And make sure that Nagasaki
Does not prevail again.
A final word to governments
To put a few things straight
Wake up and realise, you stupid lot
Before it is too late.

In September/October we were encouraging one another to attend *Gwyl Heddwch Meirion*, the Merioneth Festival of Peace, the Clwyd Campaign Committee, the CND AGM at Dolgellau and a March for a Nuclear-free zone in Cheshire. Then there was a major Colwyn Bay Rally, and between them all we could listen to speakers like Oliver Postgate, Bruce Kent, Dafydd Ellis Thomas, and E. P. Thompson. All this apart from our own monthly campaigners' meeting, and a special Press Conference in the Peace Studies Centre. By now we also had two subsidiary groups, Women for Peace, and Christians for Peace with its special focus in the Week of Prayer for World Peace before One World Week.

14. WRITINGS AND BOOKS

At this time Peter and Hilary Appleton had produced a useful leaflet, entitled *Could You Survive a Nuclear Attack?* We needed a bulk order to distribute wherever we went in the campaign. The Peace Studies Centre continued to build up other useful literature in its library. I noted the arrival of a very readable book *The Hundredth Monkey*, which, rather like Catastrophe Theory, showed how the awareness of a truth could reach a certain numerical point among its supporters and then would be a sudden switch as the truth became evident everywhere. We were urged to try to be the 'hundredth monkey' for the peace movement. Two other books came our way. E.P.Thompson's 'Zero Option' where the theme he had explored at Wrexham's Memorial Hall was more fully described. He analysed the Theory of Deterrence saying: '...by maintaining each party in a posture of menace to the other, it fixes indefinitely the tension which makes the resolution of differences improbable. It transfixes diplomacies and ideologies into a twilight state; while postponing war, it postpones also the resolution of peace.'

Then there came the remarkable book by Jonathan Schell 'The Fate of the Earth'. One relevant passage said:'The policy of deterrence does not contemplate doing anything in defence of one's nation; it only promises that if the homeland is annihilated the aggressor's homeland will be annihilated too. In fact the policy goes further than this; it positively requires that each side leave its population open to attack, and make no serious effort to protect it. This requirement follows from the basic logic of deterrence which is that safety is 'the sturdy child of terror'. According to this logic, the safety can only be as great as the terror is, and the terror therefore has to be kept relentless. If it were to be diminished, by, for example, building bomb shelters that protected some significant part of the population — then safety would be diminished too because the protected side might be tempted to launch a holocaust, in the belief that it could 'win' the hostilities. That is why in nuclear strategy 'destruction' must be 'assured', as though our aim were to destroy, and not to save, mankind.'.

The same bulletin referred to a brilliant chapter in Barbara Tuchman's historical study of the 1890-1914 period. Reminding us of the surprising offer of a peace move by the Czar of Russia in 1898, she writes:

Fear of the swelling armaments' industry was widespread. Krupp, the colossus of Essen, was the single largest business in Europe. Skoda, Schneider-Creuset, Vickers-Maxim, the distended combines of many mergers, with harsh names that grated on every year, had interests in every camp, sold their products to customers in every continent, and to both sides in every quarrel, profited from dispute. Each year one or other of them produced a new weapon more efficient in deadliness which, when adopted by the armed forces of one power, immediately required a matching effort by its rival. Each year the cost mounted and the huge piles of weapons grew till it seemed they must burst in final, lethal explosion.

The bulletin remarked: 'We've been this way before'.

15. THE CRUISE MISSILE THREAT

Our mid-October bulletin tried to rally tiring campaigners for confronting the new threat of Cruise Missiles. We suggested:

… a new sense of urgency is building up. 1983 is the likely year of the next General Election. 1983 is the year in which the first Cruise missiles are scheduled to arrive in UK We can't stop the first of these — indeed we can use it to highlight the issue. We can and must stop the second — and sufficient impact at an election could help …. Many people believe that if ground-launched Cruise missiles are sited in UK we will have reached a point of No Return.

Cruise is a new missile system which can be deployed on planes, on ships (including submarines) and on the ground. The ground-launched ones are put on mobile transporters and can be taken anywhere. They are thus more difficult to detect and increasingly difficult to 'verify'. The West talks a lot about the Soviets' unwillingness to allow 'verification' of weapons. The West is now setting about destroying any chances of this here. Cruise missiles are quite small — about 28ft. long; but their lethal power is between 7 and 10 times that of one Hiroshima bomb. They can travel thousands of miles and are supposed to land accurately within a few hundred feet of their targets.(It is reported that 50% will not succeed in their accuracy.) They are intended to centre on military targets — primarily on missile silos in USSR. They fly as pilotless aircraft with computer guidance below radar. They are bound to pose a new threat to the fears of the Soviets….They were never designed as a response to Soviet SS20s, which are equally hideous weapons targeted on Europe. But these all-American Cruise missiles threaten the inner areas of USSR. SS20s cannot reach USA. The Cruise missiles will be deployed in American bases in Britain, run entirely by USA troops, and the decision to fire them is not in the hands of the British.

'The answer is more weapons. What is the question?'

In our determination to take a stand — apart from the moral support we wanted to give to the Greenham Common women - we stressed that while we intended using every democratic method, if we failed thereby we will have to do it by non-violent direct action; and we noted that training courses in this were sprouting up all over the place. Welshpool was due to set up the first for CND Cymru at about this time. We also said: 'The arrival of Cruise incidentally proves that deterrence is not working — that we need more weapons yet (to kill people more times over); and we can be certain the USSR will do something to 'balance' the picture. Maybe total destruction and death is the only real ' balance'.'

New items on our horizons at this time were the growth of twinning schemes not only between UK and US peace groups, which we needed for wider fraternity, but at least one unusual one between Sheffield and Donetsk City Soviet in the Ukraine. October also saw the first Babies Against the Bomb rally in Westminster. And then Jack Sheppard of Pensioners for Peace visiting New Zealand reminded us that 'Since the first atomic tests at Bikini in July 1946 more than 180 nuclear bombs have been detonated in the Pacific. Only now are the long-term horror effects being revealed. We heard of still-born babies turned to bags of jelly in the womb, of babies born unlike anything human. In Hawaii 5 million gallons of liquid nuclear waste has been discharged in home waters. There are more than 3000 nuclear weapons stored ready for use.'

The same bulletin recorded that the nucleus of a good new peace group was forming in Overton, and that Farndon has its own group. We offered them a hearty welcome.

In November, apart from meetings in St Asaph on the medical effects of nuclear war, and the Clwyd Federation meeting in Denbigh I see from the bulletin that I was in debate with Keith Best MP in Llangefni, and encouraging people to attend CND's annual conference in Sheffield, and the special conference in north Wales arranged by the Welsh Centre for International Affairs to examine in detail the Second Special Session on Disarmament, and the 24 hour Vigil in Wrexham centre for the Christmas Peace message to stress the neglect of the homeless and the hungry with the wastage of resources on death and destruction.

16. UNILATERALISM AND THE SOVIETS

As we entered 1983 our local campaigning was looking at every avenue to get more people involved. The bulletin for January listed fourteen different elements of the campaign which could be taken up by individuals. The arguments in the press and elsewhere between 'multi-lateralists'(listed as 'good') and uni-lateralists (bad) were all too frequent. I made an effort in the bulletin to suggest we should not 'demonise' those who disagreed with us; we were apt to be self-righteous. On the other hand we were often mis-represented. I said:

A thousand times over we need to tell people that unilateralism is not the same as pacifism (even if many of us are pacifists); it does not propose instant and total abolition of nuclear warheads (that would be impossible anyway). It does not oppose outright the need for alternative defence postures (even if many want now to look at the effectiveness of non-violent alternatives.) Unilateralism means taking unilateral initiatives, not just talks, to get rid of some weapons. That is the only way to the multi-lateralism we all want. While multi-lateralism has been the avowed policy of every British government, there has not been a single disarmament measure in 35 years. While the USA and USSR have their Strategic Reduction talks, which are planned to last seven years, Britain is not even at the negotiating table; and in the Geneva talks, Britain and the USA continue to block the moves towards a a Comprehensive Test Ban Treaty.

I also felt it was worth publicising the speech of the Soviet President Andropov, which, while including the regular swipes at the USA had some really positive elements. It went like this:

A nuclear war, big or small, whether limited or total, must not be allowed to break out … This is required by the vital interests of all nations. That is why the unilateral commitment of the Soviet Union not to use nuclear weapons first was received with approval and hope all over the world. If our example is followed by the other nuclear powers, this will truly be a momentous contribution to the efforts for preventing nuclear war … Furthermore we are in favour of limiting conventional armaments as well, and of searching for sensible, mutually acceptable solutions to this end. We are also prepared to agree that the sides should renounce first use of conventional as well as nuclear arms … The proposals of the USSR are based on the principle of preserving parity. We are prepared to reduce our strategic arms by more than 25%. The US arms too must be reduced accordingly, so that the two states have the same number of nuclear warheads … And while the negotiations are under way we offer what is suggested by common sense — to freeze the strategic arsenals of the two sides. The US government does not want this and now everyone can understand why: it has embarked on a new considerable build-up of nuclear armaments … No programmes of a further arms build-up will ever force the Soviet Union to make unilateral concessions. We will be compelled to counter the challenge of the American side by deploying corresponding weapons systems of our own — an analogous missile to counter the MX missile which we are now testing to counter the US long-range cruise missile … If the people in Washington really believe that the new weapons systems will be a 'trump' for the Americans, we want them to know that these 'trumps' are false.

We are also prepared to consider pertinent proposals made by others including the recent ones by the US President … Something more is needed: to normalise the situation and to renounce incitement of hostility, hatred and propaganda for nuclear war. And surely the road to confidence, to preventing any and all wars, including an accidental one, is that of stopping the arms race and going back to calm, respectful relations between states; back to detente.

It seemed to me important that we should all know what was being said, however doubtful we might be as to the firm purpose of truthfulness.

It happens that on the very day of that speech (December 21st 1983) I was in the USSR Embassy in London.(MI5 please note if you didn't get a good enough photo) with another priest colleague, Oliver McTernan, registering our deep concern about the harassment of the independent Moscow peace group. The First Secretary hoped we would read Andropov's speech in full. Within a few hours we heard of the rejection of it by Britain and the USA. I remarked in the bulletin that this rejection was unreasonable for several reasons including the untruthfulness — despite Mrs.Thatcher's assertion to the contrary — that without Cruise and Pershing missiles, the Americans had no missiles in Europe capable of striking the USSR. At that time there were 1,272 American warheads (each one more powerful than the Hiroshima bomb) which are on Poseidon submarines assigned to the European station by NATO, and on its F111 and FB111 bombers. Also too much emphasis had been placed on the quantity rather then the quality of nuclear weapons now in existence and planned for the future. Pershing II missiles are seen by the USSR as possible first-strike weapons due to their speed and accuracy. Cruise is too accurate to be a 'deterrent' weapon; it must be seen as part of a nuclear war-fighting arsenal.

About this time an interesting remark of Professor Eric Hobsbawm appeared in the *Guardian*:

> One of the most sinister lessons of the Falklands is the ease with which the Thatcherites captured the patriotic upsurge which initially was in no sense confined to political Conservatives, let alone to Thatcherite ones … It is a sign of very great danger. Jingoism today is particularly strong because it acts as a sort of compensation for the feelings of decline, demoralisation and inferiority which most people in this country now feel, including a lot of workers … Symbolically jingoism helps people feel that Britain isn't just floundering; that it can still do and achieve something; can be taken seriously; can, as they say, be 'Great' Britain.

17. CHRISTIAN ASSESSMENTS

In our February bulletin I noted that I had just returned from five days of meetings and speaking events in Cheltenham and Cardiff, when the Anglican Synod's debate on its 'Church and the Bomb' document was being broadcast, and I had one ear at the radio while typing. Since the vote was 100 in favour of the report and 338 against it was evident that a little less than a quarter of Synod members were in favour of the unilateralism recommended therein. 'Of course, I said, many people will be disappointed at this; but if one reflects on the likely make-up of those attending Synod this figure is not so upsetting at this stage. The alternative amendment, put by the Bishop of Birmingham, which contained a firm declaration in favour of 'No First Use', and of trying to make our deterrence policy a purely 'defensive' one, was passed by 275 against 226. Now one may reasonably enquire what 'defensive deterrence' can possibly mean; but the general tenor of the debate showed that more than half the Synod recognises the dangers we are in, and the need to develop a much more positive approach to the problems of disarmament.'

I then attempted a summary of the report made in Christian Action, because I didn't reckon many would stump up £4.50 for their own copy.

Then I came across, and added a retrospective judgement from Father George Zabelka, who was the American Catholic chaplain to the USAF bomber crews who dropped the bombs on Hiroshima and Nagasaki. 'To fail to speak to the utter moral corruption of the mass destruction of civilians was to fail as a Christian and as a priest. As I see it, Hiroshima and Nagasaki happened in and to a world, and a Christian Church that has asked for it — that has prepared the moral consciousness of humanity to do and justify the unthinkable. I was there, and I'll tell you that the operative moral atmosphere in the Church in relation to mass bombing of enemy civilians was totally indifferent, silent, corrupt at best; at worst it was religiously supportive of these activities by blessing those who did them. I, like the Catholic pilot of the Nagasaki plane, was heir to a Christianity that had for 1700 years engaged in revenge, murder, torture, the pursuit of power and prerogative violence –all in the name of the Lord. Jesus authorised none of his followers to substitute violence for love –not me, or you; not Jimmy Carter nor the Pope, nor the Vatican Council or even an ecumenical Council … Christians the world over should be taught that to love their enemies is not optional.'

Interestingly the new Anglican Bishop of Bangor, John Mears, was a lifelong member of the Anglican Pacifist Fellowship. Indeed I later discovered he had his conscientious objector's Tribunal in Cardiff within a few months of my own. He wrote recently that 'any kind of war is incompatible with the teaching and example of our Lord Jesus Christ' And that coincided with a Lambeth Conference statement of many years earlier. Bishop Mears clearly meant it as a matter of personal conviction.

At this moment I also uncovered a statement made in

the Commons by Winston Churchill in March 1955: 'There is an immense gulf between the atomic and the hydrogen bomb. The atomic bomb with all its horrors, did not carry us outside the scope of human control in manageable events, in thought or action, in peace or war. When the chairman of the US Congressional Committee gave out a year ago their first comprehensive review of the hydrogen bomb, the entire foundation of human affairs was revolutionised and mankind placed in a situation both measureless and laden with doom.'

I'm unsure how the devastation of Hiroshima can be said to be within the scope of human control. and I prefer the placing of the watershed a little earlier, in the words of Einstein:'The splitting of the atom has changed everything save our modes of thinking, and we drift towards unparalleled catastrophe.'

18. EUROPEAN MOVEMENTS

The European peace movements were now linking up more confidently. We were well aware that some of the 'official' East European groups needed to be treated with some scepticism, but we soon discovered real peace allies. The European Nuclear Disarmament group had scholarly leaders and their Conventions — at first in Berlin — were great opportunities for widening contacts. Hungary was showing a great independent spirit as its Peace Group for Dialogue warmly commended those in Italy resisting Cruise missiles. 'Your initiative, they wrote, will increase the belief on our side that the existing schism between East and West is artificial and that European peoples are not interested in it at all. We have to work against the bloc mentality ... The nuclear weapons on your and our side are aimed at peoples who are of the same human community both in East and West. We are not enemies at all. We do not believe in any kind of such ideologies which are based on the inevitability of final and decisive wars between antagonistic blocs.... Unfortunately state restrictions prevent us from visiting and supporting you physically. Perhaps our common work will make an end to all this. Hopefully we shall meet sometime and discuss our common problems with you.'

At this time, imaginative and creative ideas were appearing, as, for instance, when Chris Spragg and Janet Barlow decided to set up a display centre in the Peace Studies Centre for Traidcraft. Their introductory notice said: 'The money required to provide adequate food, water, education, health and housing for everyone in the world has been estimated to be 17 billion dollars a year — a huge sum of money — about as much as the world spends on armaments in a fortnight' (1976 figures) ... In a world of finite resources there cannot fail to be a link between expenditure on armaments and resources allocated to economic and social development … Military outlay involves a huge consumption of resources which not only limits the amount of money available as aid from the developed world, but also severely curtails expenditure on vital 'home grown' development projects. Traidcraft is working in a small way for radical change so that Third World countries can achieve economic growth which will bring dignity and security to all ….'

So we recommended a visit to the Traidcraft Bus which was appearing in Wrexham's Beast Market on 28th February.

That month also saw the inaugural meeting of a London group TACT — Tories against Cruise and Trident — saying they were the voice of over 5 million British people who voted Conservative. They saw Cruise and Trident programmes as immoral, unnecessary, unthinking acts of unilateral re-armament, and were in favour of their unilateral abandonment as a first step towards the unravelling of the nuclear deadlock. I don't recall hearing any more of this interesting political development; but it showed that the peace movement's arguments were getting through here and there.

I ended that bulletin with a couple of American quotations: the first from George Bush (in 1981): 'You have to have weapons capacity which causes more damage to the other side than to yourself — that is precisely the way to come out on top in a nuclear war.'

And then from Admiral Rickover — originator of the US fleet of nuclear submarines:

First of all we should convene an international conference with the aim of banning all nuclear weapons. I know exactly how destructive they are. Why must we have more than everything the Russians have? What does it matter whether we have 100 or 200 nuclear submarines? With those we have already got we can sink several times over anything crossing the ocean. The Russians can do the same. So why add more arms?

Part of an answer would be that the armaments manufacturers need more production; but this aspect is rarely adverted to.

**If we've all finished talking about the Bomb,
who'd like a piece of sponge cake?**

19. CONTROVERSIES

We had all gained a good deal of experience in our campaigning. In March our bulletin mulled over the sort of thing that was being used as a challenge to the CND approach. I had myself been on platforms with a retired admiral, an MP, another Catholic priest and a schoolmaster to debate some of the issues. 'It is so easy to get dis-heartened when discussing the issues with our friends and neighbours ; but at least we have time and chance of putting right the blunders we all make by a second 'go'. After public occasions there have been many times when one wished one's responses had been different. I was beginning to see that it was wiser to follow up the positive elements of our opponents' views. They said, for instance, that our society, for all its faults, is infinitely superior to the tyranny of Soviet communism; it is therefore worth defending. In response it didn't always help to speak only of the ugly aspects of our own society, and to list the support we have shown to right-wing dictatorships, the handing over and expulsion of the peoples of Diego Garcia for a US military base. It was more important to agree that many of our national characteristics were worth defending, but stressing that nuclear deterrence defends nothing. They said that our politicians and government ministers needed support in a difficult and technical job. We should agree but suggest they needed the help of an open and honest society, not the supine acceptance of limited involvement and information. When they asserted that we seemed ready to let evil triumph by refusing to face the reality of threat, we should say we were raising the cry of people for disarmament and peace — real peace, not just the absence of war.

But as the numbers involved in the peace movement increased, so did the opposition. Bruce Kent was quoted as saying, ' That we are becoming an effective political force is evident from all the opinion polls, and indeed from the level of abuse now coming our way. The latest suggestion (and I'm sorry to say it comes from Mrs.Thatcher) is that had CND been around in the 1930s we would have had a thousand years of Hitler's Reich. This is a disgraceful perversion of history. It was precisely the right-wing groups in this country which helped to destroy the League of Nations, which obstructed any hope of an international collective security system and which broke the Disarmament Conference of 1932 — It was they who made Hitler possible. Rudolf Hess, in his extraordinary flight to this country, was not on his way to see the Peace Pledge Union, but to visit, as he imagined, a series of right-wing personalities whom he had good reason to suppose his allies.'

A TV programme revealed that a Mr John Leslie had apparently been appointed to the Ministry of Defence to head a special Unit to attack CND and the peace movement. Bruce wrote to him to complain that Mr Heseltine had declined a reasonable offer to debate with us on the grounds that we had 'closed minds'. He pointed out that Mr Parkinson on TV had lent his weight to anti-communist smears and has insinuated that we, as part of the western peace movement, are Soviet-funded — an allegation for which there is not a scrap of evidence. 'The Young Conservatives have now issued a leaflet in which they tell lies about one of our Council members in an effort to spread the communist smears. One of your fringe organisations, the Coalition for Peace through Security,, which has been praised by the Prime Minister, has even named me as the organiser of an IRA march. We want to know why our government opposes the UN nuclear Freeze proposal, refuses No First Use commitment, and a UN Test Ban proposal. We think that the deployment of Trident would be a breach of our obligations under the Non-Proliferation Treaty and that Polaris, incredible as an 'independent' weapons system, should be abandoned. We reject yet more weapons like Cruise missiles and Pershing II which, because of their extreme accuracy, signal the breakdown of deterrence. Indeed if we could get away from the abuse, we might even sit down together to discuss what a reasonable defence strategy for this country might involve. No-one can win a nuclear war and the present government, with the help of militarists, is making one very much more likely.'

In that same bulletin I reproduced a little item called 'The Responsibility.'

> I am the man who gives the word
> if it should come, to use the bomb
>
> I am the man who spreads the word
> from him to them if it should come
>
> I am the man who gets the word
> from him who spreads the word
>
> I am the man who drops the bomb
> if ordered by the one who's heard
> from him who merely spreads the word
> the first one gives, if it should come
>
> I am the one who loads the bomb
> that he must drop, should orders come
> from him who gets the word passed on
> by one who waits to hear from him
>
> I am the man who makes the bomb
> that he must load for him to drop
> if told by one who gets the word
> from one who passes it from him.

> I am the man who fills the till
> who pays the tax, who foots the bill
> that guarantees the bomb he makes
> for him to load for him to drop
> if orders come from one who gets
> the word passed on to him by one
> who waits to hear it from the man
> who gives the word to use the bomb.
>
> I am the man behind it all
> I am the man responsible.

(This came from the Peace Pledge Union)

By now we heard the idea of Nuclear-Free Zones (NFZs) was spreading. The Irish Republic now had 6 NF counties and 18 cities and towns. The Netherlands had 45 municipalities; Norway had 11 counties and 70 municipalities. In Italy Siena and several Sicilian towns had made a declaration. In the USA there were 4 NFZs. Ashland, Oregon had issued an ordinance which established a fine or gaol sentence for violations of its NF status. Christchurch and Wellington, New Zealand were NFZs — the first was publicising it with notices and festivals. They were campaigning to have the whole of New Zealand and then the Pacific as an NFZ. The Seychelles refused port access to any navy which refused to make a declaration that its vessels did not contain nuclear weapons. UK and US navies would not comply.

Edward Thompson and others reported how high Wales stood in people's estimation because of the eight counties' vote to be NFZs. Our bulletin suggested we bring our Councillors' attention to this.

The bulletin ended with a quotation from Richard Burt, the US Asst Secretary of State for European Affairs:

> If we had not entered into negotiations with the Russians, it would have been impossible to get the allies to deploy missiles on their territory. The anti-nuclear movement in West Europe keeps growing and it could jeopardise NATO's Dec.1979 decision to deploy medium-range missiles. So it was necessary to create the impression among our allies that we are making genuine progress on the limitation of nuclear armaments.' Whoops! I wonder if he should have said that?
>
> I think it was about the same time that another right-wing American, Richard Perle (dubbed The Prince of Darkness by some) said 'Democracies will not sacrifice to protect their security in the absence of a sense of danger' which was rather 'filled out' when John Foster Dulles said: 'In order to make the country bear the burden (of expenditure on armaments) we have to create an emotional atmosphere akin to wartime psychology. We must create the idea of a threat from without.

'H. M. Schools Inspector! Switch to discussing how the national economic cake is divided up.

Part of our function as people of peace was to expose the frightening manipulation of people's minds by such powerful figures. I wrote in the bulletin:

'Ultimately it is a 'mind-set' which we are challenging. People are frightened to change their ways of thinking, and the whole balance-of-power politics which has served the world for centuries with disastrous results. It is up to us to create a new approach; to say what kind of international dealings are possible; to de-militarise our whole way of living; to examine what 'defence' really could mean....What matters about the symbolic and other gestures we make — whether of protest, non-co-operation or intervention — is that they speak with a universal concern, a rooted non-violence and persistent effort to love without limit. Sometimes there is real cause for anxiety when someone (allegedly) barges Mr Heseltine or throws a chair at Winston Churchill; that is the politics of fanaticism. Dancing on roofs is by contrast what I think Helen John calls 'the politics of whimsy'. If opponents do not like such foolishness, we need to ask again and again what is so sensible about deploying Cruise missiles. The Greenham women's action is all about a different way of looking at things; and I don't see why that shouldn't be fun sometimes.'

From time to time we had to remind ourselves and others what nuclear war would mean, using "official" statements from the 50s onwards. The statement made by Lord Mountbatten some time before his murder was too easily overlooked. After a nuclear attack, he said, 'Our works of art will be lost. Radio, television, newspapers will disappear. There will be no means of transport. There will be no hospitals. No help can be expected for the few mutilated survivors in any town to be sent from a neighbouring town — there will be no neighbouring towns left, no neighbours; there will be no help; there will be no hope.'

The Home Secretary, William Whitelaw, had said in 1982 'It is right for information about civil defence and the likely effects of a future war involving the UK to be made generally available in peacetime. The public has a right to knowledge of these matters.' But I felt obliged to remark 'Perhaps it was just one of his 'off' days when he informed us that a set of simple do-it-yourself measures would help us in nuclear protection!

And still they pile up more and more of the weapons; not to use them of course; but to make sure they are not used — if you see what they mean!. Yet Lord Zuckerman (former Adviser to HM Government on nuclear affairs) wrote recently; 'While most Europeans and no doubt many Americans, who know the facts, are convinced that nuclear weapons are so destructive that their very existence deters armed conflict, there exists in the US, but not in Europe, an influential war-fighting school of nuclear enthusiasts.''

Listing the forthcoming events one could see how we continually tried to adapt our ways of working, distinguishing between the monthly meeting for support, encouragement and 'education' with a special welcome for first-timers; and the other monthly meeting for business, planning and campaigning. Apart from our own three Wrexham groups we belonged to the Clwyd Federation linking us with groups in Ruabon, Llangollen, Acrefair & Cefn, Corwen and Maelor to speak of the 'east' of the county alone. Then there was the national CND Cymru organisation which was just working up to a one-day conference to decide whether or not we should be a 'national' body rather than a 'region' of CND UK. I was still the part-time secretary for CND Cymru, due to stand down in December 1983.

20. FALSE MULTI-LATERALISM

Some of the most valuable items of information were slow to reach us, or to our awareness. For instance it was only in April 1983 that we set out the actual record of the UK and USA on multilateralism to which they both pretended to be devoted. Six months after SSD II the following votes were recorded on motions before the UN Assembly:

> That doctrines justifying nuclear war endanger peace.
> 116 Yes, 12 No (including UK)
> A call to nuclear-armed states that they will not use nuclear weapons
> against non-nuclear states 108 Yes. 17 No (including UK)

Call to the Committee on Disarmament to work out in full a nuclear
disarmament programme 118 Yes, 19 No (including UK)

Call for immediate negotiations against Neutron weapons 81 Yes, 14 No
(including UK)

Call for immediate negotiations for a Test Ban Treaty 115 Yes, 5 No
(including UK)

Stressing the importance of Test Ban Treaty 124 Yes, 2 No (UK and USA)

Outer space to be used solely for peaceful purposes 130 Yes, 1 No (USA)

The last one ties up with a statement in 1983 from E.Aldridge, (Under Secretary
of US Air Force): 'We do not have to stretch our imaginations very far to see that
the nation that controls space may control the world.'. Whatever happened to the
statement of President (ex General) Eisenhower: 'War in our time is an
anachronism. Disarmament is a continuing imperative. Every aircraft, every gun,
every warship, is a theft from those who hunger and are not fed.'

21. A NEW STAGE

The May bulletin which continued to
explain the necessary developments in
our structures also announced that it was
the last bulletin I would put together. I
needed a successor. 'It was sensibly
commented recently that the bulletin
may be interesting, but often has very
little about the Wrexham Group … The
items which Owen has provided out of
his work in the Peace Studies Centre are
going to be made into a monthly
COMMENTS AND QUOTES, and
available to people outside the area.'
Indeed this new venture continued till
1988, when I returned to work as a
parish priest

In the meantime we were filling
coaches to spend a day in support of the
Greenham Common protest, and a
weekend at Upper Heyford for Peace
Pentecost. The latter event began with a

7 mile walk; then a special service at the gates of the air-base; and an All-night Vigil for those who could stay till a dawn service. As an important contrasting event we had a Nuclear Free Picnic at the Robson's home in Glyndyfrdwy. 'Fines will be exacted for any reference to missiles or disarmament. Bring along all the friends you have alienated. Lovely hills to walk in, barns to shelter in; lambs to play with!' We realised it was important to have fun, and not take ourselves too seriously nor too pompously all the time. Here's a paragraph from my first Comments and Quotes (C&Q from now on).

'None of us can 'know it all'. In the peace movements we have more questions than answers. We do not pretend there is any single solution to the multiplicity of problems. We do not think there is any risk-free way of getting real disarmament. We do not think that nuclear weapons can be dis-invented. But we do not and will not simply accept the present situation of aggressive deterrence policies, and increasing armaments. When we discover some of the disturbing facts that lie behind the arms race and the non-negotiations, we have a right and a duty to let the public know. We soon discover that our over-worked members of parliament simply haven't time to know all the facts themselves. We must tell them. That means we must find out first. There is no alternative for some of us to be reading and researching — not everyone's cup of tea perhaps. In some measure C&Q is an attempt to get some of the facts more widely known.'

Reading Ronald Aronson's 'Technological Madness' there is a detailed account of the Cuban crisis, and what Kennedy apparently confided to his brother Robert at the time:

> War is rarely intentional. The Russians don't wish to fight any more than we do....Yet if events continue as they have in the last several days, that struggle –which no-one wishes and which will accomplish nothing — will engulf and destroy all mankind.'...'.The thought that disturbed him most was the spectre of the death of the children of this country and all the world....Kruschev too has spoken of the 'madness' of initiating nuclear war.' Then Aronson added : 'All of Kennedy's concern for the world's children cannot veil the fact that he was indeed threatening them with death if Kruschev did not capitulate.And all of Kruschev's pained awareness cannot veil the fact that he ordered the missiles to Cuba in the first place.

Earlier in 1983 Peter Hebblethwaite wrote in the *Tablet* that on 22nd October 1962 with the US ships on blockade duty, Kennedy thought that the Vatican might be able to help. Some Russians and Americans were in conference in Massachusetts — scholars and writers, and among them Father Morlion, who ran an anti-communist institute in Rome. The Russians were about to leave in a hurry because of the crisis but on consultation, since they knew Kruschev personally, thought a Vatican intervention was worth trying. They helped Fr.Morlion draft a coded message to Kruschev: 'We really believe you are a friend of peace and that you would not want the death of millions.' Pope John XXIII agreed to send his own message. He had no power but this very fact meant that both sides would be let off the hook by his intervention, and could accept without loss of face. But he would have to give Kruschev a signal that the Vatican had modified its rigid anti-communist stance. He inserted a loosely connected sentence into his next day's speech to a public audience: Hebblethwaite continues: 'The Pope always speaks well of those statesmen on whatever side who strive to come together to avoid war and bring peace to the world.' It was banal but it was what Kruschev was waiting for. It was broadcast at noon. On 26th October the papal message was on the front of Pravda under the heading 'We beg all rulers not to be deaf to the cry of humanity.' On 28th October Kennedy thanked the Pope for his intervention … Without exaggerating the importance of the papal initiative, it seems it played some part in resolving the conflict.

Soon afterwards good Pope John published his '*Pacem in Terris*' encyclical in which he declared: 'It no longer makes sense to maintain that war is a fit instrument with which to repair the violation of justice.'

In 1983 Pope, John-Paul II seemed to support the idea that the policy of deterrence could be tolerated so long as it is part of a strategy towards negotiation and disarmament. Many of us were totally unconvinced of this. Andrew White wrote (in The Terror of Balance): '… deterrence is an offensive, not defensive, strategy. Deterrence, by credibly preparing to fight and win nuclear war is bound by its intrinsic impact, to provoke the other side. Thus, as the US and USSR exchange threat and counter-threat, neither side is being deterred by the nuclear weapons of the other; each is being intimidated. Neither is being guided towards restraint; each is being prompted towards ever more grotesque counter-measures to counteract the dangers it perceives are confronting it … The underlying paradox of the arms race is that, with every new weapons system that one side deploys, it ends up multiplying rather than alleviating its own insecurity. The nuclear arms race has evolved into a self-generating process of escalating fear, response and counter-response, which has an internal upward dynamic and no ascertainable point of termination short of nuclear war or effective disarmament.'

When the UN Secretary General made his Report on Nuclear Weapons in 1980 he said: 'The concept of the maintenance of world peace, stability and balance through the process of deterrence is perhaps the most dangerous collective fallacy that exists today.'

New on the peace movement scene was END — European Nuclear Disarmament — which was not a 'membership' organisation, but, led largely by the Bertrand Russell Peace Foundation in UK, had already held a European Convention in Brussels in 1982, and was now planning another in Berlin. Here arose all the tricky aspects of the Soviet Peace Committee who claimed the event would dis-unite the anti-war movements. The idea was to gather together the non-aligned peace movements, and — perhaps through slightly insensitive wording in preparation — Mr Zhukov (President of the Soviet Peace Committee) reckoned the various east european committees, which had to have the sanction of their respective governments, would not be welcome at all, even as 'participating observers.' But the original END Appeal had simply said that international healing, and concern for peace cannot be done by the directive of governments, which harbour for historical reasons deep suspicions of each other, but only in the first place by direct citizens' exchanges. 'We must commence to act as if a united, neutral and pacific Europe already exists. We must learn to be loyal, not to 'East' or 'West' but to each other.' A direct effort was made with the Soviet Peace Committee to influence the relevant government authorities to permit unofficial groups of Soviet citizens to attend : 'We say to you in all sincerity: if the freedom of action of such groups is permitted, then we shall not respect the Soviet Peace Committee less — we shall respect you more.' The effort did not succeed; and the Soviet Peace Committee representatives and the Hungarian Independent group and others did not arrive.

I attended as an individual for Pax Christi, and found church groups, such as the Berlin Evangelical Church, had members there. It wasn't confined to Europeans; there were Japanese participants and several distinguished US activists, like Randall Forsberg (who helped found the USA Freeze Movement). I also bumped into a Soviet journalist who had come specially; and I had reason to know that he was phoning the Soviet Peace Committee in Moscow — so they were not altogether out of touch. This was my first encounter with ex-military men; two Generals to start with, Christian Krause and Gert Bastian (who helped to lead the Green Party in due course).

Our journey to Berlin from UK was by coach. I noted that we were a fine mixture: 8 teachers or lecturers, 8 students, 2 miners, 2 booksellers, a mother and a housewife, a fireman, 2 solicitors, a laser-operator, a local government officer, a secretary, a clergyman, a heavy-goods driver, a Probation officer, a shop-keeper, a hair-dresser, 2 publishers and a social worker. We were given free hospitality and warm welcomes with families. The hand-to-hand link up between the Polish Mission and the Portuguese Embassy (to mirror the END slogan 'No nuclear weapons from Poland to Portugal') didn't quite succeed, perhaps because many rushed off to their homes when the formalities were over. But we all had a good laugh and some valued exercise. I recall that I managed to see Aida at the Opera House; very cheap too!

The *Times* of 28th March had quoted Max Beloff with a new attack on CND: 'What strengthens my conservatism is that for me a CND badge and a swastika are essentially interchangeable.' Ah well, we remarked, it makes a change from the hammer and sickle image.

22. US BISHOPS JOIN THE DISCUSSION

As more and more people seemed to be taking up elements of the anti-nuclear campaign, they were looking for a clearer statement of Christian teaching. The summer of 1983 saw the publication of the American Catholic bishops Pastoral Letter — a long document of 30/40 pages. What was special about it was the consultative process which had preceded it. It did not confine itself to generalisations, or absolute principles, but made precise comments on some of the key issues of our time: I hastened to give some extracts straight away. Here are some of them.

> Traditionally the Church's moral teaching sought first to prevent war, and then to limit its consequences if it occurred. Today the possibilities for placing political and moral limits on nuclear war are so infinitesimal that the moral task, like the medical, is prevention ....We are sure of one moral imperative we should declare — a rejection of nuclear war ....
>
> There should be a clear public resistance to the rhetoric and strategies of ' winnable nuclear wars', 'surviving nuclear exchanges' and strategies of 'protracted nuclear war'. We seek to encourage a public attitude which sets stringent limits on the kind of actions our government will take on nuclear policy in our name.
>
> A justifiable use of force must be both discriminatory and proportionate. Certain aspects of both US and Soviet strategies fail both test.
>
> We do not perceive any situation in which the deliberate initiation of nuclear warfare, on however restricted a scale, can be morally justified ...the danger of escalation is so great that it is an unacceptable moral risk to initiate nuclear war in any form. The danger is rooted not only in the technology of our weapons' systems, but in the weakness and sinfulness of human communities.

The bishops repeated (perhaps they felt obliged) to repeat the papal statement to the UN. I deplored this. That had stated: 'In current conditions 'deterrence' based on balance, certainly not as an end in itself, but as a step towards progressive disarmament, may still be judged morally acceptable. Nonetheless in order to ensure peace, it is indispensable not to be satisfied with this minimum which is always susceptible to the real danger of explosion.' But at least they added: 'The Pope's words 'morally acceptable' are strictly conditioned ... They were designed to limit the acceptable function of deterrence precisely to the one positive value it is said to have had — preventing the use of nuclear weapons in any form'. Note that 'it is said to have had'; I think their disagreement lay behind that. Anyway 238 of the bishops voted for the document; nine voted against. Archbishop Hannan fought a rear-guard action throughout the 400 amendments to the Third Draft. We sensed other positive voices — surely including Bishop Gumbleton of Pax Christi –

Then the document said: 'We acknowledge that there are strong voices within our own episcopal ranks, and within the wider Catholic community in the US, which challenge the strategy of deterrence as an adequate response to the arms race today. They highlight the historical evidence that deterrence has not in fact set in motion the process of disarmament. On the contrary, under its impulse there has been almost unlimited acceleration in building arms. Moreover these voices rightly raise the concern that even the nuanced conditional acceptance of deterrence laid out in a letter such as this, might be inappropriately used by some to re-inforce the policy of arms build-up. In its stead they call us to raise a prophetic challenge to the community of faith..... a challenge which goes beyond deterrence even in its conditional form, towards more resolute steps to actual bilateral disarmament and peacemaking.'

Then to confront that difficult word 'unilateral' they said, 'While we do not advocate a policy of unilateral disarmament, we believe the urgent need for control of the arms race requires a willingness for each side to take some first steps...Certain risks are required today to help free the world from bondage to nuclear deterrence and the risk of nuclear war.' And that is largely what most of us meant by 'unilateral disarmament'! Then they added: 'Article VI of the Non-Proliferation Treaty pledged the super-powers to serious efforts of control; unfortunately this promise has not been kept. Moreover the multi-national controls envisaged by the Treaty seem to have been gradually relaxed by the states exporting fissionable materials for the production of energy … US arms sales' policies have in the last decade become more expansive. Precisely the opposite course is needed.' (As I write this twenty years on, there is no change. Indeed the US has been pulling out of several international treaties).

There were other voices on the international scene; especially a document called Ten Questions answered vigorously, challenging the continuing arms trade, 'which has an over-riding self-interest in the manufacture and the sale of arms and which possesses the financial resources to influence and manipulate policy-making — an institution more commonly known as the 'military-industrial complex. There are the scientists and physicists involved in military research who see weapons development … as an unlimited field of exploration for man to conquer. There are the militarists who believe in the time-honoured dictum that ' if you want peace, prepare for war', and whose rationale is that when war comes they must have the most up-to-date weapons necessary to defeat the enemy. Not least there are those politicians whose decision to promote the arms race stems from the obsession that it is the only way by which the threat of war can be avoided, an obsession which in recent years has become a paranoia. Add to all this is the cost, the crippling cost, for research and development, and this creates instability in the Third World. The result is the profusion of 'small wars' around the globe from which the only ones to benefit are the arms manufacturers and traders.'

This sturdy publication was written by 13 former NATO military and naval officers. It was some of these strong-minded men I was privileged to meet in the next few years.

I was delighted to quote from the various publications which were now arriving at the Peace Studies Centre when there were snippets to encourage or amuse. A Pensioners for Peace Newsletter quoted a child at Greenham: 'Unilateral disarmament is like deciding to tell the truth and not to steal all on your own just because it is right, and not waiting to see if everyone else does.' The Peace Education Newsletter reminded us how war-like some Christian hymns are. For instance, Onward Christian soldiers, Marching as to war … goes on

> Christ the royal master leads against the foe.
> Forward into battle see his banners go …

(And later)

> Like a mighty army moves the Church of God

My comment was: You can't rewrite history. Religious wars are a fact; and some of the bloodiest ever. Indeed torture of opponents, burning their books, imprisoning them for disbelief etc. was not invented by communists or other dictators. It's all part of Church history. One little effort to turn the tide of hymn words goes as follows:

> Onward Christian pilgrims
> Working hard for peace
> Day by day we're praying
> That all wars will cease.
> Christ our royal master
> Bids us love our foes
> Pray for those who harm us
> And violence oppose.

Well, it was worth a try!

The July issue of C&Q gave some more information about the growth of NVDA — Non-violent Direct Action, including the books of Gene Sharp, who uses the phrase 'civilian based defence', and others, like the evangelicals Ronald Sider and Richard Taylor. Many 'peace people' were putting themselves on the line for arrest at military bases. One woman reported in the Chester Women for Peace newsletter who was arrested one evening, and again the next morning. The arresting policeman greeted her like an old friend. He stopped her in the corridor saying: 'Two arrests are a small sacrifice to make for what you stand for. Think of the people in history who have done just that and more. You'll be strong enough to carry on'. The charging officer said: 'You people really <u>care</u> what goes on at the base, don't you?'

23. THE STORY OF 'THE BOMB'

In the August issue I gave long extracts from Peter Ustinov's new book *My Russia* which demonstrated to me an extra-ordinary balanced judgement. Then I turned to a really significant book by Robert Jungk *Brighter than a Thousand Suns* which contained the personal history of the atomic scientists 'a tragic story of a group of men with quite exceptional intellectual gifts, idealistic and single-minded in youth, but gradually seduced by a mixture of good motives and bad to the service of the devil'. The whole cycle of their work began because of the fear that the Germans would be working to produce an atomic weapon. What was later discovered was precisely the opposite. The evidence shows that the German physicists 'were able successfully to divert the minds of the Nazi Service Departments from the idea of so inhumane a weapon' They worked together to obscure and delay any suggestion of such work. They were in a strange position. Many of them., so deeply shocked by the terror and cynicism with which the Nazis had started the war '... while on the one hand they could not bring themselves to desire a German victory, on the other hand they could wish as little for a German defeat with all its frightful consequences. It seems paradoxical that the German nuclear physicists, living under a sabre-rattling dictatorship, obeyed the voice of conscience and attempted to prevent the construction of atom bombs, while their professional colleagues in the democracies, who had no coercion to fear, with very few exceptions concentrated their whole energies on production of the new weapon.'

In the 'Manhattan Project' barely a dozen of the total of some 150,000 persons eventually employed were allowed an over-all view of the plan as a whole. In fact only a very small number of staff knew that they were working on the production of an atom bomb at all.' The European war ended, and Einstein and Szilard wrote memoranda to President Roosevelt against any <u>use</u> of the new bomb. 'Any momentary military advantage the bomb might bring to the USA would be offset by grave political and strategic disadvantages'. But no warning ever came to the President's notice. They were still unopened on his desk, untouched, when suddenly he died. A later band of scientists worked hard to stop any use of the bomb. They insisted that there should be control established on a basis of mutual trust. This, they said, 'would be destroyed at the start if the US were to make a surprise attack on Japan … The military advantages and the saving of American lives … may be outweighed by the ensuing loss of confidence, and by a wave of horror and revulsion sweeping over the rest of the world, and perhaps even dividing public opinion at home.' How right they were!

After the experimental explosion at Almagordo 'many of us signed a petition urging that the atomic bomb should not be used against Japan without prior demonstration and an opportunity to surrender.' Jungk's book documents the evidence of the overtures Japan had already made for peace before August 6th. There were real chances of peace just as there were signs that the USSR might be drawn into helping in the conflict. 'But probably the main reason why the US government remained blind to the possibility of such measures was the knowledge that it possessed the atomic bomb. Instead of patiently undoing the knot, it appeared more convenient to cut it with a slash or two of the shining new weapon. General Groves (the military man in charge of the whole project) said: 'Truman did not so much say Yes as not say No. It would have taken a lot of nerve to say No at that time'. The scientists 'felt themselves caught in a vast machinery and they were inadequately informed as to the true political and strategic situation. If at that time they had had the moral strength to protest on purely humane grounds…their attitude would no doubt have deeply impressed the President, the Cabinet and the generals. Once more the 'atomic scientists' only 'did their duty'.'

Jungk also outlined the attitude of the USSR scientist Kapitza, who had worked for years in Cambridge. He made a speech encouraging scientists to resist the development of more atomic weapons for war. He was removed from his post and placed under house arrest. Other Russian nuclear experts were deported or sentenced to compulsory labour for refusing to work on atomic bombs.' It was my great pride to meet Kapitza's son, heading a Scientific Institute in Moscow, when I visited in 1985.

I did what I could to pepper C&Q with quotations from various voices. It was worth quoting a US atomic scientist, H. S. Bethe speaking out:

I believe we would lose far more than our lives in a war fought with hydrogen bombs; that we would in fact lose all our liberties and human values at the same time, and so thoroughly that we would not recover them for an unforeseeably long time. We believe in peace based on

"These are Offensive rocks, and these are Defensive rocks."

mutual trust. Shall we achieve it by hydrogen bombs? Shall we convince the Russians of the value of the individual by killing millions of them? If we fight a war and win with H bombs, what history will remember is not the ideals we were fighting for, but the method we used to accomplish them. These methods will be compared to the warfare of Genghis Khan who ruthlessly killed every last inhabitant of Persia.

Olof Palme, the Swedish Prime Minister, said: 'I have met several scientific advisers, former aides of presidents and prime ministers, who have stated publicly that they had said to their leaders that the arms race is senseless, that we only get more insecurity by searching for security through more arms. But they were not listened to.'

Dr Frank Blackaby (President of the Swedish International Peace Research Institute said: 'Nuclear weapons today represent the production of one Hiroshima bomb every 20 minutes since 1945. So nuclear balance or parity of security is not possible; and it is a demand not of the military (who know) but of the politicians. The claim that uncertainty improves deterrence is false. Uncertainty fuels the arms race.'

In these Cold War days of the 80s, it was interesting to read General Sir John Glub saying:'I would beg the British government to open talks with the USA and all NATO powers to persuade them to approach the Soviet Union with one simple statement, namely that nuclear war would result in the mutual extermination of the human race. Let us then agree to abandon all nuclear weapons. If such an agreement could be reached, it might slowly reduce mistrust and fear, resulting in the gradual growth of confidence and the slow relaxation of propaganda and subversion.' And even more starkly a retired US Navy Admiral, Noel Gayler said: 'The time has come for the two super-powers to recognise that the USA is not the enemy: the Soviet Union is not the enemy. Nuclear weapons are the enemy of both nations and of all mankind.'

24. PERSONAL INVOLVEMENT & JOURNEYS

The October C&Q began with a little personal note. 'Those who receive this broadsheet will have noticed the gap in September. The work of putting it together was crowded out by my having to travel abroad twice for CND's International Committee of which I am the current chairperson. I had to go to Bonn for the Krefeld Petition Forum, and then to Brussels to represent CND and END on the Liaison Committee of the West European Peace movements preparing for a major convention in Italy.' 'I have now ceased to be Secretary for CND Cymru. With its re-organisation I am now redundant, but anyway have too much to do elsewhere, developing the Peace Studies Centre and other activities of Wrexham Concern Trust of which it is now a part. My work as Disarmament Co-ordinator for Pax Christi UK continues also. The only trouble is that I don't have any visible means of support financially; but, Micawber like, I rather trust that 'something will turn up'. I've too much to do to go and get a job, if you know what I mean.'

The meeting in Bonn — actually just outside in Bad Godesburg — was for the Krefeld Appeal. This was a coalition of disarmament groups and others who had circulated a petition since 1980 against the deployment of Cruise and Pershing. There were now 5 million signatures on it; they reckoned 75%of Germans were against these new weapons. Yet the government took no serious account of the public's views. (Nothing new here, we might say.) The Forum was a long day, with 26 speeches from the platform. I was No.18 for CND's International Committee, and I delivered it in my best German, having found a Cardiffian to translate the text for me. Among the other speakers were ex-General Gert Bastian, and Petra Kelly, founders of the Green Party. (She gave me a warm welcome because in June this year I had 'hosted' her in Cardiff when she came to speak to a rally there. I met her at the airport, and escorted her to the BBC studio for a group appearance. Lord Chalfont was in the group and made a verbal attack on her as a most dangerous woman on the political scene. This really upset her, and I was glad to be around to let her get it off her mind before our rally).

Two of the other speakers were American Nobel Prize winners, and it was extraordinary to hear one of them referring, as an American, to his perception that it wasn't 'the government' that really controlled politics in USA, but the banks. The other was Professor Linus Pauling — Nobel laureate in 1954 for chemistry and for Peace in 1962. I travelled with him in a car from our hotel to the meeting, driven by a German lecturer. At one stage of the journey she overshot the right turn we should have made; after making a U-turn as soon as she could we re-traced the road, till she said, 'Oh dear: I've over shot it slightly again.' Professor Pauling grinned and said 'We seem to be getting there by successive approximations'.(I was happy to tell this story to Pauling's family at the opening of a special Pauling exhibition at the Palais des Nations in Geneva in 2003)

An impressive Congressman, Ron Dellums, declared the hypocrisy of the arms 'modernisation' programme as another name for a new wave of the arms race. Randall Forsberg also spoke; and a Professor from the Vatican Scientists' Association, and a retired Greek General Koumanakos. Ten days later General Koumanakos and I were together again, this time in Brussels, for a wider representation of West European Disarmament movements, laying plans for a 1994 Convention in Italy. The general, who had commanded the Greek troops in the UN force in Korea spoke of his move from fighting wars to working for peace. 'War is no longer for generals to plan, but for people to prevent', he said. Aaron Tovish, another American who had worked in Oxford, and was now with the

Swedish Arbitration organisation, had some interesting things to say about Third Party Intervention, to draw the non-aligned nations into their rightful place to influence disarmament. The way we allow the super-powers alone to be negotiating (or playing at negotiating) in Geneva really was an outrage, he reckoned, when others have signed the Helsinki Accord, and had their lives constantly at risk from the weapons of the nuclear states.

My contact with Pax Christi International was growing of course, as I made these European and other journeys for CND. My irregular visits to the London Pax Christi office as Disarmament Co-ordinator continued, and led eventually to my applying for the job of National Secretary, to follow in the footsteps of that wonderful worker, Valerie Flessati. Meantime it was good to record that our international President, Bishop Bettazzi of Ivrea, collected the UNESCO Prize for Pax Christi's Peace Education work.

In an effort to develop people's understanding I outlined in C&Q the contents of some more admirable books on Russia and the Soviet Union; particularly Hendryk Smith's *The Russians*, and Laurens van der Post's *Journey into Russia*. He said:

> The characters revealed to us in newspapers and books, or smeared on to the crowded international canvas tend to be more and more over-simplified and over-drawn until the responses of the individual suddenly acquire the dimensions of caricature. Even more than these cartoon inaccuracies, what alarmed me on my travels were the factors of impersonalisation and dehumanisation in the pictures countries painted for themselves of other nations, and years ago I cast around for correctives. I found the only effective one was holding on firmly in my imagination to such personal relationships as I had been able to form in foreign countries This scaling down of monstrous over-simplifications to their fallible, questing, human constituent proportions came to appear to me as one of the most urgent tasks for our day. I could understand possibly that a nation might be tempted to bomb a country which is regarded as filled with dire monsters. But I firmly believed the temptation could be resisted the moment it saw the potential enemy as people like itself, struggling each day to get to its office desk, factory bench or plough …

25. USA. ENCOUNTERS

October 1983 saw me off on another delegation of CND's International Committee, with Mavis Middleton of Cambridge and Dan Plesch of Bristol, to Washington. It seemed that the Congress had one more resolution to face about the possible delay in the deployment of the new weapons, so we were off to lobby some of the Congressmen. The three of us had varied programmes. I clocked up 27 events in 9 days, guided throughout by Izzy Guy, a British campaigner, now living in Connecticut. There was one event round the launching of the fifth Trident submarine at Rhode Island, where General Dynamics had an enormous factory, turning out these submarines in a grim series. Some 400/500 demonstrators had a religious service at the gates, and then an impressive 'die-in', with several priests and nuns taking part.

"S::. we find there's no way of cutting the military budget without cutting the military budget."

In Washington we lobbied the Defense Advisers of a number of Congress representatives. The Defense Aide of Claudine Schneider told us that she voted in favour of the Freeze of nuclear weapons, though she is a Republican; but because Trident is made in her constituency, she has to keep quiet. In another Connecticut town I was invited to act as a substitute proposer of a motion against Cruise and Pershing at the 600-strong Assembly of the United Church of Christ. This was one of many Christian manifestations of support for real disarmament.

The most impressive encounter we had was at the Center for Defense Information where many distinguished military (retired) officers are Directors. We had time with Captain James Bush and Arthur Kline and determined to latch onto their publication Defense Monitor for the future. One issue said this: 'Under present plans the Reagan administration will spend 450 billion dollars in the next 6 years preparing for nuclear war. This is approximately 22% of all military spending and considerably higher than the 10-1% usually cited by officials.' 'In the next decade the US will build about 17,000 new nuclear weapons.' 'Spending on nuclear weapons has more than doubled since Reagan became President' 'If it is the national policy of the US to fight and win a nuclear war, the Reagan military budget is appropriate.'

I commented: 'We wish that hesitant church leaders would take note of what is actually being prepared, to moderate their dangerous defence of deterrence as a 'temporary expedient' '

We were given about fifteen pages of this type of quotation. Like it or not, they proved that the USA was preparing to fight nuclear war, first of all in Europe, and then somehow in survivable vehicles, probably at sea, till they 'win'. The scientists have re-affirmed for us that the use of only 10% of existing arsenals of nuclear weapons will destroy all life on earth. They do not <u>want</u> to fight such a war, but they are making sure that they have the weapons to do so. My indignation was rising, and I commented: 'So are we expected to respect our leaders? Do they really think that humankind will allow such policies of terror and madness to continue unchallenged? How dare we <u>not</u> talk of direct civil disobedience to this blasphemy against God's creation?' ' Be sure of one thing. We shall owe more to the American Peace Movements in changing the minds of people and the policies of government than to anyone else.'

The latest Defense Monitor commented: 'Most of the nuclear war preparations contribute nothing to the defense of the US and are wasteful and dangerous ... The Reagan nuclear build-up will precipitate a corresponding Soviet build-up, leaving both nations less secure. A halt in the production of new nuclear weapons by both US and the Soviet Union is urgently required. It is time to begin negotiations on a US/Soviet nuclear standstill.'

The trouble is that when the US conducted Arms Control negotiations, it always managed to exclude the latest and most devastating weapons from the talks.

It is worth noting that already the development of space weapons was on line. Lt General R. Henry said: 'Space is the new high ground of battle'. Edward Aldridge, Under-Sec.of Air Force said: 'We do not have to stretch our imagination very far to see that the nation that controls space may control the world.'. General Marsh said: 'We should move into war-fighting capabilities — that is ground-to-space, space-to-space, space-to-ground' And in the US Defense Guidance for 1984–8 it said the US 'must ensure that treaties and agreements do not foreclose on opportunities to develop these (military space) capabilities.'

In a book entitled *The Deadly Connection:Nuclear War and US Intervention* Randall Forsberg concluded that the only place the new generation of nuclear weapons actually played an active role in international politics is in backing up intervention by the US and deterring intervention by the Soviet Union. I then recalled a vivid lecture given to about 35 of us by Noam Chomsky in New York in 1982. In this same book he expands his theme:

'... a prime concern for those who want to do something to avert nuclear war must be to try to reduce the tensions and conflicts that will serve, sooner or later, as the trigger for such a war'. Cold War propaganda system 'typically seeks to disguise issues of intervention in terms of great power conflict. But it is not at all unlikely that super-powers will come into conflict, even nuclear conflict, when some third world conflagration blazes out of control.'

I am glad that twenty-one years later Chomsky is still telling us the truth about US foreign policy. Now that the Middle East is again the focus of crisis, it is worth quoting Chomsky's words again: 'It is quite clear that US payments to Israel through a variety of means have reflected Israel's perceived role as a 'strategic asset' ensuring American dominance in the region. With this aim, the US has moulded Israel into the world's fourth largest military power, doing what it could to further the transformation of Israel into a militarised state, completely dependent on the US for survival and serving the interests of American power; primarily the perceived need to control or destroy radical nationalist forces. In conformity to these ends, the US has consistently blocked all efforts to solve the Arab-Israeli conflict by peaceful means in a manner that recognises the rights of Israelis and Palestinians. It has virtually been an axiom of US foreign policy since World War II that the stupendous energy reserves of the Middle East must remain under effective American control, or at least that other powers gain no privileged access to them.'

Another admirable American is Jim Garrison, and we had him as a speaker several times in various places. Together with his book 'The Russian Threat' he had as balanced a judgement on the Soviet Union as was possible. 'What needs to be kept clear', he said 'about the oppresiveness of the Soviet system, is that many human rights' violations in the USSR are not so much because of 'communism' as because of the heritage of Russian history.... What is indictable about the human rights situation in the USSR is not that the Soviets have deprived people of rights they once had, but that the Soviets have never developed the notions of the individual freedom of free speech, free religion, free press, free travel or free political expression into a meaningful part of Soviet life.'

At this time I found myself clashing with Cardinal Hume's standpoint when he said, 'There is a tension between the moral imperative not to use such inhuman weapons and a policy of nuclear deterrence with its declared willingness to use them if attacked. To condemn all use and yet to accept deterrence places us in a seemingly contradictory position.' In Comments & Quotes I continued: 'The Cardinal's ' way out' of the contradiction (which to me is real, not seeming) is to support John-Paul's words about the temporary expedient of nuclear deterrence; but there are conditions. It is conditional upon (a) solely if it constitutes a stage on the way to disarmament; (b) it implies steps to reduce nuclear weapons; (c). and to limit their deployment; (d) it must be to prevent war, not to wage it and e) the spiral of armaments must be stopped and expenditure reduced.' The Cardinal said: 'People everywhere have a right to know in what ways their governments are pursuing policies which will lead to disarmament. Without such policies, deterrence has to be condemned.'

I responded: 'My re-action is to say: 'I can overlook for the moment my horror at the apparent moral acceptance of temporary deterrence policies; but we are bound to converge in our conclusions. None of the conditions which you demand, Dom Basil, are present. Therefore deterrence has to be condemned.'

Then we had a wonderful visit from Sr Joan Chittister, the Benedictine sister from USA. She was due to meet the Cardinal on her tour. I expressed the hope she would fill in the picture for him. In her talk she outlined the psychology of authoritarianism which makes church-goers in particular so passive before the policies of authoritarian governments. She demonstrated the state of moral immaturity in which many of us live, obeying our 'betters' without question; and she called on us to cry aloud against the blasphemy of first-strike policies linked to the new Cruise and Pershing weapons.

It is a happy memory that amidst all our serious efforts for peace we had time to laugh; indeed, there is no better way to build community than to work for some ideal, and enjoy one another's company in doing so. That meant some singing from time to time; and there were those who could find us some new words to old tunes. In the WND newsletter at the end of 1983 we printed some thing that had come from 'Starmaker', whoever that was. To be sung to the tune of Clementine, there was this refrain, and about eight verses, referring to politicians like John Nott.

Maggie's darling, Maggie's darling
Maggie's blue-eyed Heseltine.
Nott is lost and gone forever,
Now we're stuck with Heseltine.

From the Min'stry of th'environment
Came the golden Heseltine
To defend us; how horrendous!
He's just shooting us a line

Not for long though, not for long though
Not for long though Heseltine
Now we've met you we'll upset you
So be careful Heseltine

Threats don't scare us. We're gregarious
And we get along just fine
You can't break us, so forsake us
You'll get nowhere Heseltine

And those missiles that you've guiding
To the Common my dear friend
Must refuse them, never use them
Or the world will truly end

In December just remember
We'll be there dear Heseltine
We'll be lying 'Stead of dying
Straight and steady in a line

Come the New Year there'll be less fear
Peace will come we hope in time
And the Good News,there'll be no Cruise
Dreadful sorry Heseltine

The final chorus ended:
Nott is lost and gone for ever
Soon we hope will Heseltine

With such songs as these many of us went by special train to Cardiff to demonstrate at the Royal Ordnance Factory in Llanishen; and then we all marched into the centre of the city for a rally outside the Law courts.

We needed to laugh because we felt the official version of the 'need' for Cruise missiles etc. was obscene. It was difficult to believe the official propaganda. At the end of 1983 David Summerhayes, (the former UN Ambassador again,) came to Kelsterton College to address about 60 of us. The rough outline of his message was a.that a diplomat alone knows how complex the whole business is. b. that the situation is nowhere near danger-point, nor as black as people paint it. And c. let us carry on and we'll have some disarmament in the next few years.

We all found this bland and patronising, and even the chairman, Professor Glyn Phillips, interposed with a challenging remark about Britain and Arms Trade. We felt that Summerhayes left somewhat discomforted.

26. HISTORIC ATTEMPTS AT DISARMAMENT

It was important to clarify the moral and religious principles concerning deterrence, war and the alternatives of non-violence, and the major part of the issues of Comments & Quotes for January–April 1984 was concerned with these. I did what I could to introduce extracts from the speeches and writings of real experts, and to look back to our history. While the specific arguments about nuclear deterrence between two super-powers is no longer the focus, there are elements which continue to be applicable

in 2003.The fundamental issue is disarmament.

The General Assembly of the UN had urged the development of disarmament education as a distinct field of study through the preparation of teachers' guides, textbooks etc. But the government was hesitant about the subject of disarmament in schools. You could talk about 'peace', but strategies for disarmament would be 'political' in an unacceptable sense. I wondered whether we could get at it by a bit of history, and was delighted to refer again to Noel-Baker's admirable reminiscences of the First World Disarmament Conference of 1932/3.

> In the struggle for disarmament for three quarters of a century the internationalists have won all the arguments, but the bureaucrats and militarists have won all the victories that count. The motives of these men were ' honourable' and according to their light 'patriotic' but their guilt before history, and before past, present and future generations is appaling.'
>
> 'The Conferences and Commissions have proved that all the technical problems of disarmament have been solved; that the further disarmament is taken, the more swiftly and completely would the difficulties disappear.......The only problem which remains is to create the popular support that will enable and compel statesmen to see us through to disarmament.

That already accords with the American Catholic Bishops Pastoral Letter of 1983., when they said: 'Peace cannot be built by the power of rulers alone. Peace can be firmly constructed only if it corresponds to the resolute determination of all people of good will. Rulers must be supported and enlightened by a public opinion that encourages them, or where necessary, expresses disapproval.'

There have been real attempts at disarmament, apart from the large-scale aims of the League of Nations and the Charter of the United Nations. In 1955 Selwyn Lloyd (UK) and Jules Moch (France) produced a First Stage Treaty of Disarmament. In 1956 the hawks had induced the Western governments to do a volte-face on this Anglo-French memorandum. Sir Anthony Nutting, a young Minister of State in the Foreign Office, had helped to persuade Moscow to accept the Memorandum. Now his work was undermined; the British and French went on to launch the Suez War. Nutting resigned, and wrote:

> The student of this melancholy piece of history must always bear in mind — as the negotiators for their part were never allowed to forget — that behind each disarmament delegation there hovers the gaunt, grey giant in the affairs of men and nations — the Ministry of Defence.

'That is', Noel-Baker added, 'the hawks'.

Another witness to this gloomy fact is Dr Bernard Feld, who worked for the US Military Research, and was later Secretary of the Pugwash Movement. He wrote:

There is a universal tendency among intellectuals to think of the world as divided into peace-loving and aggressive nations....and that the problem of ensuring peace is one of getting the aggressive nations to behave like the peace-loving ones; that the achievement of peace depends primarily on the process of negotiation between sovereign states. My experiences over the last 15 years....have convinced me that this is a dangerous illusion. In every country of which I have first-hand knowledge (and this covers nations governed by all systems and ideologies) there are people whose basic orientation is peaceful, and people who firmly believe the need for, and efficacy of, force; people who — in much oversimplified terminology, and for want of a better categorisation — can be referred to as doves or as hawks. I am firmly convinced that the achievement of peace and international order depends more on the outcomes of the continuing hawk/dove struggles in each country than it does on the confrontations between their leaders. I have accumulated enough evidence to convince me that — tacitly and without establishing any formal cabal — the military hawks of the world have learned how to act in concert, how to re-inforce each other and divide the opposition, so as to convert every international arrangement as well as each international crisis into an internal victory for their hard-line approach ... The survival of mankind demands a new approach which, with all due respect, might adopt as its new slogan, 'Doves of the world, unite. You have nothing to lose but your planet.

In spite of a number of international conventions and agreements, when the UK government has often played a notable part, there have been no disarmament treaties since 1945. The Sea Bed Treaty, the Treaty of Tlatelolco, the Convention on Environmental Modification etc; none of them were disarmament measures whatever limits were being placed for the signatories on the use of nuclear or other weapons. Some of us would have wanted to except the Convention on Biological and Toxin weapons of 1972 which called for the actual destruction of some stocks; yet Lord Chalfont, the British Minister concerned with the negotiations (and no friend of the current disarmament movements) said of all these treaties: 'They are not disarmament, and it would be wrong and misleading to say they were disarmament.' He added: 'Notwithstanding some very useful arms control agreements, the aim of the UN is disarmament: no partial agreements will do. They cannot be regarded as satisfactory as long as the means, any means of making

'I CAN'T SEEM TO SHAKE THESE RECURRING NIGHTMARES OF THE GOVERNMENT ASKING US TO MANUFACTURE SOMETHING USEFUL.'

war is left in the hands of nation states.'

Now we get into trouble for saying this sort of thing. 'Pie in the sky', 'False idealism lacking in realism' Yet this is what many hard-headed politicians have tried to bring about. The history of the efforts is a set of tragedies. Among other examples in 1957 Kruschev proposed general and complete disarmament under effective international control, and within hours there was a joint US/USSR Resolution, later sponsored by 82 nations - the whole assembly at that time. The Ten Nations Group was set up in Geneva to get to work, but there followed the U2 spy plane incident and the whole political will collapsed.

But 1961 was a remarkable year. The British Commonwealth Ministers made an amazing attempt to re-activate negotiations. Under the signature of some distinguished 'conservatives' within the commonwealth came a clear Statement and proposition:

> The aim must be to achieve total world-wide disarmament, subject to effective inspection and control.
>
> In view of the slaughter and destruction experienced in so-called 'conventional' wars and of the difficulty of preventing a conventional war once-started from developing into a nuclear war, our aim must be nothing less than the complete abolition of the means of waging war of any kind.
>
> An agreement for this purpose should be negotiated as soon as possible on the basis of the following principles:
>
> a. all national armed forces and armaments must be reduced to the levels agreed to be necessary for internal security.
>
> b. once started the process of disarmament should be continued without interruption till it is completed.
>
> c. the elimination of nuclear and conventional armaments must be so phased that at no stage will any country or group of countries obtain significant military advantage.
>
> d. at the appropriate stage a substantial and adequately armed military force should be established to prevent aggression and enforce observance of the disarmament agreement: and an international authority should be created in association with the UN to control this force.
>
> Every effort should be made to secure rapid agreement to the permanent banning of nuclear weapons' tests by all nations ... Such an agreement is urgent since otherwise further countries may soon become nuclear powers, which increase the danger of war and further complicate the problem of disarmament.
>
> Disarmament and inspection are integral parts of the same question and must be negotiated together; and both must be made as complete and effective as possible. It must however be recognised that no safeguards can provide 100% protection against error or treachery. Nevertheless the risks involved in the process of disarmament must be balanced against the risks involved in the continuance of the arms race.
>
> It is arguable whether the arms race is the cause or the result of distrust between

nations. But it is clear that the problems of disarmament and international confidence are closely linked. Therefore while striving for the abolition of armaments all nations must actively endeavour to reduce tension by helping to remove other causes of friction and suspicion.

That is not the complete document, but sufficient to sense the new spirit which was present. It was signed by Macmillan for UK, Diefenbaker for Canada, Menzies for Australia, Holyoake for New Zealand, Verwoord for South Africa — none of whom were regarded as starry-eyed idealists — as well as by Nehru, Mrs Bandaranaike, Dr Nkrumah and others. Philip Noel-Baker tells us that this Statement 'was generally understood in government and parliamentary circles in London to have been written by Earl Mountbatten.'

Later that same year, 1961, Kennedy's man (McCloy) met Kruschev's man (Zorin) who together produced an agreement which was unanimously adopted in the UN Assembly. This repeated many of the Commonwealth Ministers' points, notably the following:

> The programme for general and complete disarmament shall ensure that States shall have at their disposal only such non-nuclear armaments, forces, facilities and establishments as are agreed to be necessary to maintain internal order and protect the personal security of citizens, and that states shall support and provide agreed manpower for a UN peace force.

It went on to spell out some of the details which included:

> The disbanding of armed forces, the dismantling of military establishments, including bases, the cessation of the production of armaments as well as their liquidation or conversion to peaceful uses. The elimination of all stockpiles of nuclear, chemical, bacteriological and other weapons of mass destruction. The elimination of all means of delivery of weapons of mass destruction. The abolition of organisations and institutions designed to organise the military effort of States, the cessation of military training on the closing of all military institutions. The discontinuance of military expenditures.

So what happened afterwards? Backed up by a notable speech of Kennedy's in the UN in which he said 'We must abolish the weapons of war before they abolish us.', the UN enlarged its earlier Group of Ten Nations to Eighteen with a mandate to draw up a Treaty of General and Complete Disarmament. Dean Rusk of USA, Douglas-Home of UK, and Gromyko of USSR spent eighteen days together to start off the work and then it was left to junior ministers: and it all faded away. 1962 was the year of the Cuba crisis. It was another example of the internationalists being defeated by the 'defence' departments who seemed to continue to play with weapons and threats. By 1964 the whole process was dead altogether. We do well, however, to remind our politicians of what can be proposed and approved at top levels in the UN

A distinguished figure in the international field was Dr Homer Jack. In the 1984 issue of Disarmament Times, a publication of Non-governmental Organisations in New York, he wrote:

> Since I am leaving the UN community after observing disarmament affairs for 24 years, perhaps I may be forgiven for commenting with some dismay and even bitterness, on the voting pattern of my own government, the USA, on disarmament resolutions at the current 38th General Assembly. The US attitude and actions have been shockingly negative. I choose my words carefully and will document them. Moreover this is not the first time that the US has displayed an obstructive attitude on disarmament resolutions. The US representatives, especially Ambassador Fields, who press the 'no' votes, are nice, decent, personable men…Yet the widespread allegations that the US really does not want disarmament appear true after watching the succession of red lights flashing on the electronic board from the US chair.

Dr Jack then listed a number of the negative votes to demonstrate his thesis. In particular he noted that the USA voted against

— requesting the Committee on Disarmament in Geneva to intensify its consideration of preventing an arms race in outer space.

— re-affirming the special responsibilities of the nuclear-weapons states for nuclear disarmament, for undertaking measures to prevent nuclear war authorising a modest UN study on stimulating the adoption of unilateral nuclear disarmament measures urging the Geneva Committee to intensify negotiations on a comprehensive agreement prohibiting the development of new types of weapons of mass destruction urging the Geneva Committee to speed up the conclusion of a convention prohibiting the development and production of chemical weapons, and the possible creation of chemical weapon-free zones supporting a Swedish initiative for a two-year study on naval forces and naval arms systems.

In each of these cases the USA registered the only 'No' vote. There were another 18 resolutions with some support from Japan or Israel. The USA refused to join the consensus vote on keeping alive the effort to make the Indian Ocean a zone of peace. It voted against all three nuclear Freeze resolutions, and three resolutions to stop nuclear tests.

The USA apparently holds in contempt the views of the world community. Reading this in 2005, one has to say 'Plus ca change …'.

27. LOOKING AT THE RUSSIANS

Several valuable books on the Soviet Union came out at this time which I thought it was important to draw people's attention to. In particular a marvellously written book by Colin Thubron 'Among the Russians' Reviewers praised it. For example Cyril Connolly said 'Adventurous, observant, modest, poetical....an armchair scholar'. Richard Church said, 'Behind the sensuous prose there is a mind of probing power'. Personally I was caught wanting over 13 words in the text. Do <u>you</u> know what are moraine, galeass, mandorla, finials, mastodon, ormolued, palomine? But I didn't want anyone to be put off by my ignorance, because it was a splendid book. He had given some wonderful conversation pieces, which I knew I could trust. Here's one:

> The conversation proceeded till it turned to criticism of Soviet life. The pile of accusations went to join the pyramid already in my mind; almost everybody I met had added a stone or two. Rampaging bribery, ingrained corruption and universal political hypocrisy. The self-accorded privileges of top Party members were a rankling sore — their numberless grades of private shops, the select schools, universities and bureaucratic posts into which they inveigled their children; their permits to travel abroad, their country dachas — even their yachts. In all this my companions saw the mushrooming of a class system — both an upper hierarchy and a bourgoisie in the middle-level management — together with a lethargy and growing materialism in their own generation who did not talk of ideas any longer. The gerontocracy in the Kremlin created suffocating centralism and an inflexible fear of change.

This was of course depressing stuff; but it in no way implied Thubron's hatred for Russians or the Soviet Union. Two more paragraphs show this. In the first a student said to him in the Caucasus:

How can you imagine we all think what we're told to think in this country?' He stuffed his hand into the pockets of his frayed bomber-jacket and fixed me with the type of wide-spread Russian eyes which I had grown to trust. 'The government may try to make us think their way, but I don't know a soul who does. Not a soul! Everybody I know has ideas of his own — even the most bone-headed farmer." Of course people are affected by Party propaganda' he said, 'but they were independent of it too' The system was simply a feature of life.

Some Russians are nice

People used it or ignored it. They didn't love it or fight it.

Then a little later on:

One thing I remember with peculiar clarity. This was when I told Yury that we in the West were afraid of Russia. For an instant he stared at me open-mouthed, then burst into disbelieving laughter. It was the only time I heard him laugh, so preposterous to him, so manifestly silly, was the idea of his country's dangerousness. This disbelief had already been echoed by other Russians along my route. Twice Yury asked me if I were not joking; then gazed at me for long moments, astonished at the depth of my delusion.

Down in Georgia Thubron describes a last evening with someone from a nearby camping hut.

You've heard the news?' 'No'. It came non-commitally from the TV announcer; the outbreak of war between Iran and Iraq. We stared at one another, wondering where the Soviet and Western governments would stand, what we would be told to feel. 'It looks like Moscow and Washington are hanging back', Julian said.' It's not time to report for duty'. He tried to laugh; but we touched glasses unhappily, as if already clothed in invisible battledress. The news had momentarily reduced us….

We stopped in front of our hut doors. The noise of a radio sounded in the trees: Iraqi advance, Iranian casualties, American silence. We listened. 'I don't know how to talk about our meeting like this' — he was suddenly fumbling for phrases. 'It's important, you and I…like two people meeting in outer space…' He ran his fingers over his face, as if to order its expression, its thoughts. Outer space: his country immaterial.

As we said goodbye he clasped my hand and said: 'If in some future time I see you in the sights of my rifle, I'll miss. 'And I won't fire at all'. We laughed with deep emotion. I've never felt so brief a friendship more. In him I loved the Russian people. It was my last healing.

28. ANALYSING DETERRENCE

Disarmament was of course out of the question so long as NATO and the Warsaw Pact sustained a theory of 'security' which depended on nuclear deterrence. There were many voices challenging this. Deterrence was a kind of game played by those with state power, and which took no notice of the people. Time and again one wanted to say to national leaders, 'Who do you think you are, threatening people in our name?' The powerlessness of citizens, no less in the western democratic world than in the Soviet Union, undermined any sense of common humanity.

Yet there were also distinguished and sometimes surprising voices against nuclear deterrence. For instance Field Marshall Lord Carver wrote in *A Policy for Peace*:

> It cannot be denied that the concept of nuclear deterrence abounds in illogicalities and paradoxes. At the heart of the problem is the dilemma that if one wishes to deter war by the fear that nuclear weapons will be used, one has to appear to be prepared to use them in certain circumstances. But if one does so, and the enemy answers back, as he has the capability to do and has clearly said he would, one is very much worse off than if one had not done so, if indeed one is there at all. To pose an unacceptable risk to the enemy automatically poses the same risk to oneself. The more acceptable nuclear war may appear to be to the governments and military men of the nuclear powers, the more likely it is that it will actually come about, and, even if it is limited in some way, the effects on those who live in the countries in or over which the nuclear weapons of both sides are exploded, will be catastrophic. To call the results 'defence' or 'security' is to make a mockery of the terms.

The Field Marshal may well have sensed the inner lack of logic about deterrence, the politicians seemed to swear by it. To them it all seemed simple. Michael Quinlan, a former Ministry of Defence official put it like this:

> Deterrence meant transmitting a basically simple message: If you attack me, I will resist. I will go on resisting until you stop or until my strength fails: and if it is the latter, my strength will not fail before I have inflicted on you damage so heavy that you will be much worse off at the end than if you had never started. So do not start.

I cannot express my despondency that a Catholic like Quinlan could really believe in this as a workable, let alone a moral, policy.

Of course the theory of deterrence had gone through massive changes since the early days of Mutual Assured Destruction, through Flexible Response to Counterforce and First Strike Capability. That is both the effect and the cause of the underlying assumption that there is a Cold War in progress. I quoted Fred Halliday's helpful book *The Making of the Second Cold War* for his analysis of eight theories behind the facts. In turn he found it useful to quote Geoffrey Barraclough's *From Agadir to Armageddon*, when he wrote:

> The risk of a world conflagration arises not so much when a state deliberately provokes a general war - that is hardly ever the case — as when the great powers' willingness to compromise and find peaceful solutions have been eroded by a growing sense of crisis and the sudden emergence of problems to which the traditional solutions provide no answer. This is the situation today. What we are witnessing, as people were witnessing in 1911, is the crumbling of a system, the crisis of a society in the throes of irresistible change.

The philosopher Mary Midgley, commented in *The Dangers of Deterrence*:

The motivation of deterrence links the threatener's hardware to the activation of the person threatened in a very simple way. It treats the threat merely as producing fear, and so discouraging action. Threats, however, do not only frighten, they can also provoke.

Mary Kaldor, the political analyst, wrote: 'Nuclear deterrence can be described as the strategic expression of the bloc system … (It) is a kind of state of 'no war — no peace' that is somehow expected to be maintained indefinitely. It is an imaginary enactment of World War III (which must never actually take place) in which the antagonists are NATO and the Warsaw Pact. The raison d'etre of both blocs is based on the possibility of this imaginary war.'

It is also worth remembering the words of the Secretary General of the United Nations in 1980: 'The concept of the maintenance of world peace, stability and balance through the process of deterrence is perhaps the most dangerous collective fallacy that exists today'. But none of the great powers took any notice.

In 1982 our local Peace Group had managed to secure a visit of E.P.Thompson for a public meeting. His attitude to deterrence had already been outlined in his book 'Zero Option', where he said: '… by maintaining each party in a posture of menace to the other, it fixes indefinitely the tension which makes the resolution of differences improbable. It transfixes diplomacies and ideologies into a twilight state; while postponing war, it postpones the resolution of peace.'

All the time people spoke of the need for 'multilateral disarmament. Proponents of any kind of 'unilateral' disarmament were ridiculed as idealists without a foot in reality — indeed we were declared to be dangerous, if not actually treacherous. But Mary Midgley commented: 'The difference between 'uni-lateralists' and multi-lateralists' is not that between the foolishly self-sacrificing and the prudent. It is that between those who, apparently, think it makes sense to wait until both sides are suddenly inspired to attempt innovations simultaneously. The extreme improbability of this coincidence makes it a strange gamble for anyone interested in prudence. It is time, I think, for the claim that multi-lateralism is the more prudent and realistic policy to be properly explained.'

In almost every issue of Comments & Quotes I tried to find some helpful and even surprising bits of wisdom to prompt further thinking. One came from Reichs Marshall Herman Goering, Hitler's Deputy, who was convicted at Nuremburg:

Why: of course people don't want war. It is the Leaders who determine the policy, and it is always a simple matter to drag the people along, whether it is a democracy, or a fascist dictatorship. All you have to do is to tell them they are being attacked, and denounce the pacifists for lack of patriotism and exposing the country to danger. It works the same in any country.

This has much the same meaning as the statement of Richard Perle (who appeared once again on the scene in Bush's administration in 2003) already quoted above at the height of the Cold War in reference to the Soviet Union.(# 19)

(As I was first writing this, I noted that we were being told that we were under threat from Saddam Hussein, at least indirectly, as he perhaps passed chemical or biological weapons' material to 'terrorists'. This was another attempt to justify war, with the expressed willingness to use nuclear weapons if thought

'Must you play 'war'? Can't you play 'detente' and 'diplomacy'?'

necessary. The mind boggles; yet this is what eventuated in 2003).

29. A MEMORABLY DIFFERENT APPROACH TO INTERNATIONAL RELATIONS

It is hardly surprising that one develops a serious cynicism about the credibility or the truthfulness of political leaders. It is difficult to measure the exact influence of vested interests on policies. Now and again an important public figure will let slip a sentence that gives us a sense of integrity. President Eisenhower did just that when he warned the world of the power of the military/industrial complex'. The merest glance at military expenditure, including 'research and development', reveals how many people must be involved and would have a vested interest in its continuity and growth. That will always militate against peaceful resolution of conflicts, let alone economic health. The Commonwealth Secretary, Shandrath Ramphal, said: 'The arms trade now constitutes in itself a substantial obstacle to economic growth in developed and developing countries alike, undermining the efforts of all governments to promote the prosperity and welfare of their people. Disarmament is now an important pre-condition of vigorous world economic recovery.'

By way of contrast I was happy to uncover a totally different approach from a world leader, President Kennedy, which had a direct effect on international understanding. It was in 1963 when Kennedy made a truly remarkable speech on June 10th. There was Soviet reluctance to sign up for the Partial Test Ban Treaty, which was a genuine attempt to slow down the nuclear proliferation of that time. Kennedy said:

Some say it is useless to speak of peace or world law or world disarmament, and that it will be useless until the leaders of the Soviet Union adopt a more enlightened attitude. I hope they do. I believe we can help them to do it. But I also believe we must re-examine our own attitude — as individuals and as a nation. Every thoughtful citizen who despairs of war and wishes to bring peace, should begin by looking inward; by examining his own attitude to the possibilities of peace, toward the Soviet Union, toward the course of the cold war and toward freedom and peace here at home.

Our problems are man-made; therefore they can be solved by man. Man's reason and spirit have often solved the seemingly unsolvable and we believe they can do it again ... History teaches us that enmities between nations, as between individuals, do not last for ever. However fixed our likes and dislikes may seem, the tide of time and events will often bring surprising changes in the relations between nations and neighbours ... It is discouraging to think that (Soviet) leaders may actually believe what their propagandists write; to realise the extent of the gulf between us. But it is also a warning to the American people not to fall into the same trap as the Soviets, not to see only a distorted and desperate view of the other side, not to see conflict as inevitable, accommodation as impossible and communication as nothing more than an exchange of threats. No government or social system is so evil that its people must be considered as lacking in virtue.

As Americans we find communism profoundly repugnant as a negation of personal freedom and dignity. But we can still hail the Russian people for their many achievements in science and space, in economic and industrial growth, in culture and acts of courage ... Among the many traits the peoples of our two countries have in common, none is stronger than our mutual abhorrence of war. Almost unique among the major world powers, we have never been at war with one an other. And no nation in the history of battle ever suffered more than the Soviet Union suffered in the course of the Second World War ... So let us not be blind to our differences, but also let us direct attention to our common interests ... And if we cannot end now our differences, at least we can help make the world safe for diversity. For in the last analysis our most basic common link is that we all inhabit this small planet. We all breathe the same air. We all cherish our children's future: and we are all mortal.

I believe it is the case that this speech was on the front page of Pravda in Moscow the next day, and ten days later the Soviet Union signed up for the Partial Test Ban Treaty.

30. INTERNATIONAL JOURNEYS

Looking back on activities in the 80s I can't deny that it was a privileged time for me, and full of interest first of all because of the calibre of those I had a chance to meet and discuss things with. There were sessions in 1981 with Dafydd Elis Thomas (now Presiding Office of the National Assembly in Cardiff); a lengthy period with Cardinal Hume; hosting Lord Fenner Brockway in Colwyn Bay and then Professor Michael Pentz in Wrexham.In 1982 a session with Oonagh McDonald MP at the House of Commons, to report on my first Soviet Union visit; a day with Petra Kelly in Cardiff; and a session, (albeit rather unproductive on peace issues) with Leonard Cheshire In 1983, by which time I chaired the Disarmament Commission for Pax Christi International, I found myself in Antwerp and Amsterdam for Pax Christi, Berlin for the END Conference, Bonn as described already for the Krefeld Appel, USA for CND International Committee, and the first of three visits to Athens.In 1984 I was asked to take the Chair in Chalfont St Giles for a meeting which Tony Benn was to address. This was Tory land, and he coped admirably and courteously with direct questions from Young Conservatives in the audience who expressed their thanks afterwards. I was in Munich for the Katholikentag for Pax Christi, apart from the two other Athens visits. These were for meeting called by KEADEA, which, (in translation), stood for The Movement for National Independence, International Peace and Disarmament. It had close association with Pasok, the Greek Socialist Party. It aimed at the de-nuclearisation of the whole of Europe, east and west, and was doing its best to improve relationships between the western peace movements and the 'official' peace committees within eastern and central Europe.

My notes say: 'None of the East European Peace Committees are 'government' bodies, but because of the nature of their societies they are very like arms for government policies. There is no doubt that they contain distinguished and sincere spokespersons. They emphatically want peace and understanding; but they are totally convinced of the rightness of their governments that they certainly don't have anything like the feel of grass-roots movements. This became peculiarly clear to me in November 1983 when I shared one of the three member meetings with three Soviet Peace Committee leaders in London also. Their attitude to the deployment of Cruise missiles and Pershing II was understandably anxious. We in the western movements continue to oppose this deployment and work for reversal of the policy. But the Soviet Peace Committee believe their government is right in now deploying more missiles in western Europe in response. For a government that would hardly be surprising; but for a peace committee it seems contradictory. The Soviet Peace Committee clearly wants a change in the situation; it wants nuclear disarmament; but for the time being it believes in the nuclear deterrent without hesitation. There is a sense that the parallel 'peace' movement in the UK would be Churchill's Coalition for Peace through Strength! In no way however should this prevent us from meeting with the S.P.C. or other east European committees. We cannot impose a different way of organising their societies, but we have to be realistic about what they stand for. Meantime I think we have a right to raise our voices in support of those independent people who, without opposing their government as political 'dissidents' look for other ways of encouraging mutual trust and international exchange.' One of these, the so-called 'Group of Trust' existed in Moscow, and was the focus of one of my adventures in 1985, of which more anon.

In 1981 there had been founded a new structure — the International Peace Communication and Co-ordination Center — whose mandate displayed the new developing thinking of the world-wide 'peace movements' It said: 'Peace movements need communication and co-operation in order to become effective, not least of all on an international level … After the rise of the 'new peace movement' in Europe and the USA at the end of the 70s, the main non-aligned mass-movements in Europe, working with political campaigns, decided to meet regularly, in order to discuss politics, strategy and common actions. They met for the first time in September 1981 and agreed to establish more regularity in their contacts. To give this a start, the Inter-church Peace Council (IKV) in Holland was asked to serve as a communication and co-ordination centre of this new network IPCC. IPCC is first of all a west-European network. It establishes structural relations with political campaigns outside Europe as soon as we feel both the need for co-operation in our day to day work. On a regular basis therefore we meet and co-operate with the Freeze campaign in the USA and the campaigns against the Cruise in the USA and Canada'

It was on the basis of IPCC principles that CND was readily willing to attend international gatherings, which might well include east-european groups whose non-alignment was not always evident. When George Hutchinson and I represented CND's international committee in Athens the conference was headed 'For the Denuclearisation of Europe', so alongside the leaders of IKV (Mient Han Faber and Wim Bartels) we made contact with the Bulgarian, Roumanian, Yugoslav and Soviet Peace Committee members.

31. ARE THERE ALTERNATIVES FOR PEACE?

Satish Kumar in 1962 said 'Merely to protest achieves nothing but frustration and disappointment. To be effective a revolutionary movement, based on non-violent resistance, must derive its strength from a positive programme for living. I do not believe the western peace movements have yet learned this lesson.' Maybe that's still the case today, though we have learned something from our efforts. The April 1984 issue of Comment and Quotes took this up. I reproduce it almost in its entirety.

'One of the notable weaknesses of the disarmament movements generally is the failure to convince others that there are alternatives to nuclear deterrence. Without money or other resources it is not easy to produce a properly researched strategy;

we really could do with a Ministry for Disarmament to run alongside the War or Defence Ministry. As time goes on, however, there are clearer voices with outline plans. Among the most notable has been the report of the Alternative Defence Commission which produced the volume 'Defence Without

the Bomb'. It is a very thorough exposition, and full of interest. The Commission was the initiative of a charitable educational Trust — the Lansbury House Trust — and was supported by several other, mostly Quaker, Trusts financially, incorporating a Fellowship at Bradford's School of Peace Studies. Relating its discussion to the politics of the real world, the commission states that the aim should be ' to fashion a defence policy that is conducive to disarmament, rather than one that is likely to lead to an escalation of the arms race.' They are not afraid to develop in some detail the military strategy and list the hardware that would be necessary to a purely defensive policy. The 'Just Defence' group have also done some excellent work on non-provocative defence. There might be some hope if those with political power started looking at these options.

A standard response to those who urge the abolition of nuclear weapons is that we will have to spend excessively to improve the conventional facilities. None of those who oppose nuclear weapons simply want to make the world safe for 'conventional' war, the horrors of which would be vast and terrifying. There could be an equivalent arms-race in non-nuclear weapons, as indeed there already is with the emerging technology. So, while one recognises the validity of thinking out territorial defence in conventional terms, the attempt has been made continually to think away from weapons that are offensive and provocative, however thin the line at times. The Commission rightly stresses that this is to happen in harness with a full and active political strategy to reduce tensions and remove the causes of conflict.'

The Commission also examined the feasibility of guerilla warfare for us, if and when frontier territorial defence has failed to halt an aggressive attack. And beyond this a start is made on examining the possibilities of civilian resistance through non-co-operation with the aggressor, right through to organised civil disobedience. There were magnificent examples of this in Nazi-occupied Europe, and insufficient notice has been taken of them. There is also one story from between the two world wars. It seemed to me that it was well worthwhile drawing on this story which, as far as I knew, was little known.

The Versailles Treaty of 1919 had demanded heavy reparations from Germany for all the damage caused by the war. Germany defaulted on some of the payments because of an economic inability to keep them up. France and Belgium were unconvinced of Germany's excuses, and in 1921 occupied Dusseldorf and Duisburg as a form of territorial sanction, sequestrating customs and excise revenues there. Things got worse, and the default in payments grew, till France and Belgium decided to occupy the Ruhr. Wolfgang Sternstein tells the story in a collection of essays edited by Adam Roberts (*The Great Civilian Resistance*) Germany had to choose between 'submission, violent resistance by rioting, sabotage, terror etc., and passive resistance. They opted for the latter.' Mine owners considered the possibility of flooding the mines, but the idea was finally rejected, together with the trade union suggestion of a general strike, because it was felt that both measures would hurt the German people more than the invaders. The unions pressed for passive resistance because 'an unarmed people would still have power and opportunity to demonstrate its will and to disarm every aggressor by striking and closing plants and factories.'The German government issued a proclamation on 10th January 1923: 'Remain steadfast in suffering and in faith: be firm, be calm, be sensible. Have trust in our just cause, and face the invaders with dignity until the day dawns when justice and freedom are restored.' I wonder if there has ever been such official backing for passive resistance than is found in the further proclamation of the following day.

> You must meet the trials of this time honestly and sensibly: take no action which would harm our just cause. Anyone who lets himself be carried away and commits any rash and unconsidered action, which in the end would only serve the enemy's ends, would be deeply guilty. The public good depends on each and every person exercising the utmost self-control.

The invaders arrived in a deserted town (Essen).

> Windows were curtained; most of the shops closed. The population received the foreign invaders with icy reserve.' A commentator describes the way passive resistance built up: 'protests, strikes, boycotts, and demonstrations were organised. The military was furious, particularly about the protests, objections and complaints, which could not be dealt with by military means. The occupation forces began to break passive resistance by means of courts martial, banishment, and generally repressive measures. The refusal to obey orders became the resistance offence dealt with by courts martial.' There were other acts of defiance also: The performance of Wilhelm Tell at the municipal theatre in Essen developed into a demonstration of the national will to resist, and finally occupation troops invaded the theatre and dispersed the audience. Civil servants were arrested, tried for insubordination and given heavy fines and long terms of imprisonment. Some were detained for weeks without being charged, and were finally released without trial; most were banished to unoccupied Germany. Policemen refused to salute foreign officers and

were also banished. Occupation troops who were well provided with good money bought everything they could get hold of. Therefore shops closed down when the soldiers were off duty.

The press was attacked; banned newspapers appeared under new names; outside papers were smuggled in: leaflets and news-sheets were distributed.

The invaders tried to claim the cost of the occupation itself. They requisitioned the property, banks and workshops, and the funds of public services. 'Private homes were the first to suffer from billeting. Flats and classrooms were used as accommodation for troops, and the impoverished population was to provide furniture, vehicles, fuel and goods. Where these were refused, brute force was used to obtain them: citizens were beaten with whips and rifle butts and forced to do menial labour … Tills were raided at post offices, railway booking offices, and state and local administration offices …. Small units of soldiers frequently invaded factories to requisition motor cars, machines or other goods … Sirens sounded and workers crowded into the yards and demonstrated … In some cases they succeeded in making the foreign engineers and soldiers withdraw empty-handed.

In practice it became difficult to distinguish between fully passive resistance and active resistance when light and telegraph wires were cut, or when workers made railway engines unusable, or damaged signal-boxes. In time some resorted to sabotage, and a railway bridge was blown up with soldiers killed and wounded.Germany had to yield unconditionally in the end. But world opinion began to go against the French. The Belgian people openly condemned their government's action in the Ruhr. In France thousands of those who had gone as occupation troops 'for the first time met Germans as they really are. They met an industrious people, living in neat houses, people who were so very different from what war propaganda had led them to believe…. Many high-ranking officers had to be replaced because of their friendly attitude towards the Germans. A German historian (Erdmann) wrote: 'By the resistance of the Rhine population and the Ruhr, Germany's moral isolation was pierced. Most important of all, France failed to achieve her political goal, the separation of the Rhineland from the rest of Germany. Sternstein assessed that due to the hatred and the lack of a non-violent spirit, and to a failure in German propaganda, the Germans were unable to win over members of the occupying forces and split the occupiers' front. The outbreak of sabotage did more harm than good, and gave the invaders justification for reprisals. But an important factor in the failure was the lack of training and preparation for passive resistance.

The Germans tried prohibiting the delivery of coal to the occupation authorities. 'As a result the troops took their fuel by force, stoked their fires with tables and chairs, and beat up passers-by and forced them to load barrow-loads of requisitioned coal to their quarters … This seems to indicate that it is advisable not to deprive occupation forces of the necessities of life but, on the contrary, to provide them readily and voluntarily. Only if the opponent feels that his existence is secure may he possibly be prepared to admit he is wrong.'

32. THE SPIRIT OF NON-VIOLENCE

All this suggests that, while it is important to prepare and train in the techniques of non-violence (and we haven't even started on this in any systematic way) it is more important yet to look at the attitude of mind which underlies non-violent action. Unless non-violence stems from an inner spirit of love, it is unlikely to be persevering and strong enough to survive.

In the same issue of Comments and Quotes I had peppered the text which extracts from sayings of Gandhi, such as these:

> Three quarters of the miseries and misunderstandings in the world will disappear if we step into the shoes of our adversaries and understand their standpoint.

> Non-co-operation is not a movement of brag, bluster or bluff. It is a test of our sincerity. It requires solid and silent self-sacrifice.

> Civil disobedience is sometimes a peremptory demand of love. Dangerous it undoubtedly is, but no more than the encircling violence. Civil disobedience is the only non-violent escape from its soul-destroying heat.

> Non-violence does not mean meek submission to the will of the evil-doer, but it means the pitting of one's whole soul against the will of the tyrant.

> There are occasions, generally rare, when a person considers certain laws to be so unjust as to render obedience to them a dishonour. He then openly and civilly breaks them, and quietly suffers the penalty for their breach.

> It should be an article of faith that there is none so fallen in this world but can be converted by love. A Satyagrahi will always try to overcome evil by good, anger by love, untruth by truth, himsa by ahimsa.

> A Satyagrahi must not harbour ill-will or bitterness against the evil-doer. He may not even needlessly employ offensive language against the evil person, however unrelieved his evil might be.

Satyagraha is literally holding on to truth, and it therefore means Truth-force. It excludes the use of violence, because man is not capable of knowing the absolute truth, and therefore not competent to punish.

This fundamental humility in the search for truth is not something we can easily achieve. We must certainly stand firmly to what we believe, but an arrogant claim to know the whole truth is what closes us off from our opponents. Gandhi's way was to win over those who opposed him. Remember his words to the Viceroy of India: 'The English must of course go; but they must go as our friends.' Gandhi would not deny that there is absolute truth — indeed that might be taken as his definition of God; but our grasp of it will always be imperfect. His whole life — and the title of his autobiography — was 'An Experiment with Truth'. It might seem dangerous to get thousands of people, as he did, committed to the pursuit of non-violence unless it really was the 'absolute truth' for action. What was clear to him was that the alternative of violence was definitely ruled out as wrong. The way of non-violence is not an easy way. It does not avoid suffering; but the non-violent activist takes the suffering on him/her self, and refuses to impose it on others. 'Satyagraha in a just cause is vain if the persons espousing it are not determined and capable of suffering to the end; and the slightest use of violence defeats a just cause. Satyagraha excludes the use of violence in any shape or form, whether in thought, word or deed. 'That is nothing less than a spiritual discipline, and echoes the attitude of Jesus. Indeed, Gandhi was a profound Christian over this, though a Hindu.

It is often said that Gandhi would not have been successful in getting the British to withdraw their empire from India if the British did not share a humanity that was not too oppressive in political and military terms. First, that statement covers up quite a history of violence and oppression, although there were idealists among the imperialists, and much good also followed the take-over of India. He possibly underestimated the necessity of a significant leader to rally and train people to resist with non-violence. The British were not continuing to expand; they had taken over long before, and a basic compromise had been reached in the management of society.

Nothing like that would be the case after the outbreak of a modern war. Gandhi's way was not born out of weakness or cowardice. He preferred the use of violence to running away in fear; his judgement on the oppressed people of Central and South America would not have been harsh, even though he would proclaim a better way than guerilla fighting. It would have been interesting to see how he would have viewed the passive resistance of those of us taking a stand against the arrival of Cruise missiles. We do not have much indication of how Gandhi saw the modern horrific developments except perhaps this in1945: 'The atomic bomb has deadened the finest feelings that have sustained mankind for ages. Now we know the naked truth about war. War knows no law except might. The moral to be legitimately drawn from the supreme tragedy of 'the bomb' is that it will not be destroyed by counter-bombs, even as violence cannot be destroyed by counter-violence.'

My text also presented the Seven Deadly Sins according to Gandhi:'Politics without principle: Wealth without work: Commerce without morality; Education without character; Pleasure without conscience; Science without humanity; Worship without sacrifice.' Certainly that's a lot more stimulating than the list in our catechisms. There were three other quotes in this issue which have a continuing relevance: General Douglas Macarthur in 1957 said: 'Our government has kept us in a perpetual state of fear — kept us in a continuous stampede of patriotic fervour, with the cry of grave national emergency.... Always there has been some terrible evil to gobble us up if we did not blindly rally behind it by furnishing exorbitant sums demanded. Yet, in retrospect, these disasters seem never to have happened, seem never to have been quite real.'

Then from Ivan Selin, the US Head of Strategic Division.:'Welcome to the world of strategic analysis, where we programme weapons that don't work to meet threats that don't exist.' Now that sounds as though he was speaking out of turn; it is almost like a quotation from Bremner, Bird and Fortune.

The third is particularly sad. It comes from Lt.William Calley on trial for the murder of Vietnamese villagers at My Lai. 'In all my years in the Army, I was never taught that communists were human beings.' No indeed; but it was scarcely the role of the army to teach that; hadn't he any experience of family, neighbourhood and society?.

33. 'REMEMBER THE THIRTIES'

The issue of Comment and Quotes for May 1984 was largely based on my return to the book (already referred to several times) by Philip Noel-Baker 'The First World Disarmament Conference 1932/3 and Why It Failed' It has continuing relevance because of the 'Remember the Thirties' cry that emerges every time the politicians face a new arch-enemy. We heard it at the time of the Falkland/Malvinas war, and it has been in heavy use to justify the war against Saddam Hussein. We are told we should not forget the lessons of the rise of Hitler, of the hopeless unpreparedness of the UK for the mounting militarism of Nazi

Germany, and, above all, of the dangerous and naïve activities of the 'disarmers'. The historical reality is rather different.

There were those who, from the very start, had treated the League of Nations with cynicism and even contempt, just as many politicians today regard the United Nations Organisation, thus ensuring its powerlessness. Lord Robert Cecil, that distinguished internationalist, was not among these. He openly worked for a campaign for the compulsory arbitration of international disagreements and for general disarmament. When a Labour government came to power in 1929, Cecil was asked, without his joining the Labour Party or becoming a minister, to be the British delegate to the prospective World Disarmament Conference. He was to have a room at the Foreign Office. (Incidentally, what a model way of doing things, to bypass party boundaries!) He helped to work on a Draft Treaty, and this outline was a strong influence in the tone of developments. Noel-Baker wrote:

> It was plain that a Treaty of general world disarmament would be worth nothing unless it contained a workable and reliable system for reducing and limiting both the manpower and the budgetary expenditure of each signatory nation. If a government could cheat without detection by increasing the number of 'effectives' in the forces it maintained, or by spending larger sums of money than the Treaty allowed, the Treaty would inspire no confidence …

When Arthur Henderson was chosen to be President of the coming Conference, the hawks in several countries objected. The French Prime Minister declared: 'Henderson cannot be an impartial President; he is known to favour disarmament.' After the General Election of October 1931, Ramsay MacDonald agreed to form a National Coalition Government; but he faced a House of Commons with strong opponents of disarmament in large numbers:

> Other non-governmental categories of hawks were very active in their work against disarmament. Some private manufacturers of arms were loud in their support of Hitler, and declared that we must let him re-arm Germany, in order that he might destroy the Bolsheviks in Russia. They did not hesitate to advertise their tanks in German journals, although Germany was forbidden to own or purchase tanks by the Treaty of Versailles. When Hitler came to power they did not hesitate to sell him the latest type of British tank and the latest British aero-engine …

In Germany itself Krupps, the great armaments manufacturing firm, (forbidden since the Treaty of Versailles to continue that line) had taken to sewing machines. Its chairman, Hugenburg, then bought up more than half the daily newspapers and all the Press Advertising Agencies, and then began a sustained attack on disarmament. He particularly attacked Stresemann who was the leading prophet of disarmament, and began to support the hitherto unknown Adolf Hitler. With the growing world slump, arms manufacturers gave Hitler vast sums of money to build up the SA and SS — the Nazi forces — till the Weimar republic was undermined:

> Hitler was the creature of vested armament interests whose purpose was simple and terrible — to smash the League of Nations and re-arm Germany ... There is ample evidence throughout the whole of their campaign, the German militarists never had the support of the majority of the German people.

Thus the rise of Nazi militarist rule depended at one point on the failure of the World Disarmament Conference, which eventually began in 1932.

The non-governmental organisations had campaigned educationally for disarmament, just as many are today. For instance, two international Federations of War Veterans, speaking for the eight million of those who survived World War I, worked together to demand that the Disarmament Conference should not fail. By the time the Conference started, sadly the leadership of Robert Cecil, of Briand and of Nansen had passed to others, who did not have the commitment nor the nerve to take decisions about armaments and national defence. Cecil did in fact make an opening speech, but as a non-governmental official. He gave a concise, comprehensive account of disarmament policy:

> The function of armaments is national defence, and in a League of Nations world, that is their only justification. The object of the conference therefore was to reduce all armaments to what was needed for national defence, and to abolish forces and weapons which would help offensive, aggressive, warlike purposes.

That meant the abolition of tanks, heavy mobile guns, all military and naval aircraft. This would reduce the dangers of surprise attack and allow more time for the League to solve serious disputes peacefully.

Cecil's speech even impressed Sir John Simon, the new Foreign Secretary. Quite soon the British members of the special commissions, set up by the Conference to work out the details, were making little distinctions, to suit their own views.

> A British War Office expert argued that whether tanks were 'offensive' or 'defensive' depended on the weight of their armour and their guns. A tank of sixteen tons, he said, was obviously defensive.... By a coincidence the British Army in 1932 possessed six tanks of sixteen tons weight — the same six with which they began the war against Hitler in 1939 ... .A British Admiral refused to admit that battleships and armoured cruisers were specifically offensive ... This British stand did more than anything to delay and confuse the work of the Conference ...

President Hoover's proposals on 22nd June 1932 were most remarkable, and they were wholly based on Cecil's principles. He formally proposed the abolition of all tanks, chemical warfare and large mobile guns; of all bombing aircraft and all bombardment from the air; there were hosts of other reductions. This 'qualitative disarmament', as it came to be known, was received with enormous world-wide support, from Germany, Italy, Spain and the Soviet Union. At home Sir John Simon put it to the House of Commons, but began to pull back under pressure. 'There were more than 500 Tories in the House, and the great majority were hostile to disarmament and to the League.'

The First Lord of the Admiralty (Eyres-Monsall) had one political ambition — to keep as many British warships on the ocean as he could — never mind what other nations had. The Secretary of State for War (Douglas Hogg, first Lord Hailsham) was obstinately in favour of keeping tanks and heavy mobile guns. The Secretary of State for Air (Lord Londonderry) had the greatest difficulty, he said later, in saving the bomber because of the public outcry. There was, it seems clear, a mounting public opinion in favour of real disarmament, but it was not enough to move those in power. Sir John Simon knew that 'if the Geneva conference did not disarm the world, Germany would inevitably re-arm with the rise of Hitler. But he came back to the Disarmament Conference with a platitudinous speech, and a call for compromises and concessions. To many it seemed like an utter betrayal of the doctrine he had formerly preached under the influence of Robert Cecil. His statement killed the Hoover plan, and as events were soon to prove, he killed the Conference, smoothed Hitler's path to power and took the nations a long step further towards the Second World War.' So remember the Thirties — yes indeed!

34. THE WEAPONS ARE THE PROBLEM

It strikes me that a great deal depends on the matter of armaments. You don't need to have actual military engagement to sense the suspicion and hostility surrounding the existing weapons, standing in preparation for war. Increasingly the weapons which are produced theoretically to defend nation-states, create the hostility they are intended to vitiate. This story of the Thirties helped me to put into context the contemporary arguments about weapons. It was wholly appropriate therefore that I followed these extracts from Noel-Baker's book with three items about weapons.

The first was from the Synod of The Evangelical Church in Czechoslovakia:

> The intended deployment of the new types of nuclear weapons in European countries will radically escalate the danger of a conflict, which would mean not only the total devastation and the end of Europe, but is even a demonic denial of the creative purpose

"I MUST ADMIT THEY'RE A LOT HARDER TO SELL WITH REALISTIC NAMES......"

of God. Reconciliation is possible! It is our wish for the super-powers not to break off their contacts but to negotiate on all possible levels and to create a favourable atmosphere for this in the world public opinion.

The second came from twelve Roman Catholic bishops in the USA urging people to join a prayer vigil along the route of trains carrying nuclear warheads to Trident submarine bases. They said:

Our stand is that no further deployment of nuclear weapons can possibly be justified. Every missile and nuclear weapons shipment is both a significant step towards a first-strike holocaust and a violation of the moral stand we have taken with the support of many other US citizens, especially people of faith. What we can do all along the tracks when these shipments come through is stand in prayerful witness to the alternative power of divine love and non-violent action.

The third came from a research analyst, David Morrison, from the American Centre for Defence Information:

While much attention is currently focussed on means of bringing the superpowers back to the negotiating table to limit and reduce existing nuclear weapons, formidable technical and institutional resources and interests are being mobilised in support of a new generation of nuclear arms. Without control on these developments future arms agreements may simply become vehicles for a further round in the arms race.

It was certainly worth recording again some of the many words of wisdom from the mouth of President (ex-General) Eisenhower. I believe it was from a letter only published posthumously:

When we get to the point, as one day we will, that both sides know that in any outbreak of general hostilities, regardless of the element of surprise, destruction will be both reciprocal and complete, possibly we will have sense enough to meet at the conference table with the understanding that the era of armaments has ended and the human race must conform its actions to this truth or die.

It was also encouraging to note a quotation from the Roman Catholic bishops of England and Wales from 1978, which might have been overlooked.

> Unless we bring about disarmament we are not effectively saying 'No' to violence. Indeed, although it is appaling to contemplate, we may well be bearing some moral responsibility for allowing the most terrible and overwhelming violence of nuclear war to become possible. It is our clear duty to make every effort to get war outlawed by international agreement — and this means disarmament.

35. DETERRENCE AND THE COLD WAR

It has often been said that nuclear deterrence has kept the peace for forty years. It is stated with great sincerity; the causal relationship between nuclear deterrence and no-outbreak-of-nuclear-war is taken as self-evident. Yet the strange consequence of this is that Iran, Iraq, Israel, Lebanon, Egypt, Libya would also be much safer if they had a nuclear deterrent. The same trust in deterrence is present in the Soviet Union. In a discerning book by David Holloway, lecturer in Edinburgh's Department of Politics, and formerly visiting professor at Cornell University, (*The Soviet Union and the Arms Race*) writes:

> The Soviet leaders present their policy as essentially defensive and peaceful in purpose. The major justification they offer for Soviet military power is that it prevents war. In January 1980 Brezhnev claimed that the Soviet Union had succeeded in breaking the cycle 'World war — short breathing space — world war again'. This is undoubtedly a powerful argument, for the period of international peace that the Soviet Union has enjoyed since 1945 contrasts sharply with the wars of the first half of the century. Since 1945 Soviet forces have seen less combat than those of the leading western powers. The war in Afghanistan is by far the largest action in which Soviet combat military forces have been engaged on any scale. The assertion that Soviet military power secures peace does not therefore fly in the face of experience. The claim that Soviet military power contributes to peace goes hand in hand with military-patriotic education which helps to sustain that power.

A Russian social scientist, Feodor Burlatski, offered a more adequate explanation for me. He claimed that war was avoided because:

a. 'Mutual Assured Destruction' makes war senseless.
b. Bi-polar international system led to a balance of power which made victory by one power over the other doubtful or impossible.
c. The forces of peace have been stronger than the forces of war. 'War must be prevented not merely through the threat of destruction but by tackling the political conflict that

might give rise to it. The Soviet Union often speaks of the correlation of forces, especially to describe the power relationship between capitalism and socialism. It is a broader concept than the 'balance of power'; for it embraces not only military but also political, economic and moral elements. It is not always clear, however, what weight is being given to the different elements in the relationship ... Soviet theory does not give primary importance to military power in the correlation of force, but the very success of Soviet military effort means ...that the military instrument plays a major role in Soviet foreign policy. The Soviet Union conducts its relationship with the West from a position of military parity, but economic backwardness.

Defining 'parity' in specific terms is not a technical but a political problem. The process of negotiation presents difficulties of its own. Weapons may be developed and produced as bargaining chips, or agreements may direct interests towards technologies that are not limited. In this way arms control negotiations may actually stimulate competition. Moreover tough negotiations may draw out the process to the point where the agreement is overtaken by the development of new weapons' technologies. Arms control is deeply rooted in the East-West political relationship. It is at once an arrangement for pursuing the co-operative objective of regulating the competition in arms and an arena in which the two sides try to further their competing interests.

David Holloway concludes his book in a way that will have pleased many of us:

Too often western governments try to justify their policies by reference to what the Soviet Union is doing, as though that were a good reason in itself. Such an argument conveys the historically incorrect impression that western governments have merely reacted to Soviet actions. Similarly it is too often argued that Soviet power makes it impossible to take unilateral steps to slow down the nuclear arms race. But that is not so. There is considerable scope e.g. for western governments to reduce unilaterally their heavy reliance on nuclear weapons, especially in Europe. Not every step of this kind need be or should be made conditional on Soviet reciprocity. Actions should be judged on their merits by asking whether they contribute not only to western security, but also to the common human interest in reducing the risk of nuclear war. Only by applying that principle alongside arms control may it be possible to prevent negotiations from stimulating rather than slowing down the East-West arms competition.

Hear President Eisenhower again:'The problem in defence is how far you can go without destroying from within what you are trying to defend from without.' By comparison one shivers at the statement of President Truman:

All freedom is dependent on freedom of enterprise. The whole world should adopt the American system ... The American system can survive only if it becomes a world system.

A good deal of the material I gathered for Comment & Quotes for July/August 1984 was taken from some really serious studies of the issues. I highlighted the splendid book by Johann Galtung (*There Are Alternatives*) which has hardly been superseded even now till his joint book with Carl Jacobsen and Kai Brand-Jacobsen (*Searching for Peace*) He asked why nuclear disarmament was so difficult, what is the real nature of 'security' and how one could develop 'associative politics'.

The material in my broadsheet became pretty 'heavy' at this time, but I was pleased to receive some encouraging comments from its readers. Perhaps my digest of experts' writings saved them burying themselves in large and expensive books. I did a lot of my own reading when travelling on trains and planes; I still do. It was part of the purpose of the little Peace Studies Centre I had set up.

I also came across an important statement on 'security' which came above the signatures of former NATO and Warsaw Pact Generals — six from the Netherlands, Norway, Italy, Greece, Portugal and UK; eight from USSR, Poland, Bulgaria, Czechoslovakia, Romania, Hungary and East Germany. They said: 'The future of the peoples of Europe can be based only on the principles of equality and equal security for all peoples in the continent, bearing in mind that the solution of this vital problem depend primarily on themselves'. They realised that European security is linked with the security of other parts of the world, and that everything possible has to be done to remove the seeds of conflict in areas like Central America, the Middle East and South East Asia.

The participants in the meeting agreed they can and must use their professional influence to support the efforts of those representing European and international public opinion to resolve such problems as ridding Europe of all nuclear weapons and other weapons of mass destruction, among other ways by creating nuclear free zones in Europe.

Prevention of the militarisation of outer space.

Promotion of general disarmament.

Strengthening of confidence-building measures, and the return to détente, good neighbourliness and co-operation.

One seriously wonders why such statements are not taken into account by the politicians. It is interesting that senior military officers are far from being war-mongers. We should exempt some senior political figures from a generalised criticism. George Kennan in particular moved a long way during his career as a member of the American Foreign Service in 1926, through his service in Moscow as US Ambassador. In the 70s and 80s he was awarded doctorates by several universities as a historian, and a couple of Peace Prizes in 1981 and 1982. Small wonder for the latter when one reads:

> I am bound to say that, while the earliest possible elimination of nuclear weaponry is of no less vital importance in my eyes than it ever was, this would not be enough in itself to give western civilisation even an adequate chance of survival. War itself, as a means

of settling differences at least between the great industrial powers, will have to be in some way ruled out, and with it there will have to be dismantled (for without this the whole outlawing of war would be futile) the greater part of the vast military establishments now maintained with a view to the possibility that war might take place. The reasons for this conclusion are multiple, but among them are first, the recognition that the weapons of this age — even the so-called conventional ones — are of such destructiveness that there can be no clear line between the discriminate ones and the weapons of mass destruction; and second, the similar recognition that so extensively has public understanding and official habit been debauched by the constant encouragement given to it to perceive the military balance primarily in nuclear terms, that it would probably be incapable of making these fine distinctions between one kind of weapon and the other in time of war and those of the immensely destructive 'conventional' weapons would in all probability slip over into the use of those to which the term 'conventional' could not properly be applied.'

This extract came from the publication of various Kennan papers dating back to 1950, though the book is dated 1984. His remarks should have been better known at the height of the Cold War. The following passage challenges the whole notion of the 'evil empire'.

Great masses of people in the USA and in Europe have now been taught to believe that the Soviet leadership has been obsessed ever since World War II with a desire to invade western Europe, and has been deterred only by the threat of nuclear retaliation. A variation of this supposed verity, very common in western Germany, is the belief that the Soviet side, in the event that the threat of a nuclear response were to be removed, would not at once attack, but would subject the western European countries to various forms of nuclear blackmail, in the face of which those countries, confronted with an overwhelming Soviet superiority in conventional strength, would have no choice but to surrender. A subsidiary myth, equally widely believed, is that the Soviet superiority in conventional armed strength has now reached such vast dimensions that there is no way the NATO powers could conceivably match it.

All of these assumptions and scenarios are either quite incorrect or highly improbable, but they are now so widely implanted in the public mind that in all probability nothing I could say, and nothing any other private person could say, could eradicate them. Only a senior statesman and political leader, speaking from the prominence and authority of high governmental position (in our country a president presumably) could have a chance of re-educating the public successfully on these various points, and this is something for which one sees, at this present juncture, not the slightest prospect.

How one wishes that political leaders in our time would re-examine their statements about 'rogue states' and the 'axis of evil'. Are they willing to learn anything even from recent history?

As mentioned earlier, Pax Christi had published the personal story of Father George Zabelka, who had been the Catholic chaplain to the bomber crews at Hiroshima. In 1984 he was on a long pilgrimage across Europe; I met him briefly when a number of us were on a demonstration visit to a bomber's base in Norfolk. I think it was at this time that he addressed a letter to all military chaplains in the south of England, as he related his story of 1945.

It was not the 'Enola Gay' and 'Bok's Car' that dropped those first atomic bombs. It was Paul Tibbits, Charles Sweeney and their crews that guided those planes, pulled the levers, pushed the buttons. I was one of them. I co-operated with them. I was part of that system that directly slaughtered 200,000 people, most of whom were innocent non-combatants. St.Augustine said seventeen hundred years ago that a just war could only be fought as long as non-combatants were not harmed. I think of those little children in the makeshift medical centres suffering, dying. Is this the collateral damage we are preparing for by the tens of millions?

You have time and the obligation to search your conscience on these questions. I wish in 1945 someone had urged me to examine my conscience then on the immorality of slaughtering innocent people. I was brain-washed by my country, by my Church and family. So are you now. No; not by torture or force but by a millennium of propaganda glorifying war, romanticising it, justifying the wholesale slaughter of civilians. Einstein was right when he said, 'With the splitting of the atom, all things have changed except our way of thinking, and so we drift hopelessly towards unparalleled destruction…'. I urge you as spiritual leaders of your flock to examine seriously the morality of nuclear and bio-chemical war. You know, I know and 'they' know that if necessary those 'deterrent' bombs will be used. You have studied moral theology. It is intrinsically evil to kill directly innocent human beings, and that is all that modern nuclear weapons can do. Collateral damage and just war language belong to another past era, an era that has gone for ever.

36. GOOD NEWS; GOOD IDEAS

It seemed important to me to draw attention to some of the good things that were happening across the world, even if they didn't cancel out the obscenities of war preparation, which was what the continuing arms race seemed to be.

In C&Q for September and October 1984 I noted that Canada was just about to establish an Institute for International Peace and Security: that seven more Massachusetts' towns had voted to become Nuclear Free Zones; that France, in spite of the stance of the Socialist government towards nuclear weapons, was giving institutional recognition to 'non-violence' as a working hypothesis for defence. It had signed a contract with Christian Mellon, (the priest who had fostered *Le Mouvement pour la Non-violence)* and two other researchers to conduct a study of how the principles and methods of non-violent resistance might be used in the global defence strategy of France. This possibly owes something, I suggested, to the long-standing influence of General de la

Bollardiere who has long recommended a policy of non-violence also.

Then in West Germany there had appeared an Appeal from 140 German soldiers and army employees against the deployment of Cruise and Pershing II missiles. Among the first twenty signatories were three majors and four captains. They urged stopping the arms race, taking real disarmament steps; they urged the west to be willing to make initial concessions by dismantling mass-destruction weapons, creating nuclear-free zones in Europe, and ending arms exports.

The thirteen ex-NATO Generals and Admirals, to whom I referred above, challenging current NATO defence policies produced a book at this time (*The Arms Race to Armageddon*) The *Daily Telegraph* censured it, suggesting communist influence. The book had referred to the denunciation of CND and referred to the organisations which had been largely set up to make these attacks, saying:

> Officially these groups are independent of political parties but in reality they include influential members of the Conservative party. They include Coalition of Peace through Security, the Committee for Peace in Freedom, and the British Atlantic Committee. They receive financial support directly from the state budget. Thus without any objective discussion, state finances are being used to wage the secret psychological war.
>
> It is significant that those who voice their protest against the nuclear arms race most determinedly come from the ranks of the military experts with the greatest knowledge of nuclear weapons and their effects … Those high-ranking military leaders who help to develop their countries' defence strategies should look for ways of preventing conflicts, and work for nuclear disarmament. If politicians hesitate to consider disarmament, they should be warned and, should they not listen, the military has a responsibility to warn the general public.
>
> We believe that US policy is placing at risk the whole structure of civilisation not only in Europe but also in the world. That is why we cannot agree with the present administration's over-simplified world view that suspects the hand of Moscow behind every evil.

It was also worth quoting the historian Professor Michael Howard: 'It is no longer just a minority of ant-militarist intelligentsia who question the validity and credibility of a deterrent posture which would , if activated, destroy everything it is concerned to defend.'

Another historian, A. J. P. Taylor at this time wrote in a *Guardian* article:

> The Alliances were supposed to promote peace and to protect their members. The first World War and its outbreak demonstrated that the alliances were the cause of great wars. This was not the last time that this was shown. The deterrent is the contemporary version of the alliances. It too will be the cause of great war. Men will ask afterwards, 'Why did they do it?' There will be no convincing answer.

I also found one could put alongside one another some telling quotations, like these: 'We have a different regard for human life than those monsters (i.e. the Soviets) do' That came from President Reagan. The historian E. H. Carr in his book, *The Twenty Years Crisis* said: 'Theories designed to discredit an enemy or potential enemy are one of the commonest forms of purposeful thinking. To depict one's enemies or one's prospective victims as inferior beings in the sight of God has been a familiar technique at any rate since the days of the Old Testament.'

That didn't deter Jerome Wiesner, scientific adviser to Presidents Kennedy and Johnson from saying: 'President Reagan should declare an open-ended unilateral moratorium on new nuclear weapons and delivery systems. He should invite the Soviet Union to respond with a parallel declaration of purpose.... The call is for action, not negotiation. The unilaterally agreed moratorium should be just a first step in global psychotherapy.'

The Generals for Nuclear Disarmament were ready to expose deceptions also. British government supporters kept telling us that the advent of Cruise and Pershing II missiles into Europe was 'in response' to the Soviets' SS20s. The generals said:

> As early as May 1978 the US army announced its intention to deploy a brigade equipped with Pershing II missiles in West Germany — eighteen months before SS20s were held to be responsible for NATO's decision to step up the arms race. One brigade is made up of three battalions with 36 missiles each — a total of 108 Pershing II missiles. Eight months later in February 1979 the American armaments company, Martin, received a 360 million dollar contract to produce Pershing IIs. The company made sub-contracts with Bendix Corporations, Goodyear, Hercules and Singer Kearfoot. Recall what that meant for industry and congress members in local industry, employment and profits; and still in advance of NATO Planning Committee's acceptance (without parliamentary consultation in UK) to deploy these weapons 'as a response to SSD20s.

For those who still didn't believe that the US forces actually envisaged the use of nuclear weapons, the Generals quote the US forces Manual FM 100-1. 'The US must prepare itself for the use of military power across the entire spectrum of conflict, from relatively mild policy disagreements to fairly intensive non-warfare confrontations of an economic or political nature, leading to a range of military situations which could conceivably include nuclear war.' The document continued, saying that 'The relatively new Air-Land-Battle doctrine is the first US army doctrine which comprehensively integrates conventional. Chemical and nuclear warfare in an offensive strategy. This doctrine became official, to be reinforced by the Army Forces Manuals 100-5 and 101-3 in 1982.

The Generals commented ...To disregard these plans as pure nonsense is dangerous because they make detailed demands of the US armaments industry which are intended to ensure that America retains the initiative in military matters.

What is particularly impressive in the book is the whole approach to the principles of negotiation — something one does not immediately associate with the military:

> These principles, which must be respected for the sake of credibility include
> – an acknowledgement of the legitimate security interests of the other side, and of the equality of both negotiating partners.
> – an awareness that security cannot be guaranteed by armament, but only destroyed by it, and that security cannot be achieved in opposition to the other side but only in co-operation with it.
> – the limitation of military power as an element of foreign policy, and the rejection of a policy which attempts to achieve security primarily by military means and therefore strives for military superiority.

I see that I added another inserted quotation from Professor Michel Howard at this point: 'One of the oldest lessons of history is that the armaments of an adversary always seem 'brutal' and threatening — adjectives that appear tendentious and absurd when applied to one's own.'

37. COMMEMORATING THE DEAD

Those who are active in various disarmament groups debate each year whether or not to make their mark on Armistice Sunday. We all have a duty to commemorate with respect and sorrow the deaths of those who fought in the World Wars according to their consciences; but that applies to those on both sides of the hostilities. It has been interesting to note that the sons of Field-marshals Montgomery and Rommel were able to stand together recently on one occasion; somehow or other the war in N.Africa was 'respectable'. But wars have not ceased and we have been involved in another in Iraq. We have to remind people that nearly half of the 50 million who died in World War II were civilians, not troops at all. In Vietnam the civilian deaths proportion was over 80%. In C. & Q. for October I reproduced Siegfried Sassoon's cynical poem:

> AT THE CENOTAPH
> I saw the Prince of Darkness with his staff
> Standing bare-headed at the cenotaph,
> Unostentatious and respectful there
> He stood, and offered up the following prayer:
> 'Make them forget, O Lord, what this memorial
> Means. Their discredited ideas revive:
> Breed new belief that war is purgatorial,

Proof of the pride and power of being alive,
Man's biologic urge to re-adjust
The map of Europe. Lord of Hosts, increase,
Lift up their hearts in large destructive lust
And crown their heads with blind vindictive peace.'
The Prince of Darkness to the Cenotaph
Bowed. As he walked away I heard him laugh.

Now that's a pretty unrelenting view. Less cynical was the decision this year for the Peace Pledge Union's annual wreath to be laid with these words attached:

For all who have died or are dying in war.
For all those who have died or are dying as resources which could be used to feed or house them have gone into military preparation.
For all those who will die in war until we learn to live in peace.
When will we ever learn?

I ended that issue of C&Q with words attributed to a former US Ambassador (somehow I omitted his name — perhaps Kennan again?)

When it comes to the more normal and permanent problems of foreign policy, both of the super-powers could serve the cause of peace by developing a bit more humility in their view of themselves and of their relationships to the world environment, particularly the Third World. Both could take better account of the bitterness of their own domestic problems and of the need for overcoming these before indulging themselves in dreams of external grandeur and world leadership.

That summer I went on holiday as a chaplain for a Pax Christi organised group at Palazzola, a villa on Lake Albano. The duties were light and I had plenty of time for reading. I had determined to leave aside the issues of nuclear war temporarily, but somehow several of the books I tackled had implications not far from the issues of war and peace. Till now I had not read the 40-year-old book by R. H. Tawney *The Acquisitve Society*, and I found him saying some pretty important things. For instance:

Militarism is the characteristic, not of an army, but of society. Its essence is not any particular quality or scale of military preparations, but a state of mind which in its concentration on one particular element in social life ends finally by exalting it until it becomes the arbiter of all the rest.

What the military tradition and spirit did for Prussia with the result of creating militarism, the commercial tradition and spirit has done for England, with the result of creating Industrialism ... When a Cabinet minister declares that the greatness of a country depends upon the volume of its exports, that is Industrialism. It is the confusion of one minor department of life with the whole of life ... When the Press clamours that the one thing needed to make this island Arcadia is productivity and more productivity and yet more productivity, that is Industrialism. It is the confusion of means with ends.

I thought I might send that passage to the Chancellor of the Exchequer.

38. LOCAL CAMPAIGNING CONTINUED

While I spent much time putting together Comments and Quotes, the local WND Newsletter was in the hands of Richard Andrews, one of the several residents at the Peace Studies Centre, and it had become much more attractive in its presentation. Looking back at the issues for the spring and summer of 1984, I am reminded how many things were now going on. A new element was tracking the Cruise convoys, so the report brings back the whole spirit of our campaigning.

At 12.30 on March 9th a Cruise Missile launcher left Greenham Common and travelled for 55 miles through the Berkshire and Wiltshire countryside. Where were we? Certainly campaigners had a lot to contend with; after days of harassment the women at Greenham were rounded up as the missiles left. Motorists along the route were stopped and interrogated. Wrexham did not in fact hear of the departure of the convoy till the radio news at 6.0 am. Indeed it is rumoured that the telephones on the Newbury area were out of action at the time. So where were we? Despite all the problems a group of 8 or 9 from Wrexham, Ruabon and elsewhere met at Chirk and distributed leaflets to householders and passers-by from 12 noon till 1.00 p.m. They found people very responsive to the fact that the Essential Service Routes would be closed at the time of emergency and reflected on the event as being successful. A major leafleting exercise occurred on the A495/A550, outside Queensferry. About 60 people in all, from Mold, Holywell, Rhyl and St.Asaph distributed to motorists entering or leaving Wales. They picked an excellent site where there are three sets of traffic lights close together and slowed the traffic down even more by driving slowly up and down this stretch of road. The group was there en masse between 6.15 and 6.45 p.m. and were able to chat politely to a very placid bunch of policemen.

Friday's operation was a training exercise for us as well as for the military; what have we learned from it? Firstly the Queensferry experience has shown us that the police can be quite agreeable provided we organise ourselves sensibly and don't cause too much

Milton Keynes Peace Campaign News   June 84

disturbance. Secondly it showed we didn't need to form into affinity groups (which may become essential if they try to bring Cruise into Wales).

So that was one focus of interest. Another was the growing research on the Arms Trade. Richard attended the national meeting of the Campaign Against the Arms Trade on behalf of our local group, and reported:

'We know that there is a nuclear arms race, escalating to the point where a nuclear holocaust seems the almost inevitable result unless it is stopped soon. What we are less aware of is that the global arms race is fuelled by the ever increasing international trade in conventional arms. These weapons have already resulted in 65 major wars since 1960. With about 50 others from peace groups across the country, we were involved in role playing, quizzes and workshops on organising events, leaflet production and using the media. It was an intensive and very useful weekend which educated and inspired us, and yet still retained that all important element of fun.'

The programme for March 1984 included the local planning meeting in Wrexham (14th),the Clwyd Federation meeting in Ruthin (15th) the CND Cymru AGM in Llandrindod Wells (17th) A public meeting arranged by Ruabon group in Johnstown (21st) A public session with Ron Todd of Transport & General Workers Union (22nd)

A Video & Discussion meeting in Overton (22nd) Our General meeting in Wrexham (28th). Then the Wrexham Christians for Peace sub-group filled April with Peace Prayers evening (3rd) A Biblical Study at the Baptists church (13th) A silent Vigil and leafleting in the town (14th). A witnessing procession to the Parish Church (15th) and a fine public meeting at Capel y Groes (16th) addressed by Jim

Forest, the secretary of the International Fellowship of Reconciliation.'

We were really impressed with Ron Todd's commitment to the cause of disarmament. He related what he had to say to unemployment by speaking of the outline plans for 'conversion' to civilian and useful products instead of armaments-related work with which many of his own and other trade union members are involved.

The May bulletin was the 4th birthday edition, and started: 'Sometimes it feels as though we've been campaigning all our lives. What was life like before we gave so much time and energy to challenging the conventional wisdom about nuclear deterrence.?' It then gave a summarised history of the Wrexham groups, and ended:

> We've all learned a lot since the start, and sometimes it may seem we make little headway, but when we're on the street there is no doubt at all that our stand, and that of a quarter million others all over the UK, have helped to change public attitudes. Government policies have not changed however and with a huge parliamentary majority it often seems that nothing will ever change. We need unflagging perseverance, better communication and endless hope. Meantime we have got to know a long list of delightful people. Here's to the eventual time when we won't be needed any more because governments will have found a new way of living.

In May also there was a Ride for Life, when 24 cyclists from all over the UK rode into Wrexham from Colwyn Bay to complete a leg of their ten day and over 600 mile journey round the coast and border of Wales. The colourfully dressed riders certainly turned heads as they rode through the town centre escorted by a group of not so athletic or sun-bronzed Wrexham cyclists on their way to a well-earned cup of tea and a mountain of cakes prepared by Wrexham members at the Prices Lane Community Centre. Thus refreshed and re-vitalised, the riders were despatched in twos, threes and fours to homes all over Wrexham where they showered and ate before meeting in local pubs for an evening's get-together. This was an unusual and excellent publicity event, attracting a full complement of press people and the Community Video in attendance.

We also made strenuous efforts to influence the Dutch parliament on its vote to accept or reject having Cruise missiles stationed there. We provided the names and addresses of those Christian Democrat members who were still 'on the fence' for people to write letters urgently.

The next bulletin reported the London demonstration this year as a success with 200,000 taking part. We had sent a coach-load, many of whom risked arrest by taking part in the 'blockade'. We congratulated all the demonstrators and the police who were described as having 'behaved impeccably'. That same day (June 9th) a well-organised gathering led by Chester's Christians for Peace, celebrated a 'Peace Pentecost' at Burtonwood, when 350 people walked some three or four miles to the gates of the nuclear storage base. 'We stayed here for a while in prayer, and then took a flower-decorated cross to leave for the base commander, but he wasn't at home; nor was his deputy. The slightly bewildered but friendly police inspector said there would be no-one there till Monday, only the British police on guard. He was willing to receive a written message; but we said the decorated cross was our message. We left it in love and the spirit of reconciliation, and suggested that world understanding would benefit if the base was closed down.'

Ruth Hughes from Llangollen was just back from a Pensioners for Peace visit to the Soviet Union, which made quite a splash in our local papers; and I had my third visit to Athens with KEADEA as before. The Smiths attended the important conference in Sheffield led by scientists from USA and USSR on the details of a 'nuclear winter' in the event of the use of nuclear weapons. 'The ecosystems effects alone resulting from a large scale thermo-nuclear war could be enough to destroy current civilisations in at least the northern hemisphere.' Their report in an abridged form was the basis of a fine letter in the local paper.

I also reported on my attendance at West Germany's Katholikentag festival in Munich — three days of lectures, seminars and workshops in a biennial event. 'It was good that so many were wearing the purple scarf which was the sign of an emphatic NO to weapons of mass destruction. It was also good to find a city taken over so massively by thousands and thousands of mostly young people, singing, and dancing everywhere. The visit was no chore therefore, though I did go out with Belgian and American Pax Christi members to Dachau concentration camp to be reminded of the ugly potential of human beings taking millions of people to the incinerators. Now, however, as is often pointed out, we are ready to take the incinerators in the form of radiation bombs to the millions.'

The July bulletin also noted the arrival of Mark Brown as another resident at the Peace Studies Centre. He was plunged immediately into the task of indexing, sorting and filing the endless piles of paper which needed organising as a useful resource in the reference library. He was also asked to concentrate on another issue which was coming to the fore — that of Civil Defence plans. In September there was to be a national week of action; and we were being encouraged in Wrexham to put pressure on our council to join the 150 local authorities who are refusing to co-operate with the government's new emergency planning regulations; they were designed to prepare for the 'day after'. The Home Office circular described the first aim of civil defence as securing the UK against internal threat. That, we supposed, included us! More fundamentally we reckoned that civil defence is meant to persuade people that nuclear war is survivable. It had to be exposed as a lie. Fred Starkey of Mold had prepared a display on 'the nuclear winter' to be on show at Theatr Clwyd's foyer and we were asked to help staff the event.

39. A STORY FROM GREENHAM

While building up for a truly massive women's event at Greenham Common for 20-30th September, our bulletin included a report from Janet Tyrrell (one of the original Greenham marchers) who had so inspired us. This helped to record the Greenham phenomenon for what it really was.

'We camped for nine days in early August; six of us with five small children, with other women joining us at two weekends. We chose the Orange Gate because of the woody common and space off the road for the children. We had a 'good' time, which seemed a contradiction because we were aware all the time of the horrors beyond the fence. There is a permanent camp at the gate, as at all the others, with a core of a few women, but a considerable number of others passed through while we were there.

During the week several times we attempted to stop cruise convoy support vehicles from leaving the base; it was a gesture. There were not enough of us to stop them effectively; we could only delay them. We were moved once by MOD police on the gate (two weeks later I still have a bruise). Once warned by civil police that we would be arrested, we got up out of the way, and once we were moved by Americans with some pretty crude invective, who jumped off the vehicles waiting to go back into the base and threw us out of the way themselves. Heseltine said this shouldn't happen; but it does. One of the changes at Greenham is that there is now an armed American serviceman in control of each gate at opening and closing times. It is not difficult to sense that MOD and RAF personnel are unhappy about that.

We held a 24 hour vigil in shifts at the gate on Hiroshima Day ('Instant Sunshine Day', 'the Day of the Big Flash') gives a taste of some of the soldiers'

jokes). From 11.30 to midnight we all stood silently facing the gate holding candles. Silence is stronger than almost anything else I know. One lone RAF guard stood facing us, and after a time he wrote something on his notepad and stuck it in the gate. It read 'God bless you all. May you get through God what you want.'

We took turns to do the night watch, both for cruise convoys coming out — creep across the common, avoiding police in the bushes, and try to get the message to a house half a mile away— or for carloads of young men after closing time, coming to buzz the camps. The week remains for me a series of images: a police car in the night, nose-down in a ditch the authorities had dug to stop cars driving from the side to block convoys, with the police driver being taken up the road by a diminutive camp woman for a cup of tea by the fire. Group of orthodox Jews, pale and black, strolling round the fence. The crouching soldiers on the convoy supporting vehicles, their faces criss-crossed with black and green camouflage marks — you go out to practice launching a cruise missile and you try to look like a tree. Julia got up as Ms Greenham 1984 in a pink frilly bikini, gumboots, a crown of rowan berries in her spiked hair and bright red paper lips with a roll-up stuck between, approaching the fence with a pair of cardboard bolt cutters while the soldiers on the gate dashed around to prevent a breach of security.

What was most positive about the week was our sense of community, and out of our anger a renewed determination to do whatever we can not to be defeated by a feeling of impotence in the face of all that organised insanity'.

40. HIGH POINTS IN OCTOBER

The energy of the several Wrexham groups was in no way flagging. Kevin Proctor had joined Richard Andrews and Mark Brown as residents at the Peace Studies Centre, and a new Youth CND was being formed. There were some real tensions growing among the campaigners about the methods and emphases we should be using. It was good that several of these, especially the support for the Freeze campaign, were debated openly in the monthly newsletter. There were anxieties expressed also about the extent to which we should be showing support for the miners at the time of their strikes. October 1984 had a real end-of-the-month catalogue of events for One World Week, starting with an Arts Centre launch with the Mayoress, and a United Service at the Methodist church. The Women-for-Peace group held a discussion, music and film evening. Another evening followed with Bishop Dumper at the Congregationalist church about El Salvador. John Roberts of Oxfam led an evening at the Arts Centre called 'Hungry for Change' and another evening was designed to introduce co-operative games for parents and children. All this showed that our peace groups were linked with a range of much wider issues. Indeed, even though the CND-based issues seemed to fade away in the next few years, most people kept up their interest and concern for some important issue.

Nationally the focus in late October was on Barrow, where the Trident nuclear submarines were made, and a coach-load was arranged from our groups. There was considerable interest also about the Labour Party's detailed defence policy document which started on the Trident issue. There had been a special meeting in Birmingham on 15th September for the 'Peace Movement' to respond publicly. Our bulletin read:

> The policy is as agreed by the NEC and will be put before the Labour Conference this month. To be brief Labour will Cancel Trident — Dismantle Polaris — Get rid of US nuclear and Cruise bases — Stay in NATO — and Develop defensive conventional weaponry. Denzil Davies (Defence Spokesman) defended the decision to stay in NATO while recognising the enormous problems of staying non-nuclear in a nuclear alliance. Robin Cook (Labour front bench) also defended the NATO stance but less happily. He made further detailed proposals such as working hard in NATO for 'no first use', and de-coupling nuclear from conventional weapons. He warned of the dangers of some of the recent very nasty conventional offensive weapons.
>
> Joan Ruddock in a brilliant address welcomed the strategy for its strengths — its clear unilateral stance. She confirmed, however, that CND will never assume party political colours and advised the Labour Party to understand that clearly. CND's strength is as a grass-roots movement. To much applause she told Labour that they had done well to come so far, but they still had a long way to go in particular over NATO. CND opposed NATO simply because it is a nuclear alliance and for many reasons CND argue that we cannot compromise with NATO. Finally she warned that the next election will be fought on questions of defence and disarmament, and therefore the Labour Party had better get its political education train on the rails if it wanted to have a voice.

Looking back on that report nineteen years later, there are several points of interest.

Mark Brown contributed an item arising from his experience as a door-to-door collector for the Bersham Miners Relief Fund. He wrote:

> Approaching people directly is often scary, and to be seen handing out leaflets is to be a target for indifference and even abuse. Yet they are skills that can be learned together, and must be learned, for if we are not prepared to go out on the streets of Wrexham week in and week out just as the miners do, then we are not members of an organisation committed to disarmament, but members of a small, select club which meets twice a month to discuss disarmament. There are many ways of spreading the message; canvassing is only one of them. It's not to everyone's taste, and people may feel themselves more suited to lobbying the MP or letter-writing. Door to door leafleting is also invaluable, but it is still no substitute for knocking on people's door and talking to them. Personally this last idea scares me stiff. I'm not given to arguing on doorsteps (especially if the owner has a large dog!) but I'm prepared to do it and I think everyone who receives this bulletin ought to be prepared to do it.

The end-of-the-year bulletin recorded items which I had completely forgotten. I am indeed surprised to be reminded that some schools were not so defensive about 'political' issues being raised, because I had two one-hour classes of 70 pupils at Ysgol Rhiwabon on 'Objections to Nuclear Deterrence' and a general session on 'Peace' with 300 pupils at St David's School, Wrexham. The December issue also noted that for the third successive year Christians for Peace planned a 24 hour outdoor vigil in the centre of Wrexham on December 21/22nd. I do remember the interesting conversations at our stall base with Revd.Pryderi Llwyd Jones of Capel y Groes, especially in the difficult post-pub-closing hours in the night. I also remember that Richard Andrews called along with his bags , as he left the area to start at College in Cardiff soon afterwards. We were really sorry to lose him from the group, not least because he had been editor of the bulletin for the last year or more.

41. RAYS OF HOPE

1984 ended with the surprising but welcome note that Mrs Thatcher had had some friendly exchanges with Mr Gorbachev, new on the Soviet scene. At another level there was the appointment in Canada by the new Progressive Conservative Government of Mr Joe Clarke as head of external affairs, who had open disarmament sympathies and Mr Stephen Lewis as their ambassador to the UN who had a record of opposition to Cruise missile testing in Canada and opposition to US foreign policy. A third appointment was of Mr Douglas Roche as Ambassador for Disarmament; he had been an active peace movement supporter. At least this meant that there was a peace movement lobby to be placated.

Australia now had a Peace and Disarmament branch in their Department of Foreign Affairs, and the Australian UN Association was pressing every government to establish a Ministry for Peace. Even more surprising there had been a take-up in West Germany especially of the American, Bill Moyer's, 'People to People' Campaign founded to help link up individuals and groups in Europe and USA. The Berlin-Americans staged a public event, and then were invited to attend the City Council meeting for a debate on anti-

'So much for the international news. The facts will be along later.'

Americanism in the West German Peace Movement, put on by the Christian Democrats (CDs). The CDs argued that the peace movement was anti-American; the Greens the opposite. In fact, the Greens said, there were many Americans against the US European military policy; whereupon the Americans in the audience stood up and unfurled their peace banners, and the Greens won the day. The new American Peace Network in Europe was helping with an educational programme on the US movements, and contacting military on the US bases, and the American tourists.

Next in the East German Republic there appeared a joint declaration by some Independent Peace Defenders together with some from Czechoslovakia who protested against the arrival of Warsaw Pact missiles on their soil. They said that their criticism

> … is addressed to all states which are preparing for a new world war, threatening their neighbours, and often ordering about their own citizens to whom, however, they deny participation in decisions about truly fundamental questions of their own lives….We therefore protest against the siting and extension of nuclear complexes on our territory; we are in solidarity with the peace movements in the West which in their own countries protest against militarism and nuclear armament. …Those who think in terms of 'blocs' and 'enemies' render an honest dialogue impossible. Those who tolerate social inequality or even widen the gap are responsible for hunger and poverty. Those who deny the dignity of individual human beings, who deny freedom of opinion, necessarily also tend to resolve national and international problems by means of violence.

This was strong stuff and very brave, considering the restrictions on free speech which was one mark of eastern European regimes. This sort of evidence, which gave hope to so many of us, did not become common knowledge amidst the standard propaganda of our own country; it needed the peace movement at least to tell those who were ready to listen. Here is another item from East Germany (GDR) in an open letter to Mr Honecker from the Evangelical-Lutheran Ecclesiastical Office of Dresden-Loschwitz. It is a model of constructive protest.

> We are filled with horror at the thought that the stationing of American nuclear missiles in W.Europe, which we have all condemned, is to be accompanied by the introduction of corresponding counter-measures on our own territory as well, and that we and our children will have to live alongside nuclear missiles. You yourself on numerous occasions have expressed the thought that more weaponry does not mean more security … You have also adopted the concept of 'security partnership' as a token of perpetual willingness to engage in negotiation and dialogue … You have spontaneously endorsed the Swedish Proposal for a zone in Europe free from battlefield nuclear weapons. We are most grateful to you for all of these statements … It seems to us that a willingness, coupled with trust to make unilateral prior initiatives (in other words not to seek to repay like with like) could today be the only way to secure peace. This conviction we derive

from the New Testament, in particular from the Gospel of Jesus.

Comments & Quotes added two other statements from American sources:

> Beware of people who talk of modern war as total. It is total not because all the civilians wage it, but because all of them are its targets. (John Ford)

> Only the erosion of the tradition of civilised or just warfare could bring it to pass that non-combatants are regarded as the justifiable targets of direct military action….In this regard, the just war theory has not become inapplicable; it has simply not been applied. That is the measure of our barbarism, and not a factual report of the changes brought about by modern warfare in placing all the people in the position of making war. (Paul Ramsey)

So the official hegemony of the Soviet Union over other countries was not preventing some real items of autonomy, the practice of independent thinking and even occasional organising. It was going to be a delicate matter to recognise this while interacting with the official government- recognised 'Peace Committees' and there were different views about how far we could and should co-operate with them.

Now and again there were signs that the Soviet Peace Committee had some influence on Soviet policies, even though the members were not at liberty to give formal criticism of government policies. I remarked 'I have found several of these people very good company, and often well-disposed to hear criticism of their own stated view, especially over the coffee-breaks and dinner-table. We hoped that they might take back some of these criticisms to a useful forum, but it remained a great mistake to expect them to give an inch of ground in the discussions. I was not in favour of a softly-softly approach in argument; that did not win their respect. 'They do respect honesty and firmness, and this can be practised without losing any of the personal warmth that is generated at some meetings … taking what they put forward at its face value only did them a great dis-service.' Clear speaking even elicited a joking remark from Georgy Arbatov once: 'We know our public relations are lousy.'

Our concern for the Moscow Trust group was real. This was founded in 1982, in Brezhnev days, and had several sister organisations in other Soviet cities; altogether about 2,000 known activists. Their basic idea was to build trust between East and West, to breakdown

the enemy images, and oppose the nuclear arms race. They wanted to see new base groups arising to work for proposals for the building of international trust. They wanted greater popular participation in disarmament negotiations. They took care to do nothing illegal under the Soviet constitution, and even kept the Soviet Peace Committee informed, but they were harassed and some members were penalised from the early months. The government said there was no need for independent organising, since the Soviet policies were peaceful already. The trouble for us was that if we made contact with them we were to be regarded as interfering in the internal affairs of the Soviet Union. Yet we could not ignore them.

Our idea was to persuade Soviet officials that they will go up in our estimate when they feel mature enough to let these independent voices be heard openly. CND had noted their existence, and, as my story unfolds, our next delegation to the USSR included making direct contact.

At the AGM of the National Peace Council, Canon Paul Oestreicher stressed the need not only for 'people to people' contact but 'people to power' also. Sheila Oakes, the indefatigable General Secretary of NPC remarked: 'I spend a lot of time and energy dealing with and often condemning the policies of my own government, and that of the USA and its other allies. I object to and resent being accused of being a NATO agent if I also have the temerity to criticise the policies of the USSR, particularly if they are the same policies that I criticise in my own government.'

'Peace people' were often piggy in the middle; maligned by the British and Soviet governments for different reasons. Harking back to the 'Thirties' comparison again, I reminded readers of the explosion of Bruce Kent a year earlier when Mrs Thatcher suggested that CND members were the 'appeasers' of the thirties. He said:

> Dr Goebbels it was who believed in the really big lie. I am sorry that Mrs Thatcher has followed his road. It was not our predecessors but hers who made Hitler inevitable. It was they who imposed the crippling Treaty of Versailles on Germany, and then failed to keep our disarmament obligations under it. It was the British militarists of the day who wrecked the 1932 disarmament conference, who opposed sanctions against the Japanese in 1931; who opposed (despite French requests) resistance to the German occupation of the Rhineland in 1936. The famous League of Nations' Peace Ballot was not a pacifist ballot. It was a ballot for collective security and over 60% signing approved and wanted collective military security. The papers today who so brutally and actively misrepresent us (especially the Times and the Daily Mail) were pro-appeasement, and, in the case of the Mail, pro-Hitler. If there is a lesson today it is that the great defence of the West, the Maginot line, was actually entirely useless. We were frozen into out of date military thinking then as we are now. Mrs.Thatcher should realise that we are now in a new age of history. It is she who refuses a nuclear freeze, who opposes a 'no first use'

commitment, who urges the massive unilateral increase represented by Trident, who does not understand proliferation or 'first strike' technology, and who makes nuclear war very much more likely.

I then added three more interesting quotations from respectively 1931, 1932 and 1934. Sir Arthur Balfour: ' Will the Germans go to war again? I don't think there's any doubt about it. I am almost persuaded that we shall have to let them arm, or we shall have to arm them …. With the Russians armed to the teeth, and the tremendous menace in the East, Germany unarmed in the middle is a plum waiting for the Russians to take. One of the menaces to peace in Europe is the unarmed condition of Germany.'

S. F. Jonas of the Federal Laboratories in South America: 'The unsettled conditions have been a great thing for me, as I sold a large order of bombs to Brazil. I also sold large bomb orders for Columbia, Peru, Ecuador, Bolivia and now have made up all my losses. It's an ill wind that does not blow someone some good.'

President Roosevelt: 'This grave menace to the peace of the world — the arms race — is due to the activities of the manufacturers of, and the merchants in, the engines of destruction'.

That took me back again to President Eisenhower, who was recorded more fully in Ken Coates' book 'The Most Dangerous Decade' in his farewell address in 1961:

> This conjunction of an immense military establishment and a large arms industry is new in the American experience. The total influence, economic, political and even spiritual, is felt in every city, every state house, every office of the Federal government. Yet we must not fail to comprehend its grave implications. Our toil, resources and livelihood are all involved: so is the very structure of our society. In the councils of government, we must guard against the acquisition of unwarranted influence, whether sought or unsought, by the military-industrial complex. The potential for the disastrous rise of misplaced power exists and will persist. We must never let the weight of this combination endanger our liberties or democratic processes. We should take nothing for granted. Only an alert and knowledgeable citizenry can compel the proper meshing of the huge industrial and military machinery of defence with our peaceful methods and goals, so that security and liberty may prosper together.

I remarked, 'When one reads that Mr Heseltine is responsible for another high-salaried post (£90,000 per annum) for a civil servant to sell arms, one wonders if the disease is not rampant in the UK establishment already. The close relationship between some government officials and the arms industries is extremely sinister.'

42. THE BIG POWERS AND UNILATERAL INITIATIVES

Although there was some reduction in the rhetoric of East and West at the start of 1985, the USA and USSR seemed determined to keep up their Cold War stance. This was beginning to irritate smaller nations and the last effort at a UNresolution for a Comprehensive Test Ban Treaty from Mexico received 111 'Yes' votes; but UK and USA. voted 'No'. There were three Resolutions on establishing a Nuclear Freeze with 'Yes' votes given as 111,110 and 95; but France, UK and USA. voted 'No'. A Third World diplomat remarked: 'The two super-powers aren't really interested in disarmament or arms control. It's not in their national interest.'

The Five Continents Initiative — from the Presidents or Prime Ministers of Argentina, Greece, India, Mexico, Sweden and Tanzania — was known as the Delhi Declaration. It read:

> Almost imperceptibly over the last four decades, every nation and every human being has lost ultimate control over their own life and death. For all of us, it is a small group of men and machines in cities far away who can decide our fate … We find ourselves in this situation because the nuclear weapon states have applied traditional doctrines of war in a world where new weapons have made them obsolete … But nuclear war can be prevented if our voices are joined in a universal demand in defence of our right to live.

It was already the third anniversary of our Nuclear Free Wales Declaration, which we recognised was a statement of hope more than anything. We had a Happy Birthday sheet on which we repeated some of the wording: 'We seek to grow in recognition and respect of our differences and similarities, and know that it is possible for us Europeans as to all the people of the world, to live in tolerance and understanding, rather than under constant fear of a nuclear war.'

The UN Secretary-General commissioned a Report at this time to be made by a Group of Governmental Experts on Unilateral Disarmament measures, which concluded among other things that 'during the past four decades the arms race has developed as the result of unilateral decisions by States, taken in the name of national security', and that therefore 'the process of de-escalation and reversal of the arms race … could be promoted by unilateral initiatives of States aimed at reducing the level of international tension, gradually creating an atmosphere of mutual trust and confidence and in general improving the environment of negotiations on arms limitation and disarmament.'. The Report then added most significantly:

> Unilateralism, as developed in the literature, is not one-sided disarmament but it is a way in which through unilateral, or more precisely graduated and reciprocated initiatives

in tension reduction, two or more countries can promote genuine arms limitation and disarmament agreements … Unilateral initiatives do not require confidence and mutual trust. On the contrary, confidence and mutual trust come about as a result of unilateral actions.

On December 17th 1984 the Report came up for a vote in the UN General Assembly. 126 votes in favour; 13 abstentions (including the UK and most of the NATO states). Votes against? One, from USA.

43. JONATHAN SCHELL ON DETERRENCE

Having just read Jonathan Schell's powerful book *The Abolition*, I showered Comments & Quotes with extracts like these:

Deterrence theory is indeed a marvel of circularity and contradiction. To obtain the benefit of the policy, we must perform an insane action. But the benefit we seek is precisely not to perform that action. We thus seek to avoid performing an act by threatening to perform it.

Whatever government spokesmen might say about possessing nuclear weapons only to prevent their use, the inescapable truth was that possession inevitably implied use, and use was irredeemably senseless, since it threatened to bring about the destruction of whatever one might think one was trying to defend.

Sometimes our performance in the post-war world is called a great success on the ground that we have so far avoided a nuclear holocaust, and much of the credit is given to the policy of deterrence.
What this reckoning overlooks is that in the same period the world has built up arsenals of more than 50,000 nuclear warheads — that behind the screen of deterrence policy we have built the means of our annihilation.

When politicians speak of what is 'possible' or 'impossible', they are often referring to nothing more that what is or is not acceptable to current public opinion. What they often really mean when they say something is 'impossible' is that they cannot win the next election if they advocate it. But if public opinion changes then their opinion changes too and all of a sudden yesterday's impossible thing is possible.

44. FORTY YEARS ON: 1945–85

It was to be expected that we would hear much about the great anniversaries: VE Day, the founding of the United Nations Organisation, VJ Day (in that order). By now the whole meaning of the Yalta agreement to 'settle' post-war Europe was being called in question We were having to look at the origins of the Cold War, and I picked on John Lewis Gaddis's book *The United States and the Origins of the Cold War* for some interesting details. One summary seemed to me to be valid. 'Both Moscow and Washington wanted peace, but strong internal influences caused each to conceive of it in contradictory ways. These clashing perceptions of a common goal wrecked the Grand Alliance at the moment of victory, creating an ironic situation in which simultaneous searches for peace led to the Cold War.' The steps towards this conclusion contain many mistakes, some ghastly, some innocent. Roosevelt himself was an optimist: he said 'I think the Russians are perfectly friendly; they aren't trying to gobble up all the rest of Europe or the world … They haven't got any crazy ideas of conquest.'

The hopes for the new planned United Nations were high. Secretary Cordell Hull thought that once it was set up, 'there will no longer be need for spheres of influence, for alliances, for balance of power or any other special arrangements through which in the unhappy past the nations strove to safeguard their security or to promote their interest.' The wartime euphoria hadn't worn off generally. Just look at this extract from *Life* in 1943. 'Lenin was perhaps the greatest man of modern times' The Russians were 'one hell of a people who to a remarkable degree look like Americans, think like Americans. The NKVD was a national police force similar to the FBI'.

Roosevelt's entire 'grand design for post-war co-operation with the Soviet Union rested on the assumption that Moscow had stopped trying to impose communism on the rest of the world '. But (Gaddis writes) 'Americans recoiled in horror as they gradually became aware of Moscow's intention to dominate the post-war governments of East Europe. The resulting tension between the American principle of self-determination and Russian security needs became the single most important cause of the disintegration of the Grand Alliance.'

The Catholic Church — a powerful factor in the USA — was another vocal centre of scepticism. Traditional hostility towards communism, the Soviet persecution of religion, and memories of the confrontations in the Spanish Civil War between Catholics and communists, led to occasional excessive statements like this, from one priest-editor: 'Fascism, Nazism, Imperialism combined, if that could be, would not be so serious a threat to peace and to international co-operation as Russian Communism.'

On the other side, the Soviet Union had some of their underlying suspicions confirmed by the military delays in the war. 'The long delay in establishing the

Second Front confirmed Soviet fears that their capitalist allies had deliberately let communist Russia bear the brunt of the fighting.' Roosevelt was for 'dealing'. He 'cautiously indicated to the Russians that they could have a free hand in Europe… but hoped

Stalin would be discreet, for any appearance of abandoning self-determination would cause FDR serious political problems inside USA.' But he also told Cordell Hull that 'neither England nor the US would fight to save the Baltic states….but Russia's standing would improve in the eyes of the world if it would hold plebiscites in the territories it planned to take over.'

People like Senator Vandenberg had found Yalta hard to swallow; but he knew that 'the American people would not go to war with Russia to change this. The only alternative was to use the San Francisco Conference (on the UN) to turn the world against the Soviet Union. 'I have great hope that we can mobilise the conscience of mankind against the aggressor of tomorrow. It may not prevent World War Three one day; but if it fails it will at least unite civilisation against the new aggressor.'

Meantime Stalin, from his perspective, was telling Secretary Hopkins that 'twice within the last 25 years the Germans had invaded Russia through Poland. The Poles had either been too weak to resist or had led the Germans through because they hated the Russians so much … Russia had a vital interest in seeing to it that Poland was strong and friendly in future. Stalin admitted he had taken unilateral action in Poland, but said that this had been done for military reasons, not from any desire to exclude his allies from participation in post-war Polish affairs.' Harriman said 'It is difficult for Stalin to understand why we should want to interfere with Soviet policy in a country like Poland, which he considers so important to Russian security, unless we have some ulterior motive.'

Gaddis recorded some careless and clumsy statements made by leading political figures. For me the one that 'takes the biscuit' came from Senator Johnson in 1945: 'God Almighty in his infinite wisdom has dropped the atomic bomb in our lap. With vision and guts and plenty of atomic bombs the US could compel mankind to adopt the policy of lasting peace, or be buried to a crisp.' Gaddis added 'No responsible official in the Truman administrations wanted to go that far, but the President and his advisers did expect that the American nuclear monopoly would improve the West's bargaining position with the Soviet Union. Stimson was saying 'Development of this weapon has placed a certain moral responsibility upon us which we cannot shirk'. Truman himself rather more pompously said: 'The possession in our hands of this new power of destruction we regard as a sacred trust. The thoughtful people of the world know that this trust will not be violated, that it will be faithfully executed.' Gaddis reports that 'this address led the editor of The Nation to comment that Truman had assumed the ambitious task of conducting American foreign policy according to the principles of Theodore Roosevelt and St Francis of Assisi.'

One has heard other political leaders proclaiming St Francis as patron on the very steps of Downing Street. Some of us were not impressed!

Gaddis quoted Reinhold Niebuhr in 1943 as saying: 'Ideally collaboration between the communist and the democratic world might lead to a wholesale exchange of political experience. We have on the whole more liberty and less equality than the Russian has. Russia has less liberty and more equality. Whether democracy should be defined primarily in terms of liberty or equality is a source of unending debate.' In fact of course international politics are more pragmatic; not really concerned about ideology so long as they can 'get along'. George Kennan in 1944 wrote: 'It is a matter of indifference to Moscow whether a given Area is communistic or not. All things being equal Moscow might prefer to see it communised, although even that is debatable. But the main thing is that it should be amenable to Moscow influence, and if possible to Moscow authority.' The same may be said of the USA; only in this way can one understand the acceptance of military tyrannies all over the world. What they do doesn't seem to matter, so long as they fit in with the USA. Kennan also wrote that 'more important than the observable nature of external reality when it comes to the determination of Washington's view of the world, is the subjective state of readiness on the part of Washington officialdom to recognise this or that feature of it.' In other words you see what you choose to see.

45. JUDGEMENTS AND ASSESSMENTS

George Kennan was quoted as saying in 1946 that 'for Stalin and his associates Marxist ideology provided the justification for the dictatorship without which they do not know how to rule, for cruelties they did not dare to inflict, for sacrifices they felt bound to demand. Marxism is the fig-leaf of their moral and intellectual respectability. Without it they would stand before history at best as only the last of that long succession of cruel and wasteful Russian rulers, who have relentlessly forced their country on to ever new heights of military power in order to guarantee external security for their internally weak regime.'

In the same year Secretary Acheson spoke of 'the difficulty we have in using our great economic power in our own interest to hasten recovery in other countries along lines which are essential to our own system' He regarded a nuclear armaments race with Russia as futile. 'because there could be no defence against the bomb, and use of it might destroy civilisation. Under these circumstances the advantage of being ahead in such a race is nothing compared with not having the race.'

Gaddis winds up by saying: 'The Cold War grew out of a complicated interaction of external and internal developments inside the USA and the Soviet Union. The external situation — circumstances beyond the control of either power — left Americans and Russians facing one another across prostrated Europe at the end of World War Two. Internal influences in the Soviet Union — the search for security, the role of ideology, massive post-war reconstruction needs, the personality of Stalin — together with those in the US — the ideal of self-determination, fear of communism, the illusion of omnipotence fostered by America's economic strength and the atomic bomb made the resulting confrontation a hostile one. Leaders of both super-powers sought peace, but in doing so yielded to considerations which, while they did not precipitate war, made a resolution of differences impossible.'

46. VOICES OF DISSENT

While it seemed to me to be important to keep track of the wisdom and analyses of writers such as Gaddis, there was value in expressing an entirely different set of values. It is inadequate to refer to these as 'pacifist' — which always has a negative ring about it. There is a positive message in all of the following quotations.

Nobody was born non-violent. Nobody was born charitable. None of us comes to these things by nature, but only by conversion. The first duty of the non-violent community is helping its members work upon themselves, and come to conversion. (Lanza del Vasto)

The peace process starts with belief that peace is possible, gains support in moving towards it, increases in hope that it will be, and

132

results in the assertion of the reality of peace. The violence process begins with doubt that it is possible, mockery of the proposal, scepticism that it can ever be, and finally denial that it can be. [Pope Paul VI,1973]

I refuse to accept the cynical notion that nation after nation must spiral down a militaristic stairway into the hell of nuclear destruction. I believe that unarmed truth and unconditional love will have the final word in reality. (Martin Luther King)

'In the past it was possible to destroy a village, a town, a region, even a country. Now it is the whole planet that has come under threat. This fact should compel everyone to face a basic moral consideration; from now on it is only through a conscious choice and then deliberate policy that humanity can survive. (Pope John Paul II)

and Jonathan Schell adds:

The Pope's deceptively simple statement contains an invaluable anatomy of the challenge that the invention of nuclear weapons has placed before mankind. In distinguishing between 'a conscious choice' and 'deliberate policy' he defines two stages, one individual and spiritual, the other public and political — that we must pass through if we are to resolve the nuclear predicament.

47. POSSIBILITIES FOR CHANGE

The arms race was regularly criticised, but new opportunities arose with the change of leadership in the Soviet Union. David Holloway (in *The Choice*) wrote:

This is a time for Western governments, and especially for the USA, to work out the basis for co-operative efforts to bring the nuclear arms race under control. In spite of the present poor state of Soviet-American relations, there are several important features of Soviet policy that suggest that this is an opportune time for pursuing serious arms limitation and reduction agreements. The changes in Soviet doctrine, the setbacks in Soviet foreign policy, the problems of resource allocation, and the continuing uncertainty about the political leadership, all point in this direction.

He wrote this in 1984, and now Chernenko had died and everyone wondered whether Gorbachev wanted or intended anything new. Holloway recommended western changes:

…for the West to take advantage of these developments, a political strategy is required that aims at co-operation and agreement, and directs the normal techniques of foreign policy — both toughness and conciliation — towards that political goal. The mere application of pressure, if it is not directed towards a realistic political goal, is likely to do little more than produce hostility and truculence on the part of the Soviet Union. The mere assertion of the desire for better relations, if it is not accompanied by concrete measures, will do little more than add to the suspicion and cynicism that characterise East-West relations at present.

He went on to suggest firmly that there should be unilateral (i.e. non-negotiated) measures that could immediately be taken by the West, such as the adoption of a 'no first use' climate.; 'but in the end,' he added, 'the prevention of nuclear war and survival of the human race cannot be secured without the co-operation of the Soviet Union.'.

On both sides, it seemed to me, we could do with less rhetoric, more truth, less words, more action. Secretiveness by the Russians only fuels the hostile imaginations of many Americans; new faces among the negotiators from USA only confirm the opinion expressed to me once on one of my USSR visits that 'the USA does not have a foreign policy; only the whims of changing administrations' A harsh judgement, but not too far off the mark, I think. George Kennan once wrote: 'the American establishment has a long-standing, almost traditional, aversion to professionalism in diplomacy. The principle on which it proceeds is that experience in any other conceivable walk of professional life — the law, business, journalism — would obviously be a better qualification for senior responsibility in the diplomatic field than experience in the Foreign Services.' That seems sadly to be true even today.

But we have to go back over and again to Eisenhower's remarks: 'In the councils of government we must guard against the acquisition of unwarranted influence, whether sought or unsought, by the military-industrial complex'. Is it altogether surprising that during the Iraq invasion and subsequently we find ourselves critical of the parcelling out of tasks to American companies, and the extremely doubtful focus on the protection of oil production in the light of the background of the neo-conservatives around George W.Bush?

48. 'RUSSIA, AMERICA & THE FALL OF WESTERN EUROPE'

I decided to review (again for Comments & Quotes) Brian May's book under this title who had some interesting facts and opinions to offer. In particular, 'Twice as many American films are screened in the USSR as Soviet films in the USA. In 1980 the Soviet Union staged 130 plays by present-day Western writers. It has more teachers of Western languages than there are students of Russian in the USA.' For one awful moment I could see British hawks seeing this as evidence that the Russians are coming west. We don't need to speak Russian, of course, because we have no expansionist interests!

Brian May also suggested that 'if the West wants to see a transformation, or modification (in Russian attitudes) it should realise that any official statement it makes about Soviet internal behaviour will be counter-productive; for it will be resented not only by the Kremlin, but by the whole of society with the exception of a few dissidents. In general Soviet citizens distrust the West. Criticism of sub-standard practices such as the incarceration of dissidents in mental hospitals, should never be used as a political weapon, but should be left to impartial bodies such as Amnesty International.'

Of course we must uphold the rights of persecuted individuals; but there's a time and a place for doing this, if it is not to be counter-productive. Many of us visiting the USSR have found people of impeccable Soviet loyalty, who are able to admit that things are not always as they ought to be. As explanation (not as excuse) they refer to the relative 'youth' of their revolution — 60 years under heavy outside pressure. Mature internal political treatment will come when they do not feel threatened from outside, and less frightened of moderate pluralism within their socialism.

Having outlined the significant failures of Soviet communism to expand across the world, Brian May concludes with his recipe towards world peace: 'It is of little use calling for unilateral nuclear disarmament by a society that is content to enjoy luxuries made possible through the selling the means of destruction to backward peoples. The moral strength needed to abandon nuclear weapons could only arise from a consensus sufficiently wide and profound to encompass responsibility towards the entire world … Europe is therefore divided into two rotting halves, one with a bogus ideology, and the other with no effective values except consumerism.'

A chilling judgement indeed.

49. JONATHAN STEELE ON THE SOVIETS

The Limits of Soviet Power made a serious effort to explore the Russians' own perception of the problems of their security. Steele saw three factors behind Russian fears — 'a sense of geographical encirclement; the knowledge that their ideological enemies have invaded them twice, and have the power to do so again; and awareness that the next war is likely to be the last.

With scrupulous fairness he went on: 'The Soviet Union bears some responsibility for the nuclear arms race. Its early emphasis on rocketry, its decision to MIRV its heaviest missiles, its research into laser weapons raised the prospect of a first-strike potential. In the early 1960s Kruschev foolishly boasted of having an anti-ballistic missile system which could knock out incoming American missiles as accurately as 'hitting a fly in outer space' The boast was spurious and was probably designed to conceal Soviet weakness in strategic weapons, but it played into the hands of Pentagon hard-liners who used it to justify their own plans for

THEY'RE TRACTOR PARTS FOR EAST TIMOR... ....HONESTLY!

new weapons.' But while Kruschev's posturing is accepted and acted upon, his words are more quickly forgotten.: 'We have not sought and do not now seek, military superiority over the other side. That is not our policy.' (26th Party Congress)

'He never pretended the ideological struggle would not continue, but in 1972 he had said, 'We will strive to direct it into a channel which poses no threat of war, dangerous conflicts and an uncontrolled arms race.'

Steele remarked as the arms race continued nevertheless: 'The differences of emphasis between the political doctrine that nuclear war is futile and the military view that victory must be prepared for remained valid in the Brezhnev era. Soviet policy was as contradictory as Western policy in trying to justify the value of what were admitted to be suicidal weapons.'

50. THIS WAS NOW MARCH 1985

It was difficult to keep track of all the international developments. It wasn't till April that I found the relevant findings of the General Assembly of the United Nations at the end of 1984. These certainly undermined the government's false claim to believe in multi-lateral negotiations.

The following resolutions had been passed:

1. (The Assembly) affirms its conviction that the conclusion of a multi-lateral treaty on the prohibition of nuclear weapons' tests by all states would constitute an indispensable element to the success of efforts to halt and reverse the arms race. UK voted against.

2. (The Assembly) because the UN Committee on Disarmament is the most suitable

forum for negotiations on nuclear disarmament, calls on the C.D. to proceed without delay towards negotiations for nuclear disarmament. UKvoted against

3. (The Assembly) believes efforts should be intensified with a view to initiating multi-lateral negotiations, because it is necessary to halt all testing, production and deployment of nuclear weapons and their delivery systems. UKvoted against

4. (The Assembly) calls in all nuclear states to agree to a freeze in nuclear weapons, which would inter alia provide for a simultaneous total stoppage of any further production of nuclear weapons, and a complete cut-off in the production of fissionable material for weapons' purposes. UKvoted against

5 (The Assembly) invites nuclear states to consider holding multi-lateral talks on the limitation and reduction of naval armaments, and the extension of confidence-building measures to seas and oceans.UK voted against

5. (The Assembly) deplored the fact that the bi-lateral negotiations were not producing the desired results, and urges the governments of the USA and USSR to find a way out of the present impasse. UK voted against.

We all wondered how many members of parliament knew about all this. Meanwhile we noted that 'Every 15 seconds, someone dies of malnutrition; while every 15 seconds, the world spends more than £75,000 on armaments.

51. MORE THAN INFORMATION WAS NECESSARY

Alongside my scattered attempts to produce items from my own reading to inform people in the monthly Comments & Quotes especially for those who had less time to explore issues in depth, the local and regional activists were hard at work keeping up the momentum of the peace movement. The Wrexham for Nuclear Disarmament newsletter was full each month of events and activities.

At the end of 1984 the twenty-four hours vigil by Christians for Peace was held again in Queen Square. This included three special 'services' which had the support of ministers from the, Baptist, URC and Welsh Presbyterian churches. Bishop Hannigan joined us for the final service, and we were specially pleased to welcome the new Anglican Rector, Barry Morgan — who is now the new Archbishop of Wales, since Canterbury has stolen Rowan Williams. The report said: 'Many passers-by willingly signed the petition urging the government to give more substantial aid to the world's famine areas, and — without our proffering any money-boxes — we were able to hand over £62 to Christian Aid. The not-too-cold night round the fire was spent singing, reading, reciting and talking with various people, mostly quite young and rather boozy, who came out of curiosity, and for a warm at our fire, and who often stayed to ask us what exactly we thought we were doing there.

While I now remember very little of the details, I see that I was buzzing about, like many others, giving talks to encourage groups all over the place. One rather interesting one had been at Rhyl, where a faithful peace group met regularly. On this occasion 'about ten wives of striking miners attended, partly to express their gratitude for the financial support which the group had given to their Christmas party fund. But they also entered into the meeting with enthusiasm. They absorbed some of the story of our early years (1979/80) because they'd never heard of it before, and though they knew the deadly connection between nuclear power and nuclear weapons (and thus the need for more, not less, coal) they had not previously sensed the demands we were making in the peace movement for control of the questions of human survival. It did us all good to have such lively, intelligent and eager listeners, who promptly bought badges and literature and went out to convert a few others.'

52. GROWING EXPERTISE

The Wrexham Group's Newsletter made clear that several members of our group really had been doing their homework. Peter Appleton had written an important article for the SANA Newsletter, so we made an abbreviated form of it. Its theme was 'The New Generation of space weapons'; and he helped us to distinguish between Laser weapons, Particle beam weapons, Kinetic energy 'hit and kill' devices, Self-propelled missiles. Having outlined their technical difficulties, he ended up saying:

> In the absence of any arms control the most likely consequences of these developments will be an increase in the arms race on earth, and its extension to outer space. The size of the nuclear arsenals could be expected to increase, particularly the numbers of difficult-to-verify Cruise missiles in an attempt to ensure that there were enough warheads for some at least to get through. Furthermore, unilateral deployment of these systems could lead the opposite side to suspect a further advance towards first-strike capability and immunity from retaliation. This can only lead to greater instability.

In an effort to get people to write with alarm to the Director-General for Guided Weapons Electronics at the Ministry of Defence, we pointed out that 'Accidents will Happen' First we noted that a Russian Cruise missile accidentally went off course and landed in Finland. A Polaris missile blew up in West Germany killing three and injuring seven. In the first 107 test flights, the ground-launched Cruise missiles failed to function correctly 28 times — a failure rate of 26%. Indeed, on its 107th test it fell out of the sky after only 20 minutes in flight. I am not sure any letters were answered.

Chris Spragg at this time was flagging up the Peace Tax Campaign. 'When we spend £12,500 million a year on military preparations and only £5 million on the diplomacy of disarmament, what chances does Peace have? It is our taxes that produce the £12,500 million so why not demand the right for our taxes to be spent for Peace and not for War? We were asked to challenge our Member of Parliament on this. Our bulletin contained a very frank and lengthy personal interview with Dr John Marek MP, whose views on the whole deterrence, Cold War and disarmament issues accorded very much with ours. He is now our Assembly Member where we trust he holds the same views, even though the Assembly has less opportunity or right to raise such issues of peace and war.

In February we reported the attack on the peace camp at Rainbow Fields Village, keeping a peaceful eye on Molesworth — entitled RAF Molesworth, but actually an American nuclear plane base. Suddenly there was an unprovoked attack on the Village involving 1,500 Royal Engineers and hundreds of MoD police. Michael Heseltine flew in wearing a combat jacket, and gave us a callow piece of newspeak about his 'concern' for the children of Rainbow Fields in order to play down the overkill tactics of the eviction. Hundreds then started making their presence felt. Christian CND held a gathering led by Bruce Kent, with over 700 people; and we organised ourselves to travel to join them on various days. We also circulated a little poster which read: IT TOOK MORE BRITISH TROOPS TO EVICT A PEACE CAMP AT MOLESWORTH THAN IT DID TO CAPTURE GOOSE GREEN!

Friday March 15th (still 1985) was designated as an All Wales Day at Molesworth. CND nationally set Easter Monday April 8th as its Rally day there. Our bulletin listed eight different ways in which we could take part in this new focus for disarmament.

We continued to give publicity and support to the great women at Greenham; the peace group arranged monthly public sessions to raise more awareness, and we sent out another little poster saying: TRIDENT WILL COST US £30,000 EVERY DAY FOR THE NEXT THOUSAND YEARS … SO SCRAP IT!

One particularly imaginative item among the Molesworth events was an Easter Wheat Fund to send grain to starving Eritrea which was grown on MoD land (£7 would buy 1cwt of wheat grain) to make the link between poverty and weapons in a practical way.

The peace group's bulletin for April 1985 had a fine article by Mark Brown under the title of 'Impressions of Molesworth' after the Easter visit.

I first visited Molesworth in the New Year to spend a few days in a caravan on the edge of the base. Trudging along the flat open road that led there from Titchmarsh, feeling like one of Thomas Hardy's human specks on the horizon. Every time I have been back my perspectives have been altered: painting rainbows in the office windows of the military; seeing the American newspapers on the desk of the commander, the photos of his family, a pool table nearby — familiar but strange. On returning after the evictions, the sharp coils of razor-wire destroying the comforts of fantasy; hooded policemen in the half-built chapel. How do I begin? What are the roots that clutch; what branches grow out of this stony rubbish?

I am back at the fence again, weaving wool into galvanised steel. No longer a sight-seer, I help Julie and Sid from Rainbow Village fix a new door to their caravan. Our minibus is photographed by police every time we visit there to share a cup of tea, a smoke in front of their fire. Little Emmy snuggles up on the bed beside us. I wonder where they are now.

Easter brings the army helicopters swooping and buzzing over our heads. I am reminded by an MoD policeman of the military bye-laws as I weave another web into the fence by the chapel, and point to the daffodils beside me growing in the wire. The military tigers stand motionless in a cage of their own making. We are the hollow men; we are the stuffed men, leaning together, headpiece filled with straw.

Then a ribbon of people as far as the eye can see; pennants, streamers, bells, whistles, drums, coke-cans and saucepans banging on the fence. A policeman snatches my tin-whistle, mistaking it for a steel bar; he returns it when I show him the holes in it. We lean against the perimeter fence, shaking it with our bodies till the wire trembles and dances above us. Here come the clowns; no slogans this time, only music and the beat of the drum. It is Easter and carnival.

A loud-hailer warns us that we are all committing an offence (obstruction?) and would we kindly move on, before it is drowned in whistles. Suddenly snatch arrests in front of us: not all those wearing red and black are anarchists; and not all anarchists wear red and black. Lines of police form up and push hard, into the mud, onto the ground and into the fence. They have learnt much from the miners' strike — road-blocks, disciplined waves of blue. Did we learn, I wonder? A few of us did — when the miners went back at Maerdy in the Rhondda, there were CND banners beside them. Threads between miners' wives and the 'wimmin' at Greenham. (She who isolates her struggle has lost it).

Thousands planted flowers and ribbon into the fence — a mass act of civil disobedience — affirming commitment to dismantle these bases — and the wheat goes out to Eritrea, grain by the sackful. A policeman tears down one of my webs by the chapel, but another goes up on the fence opposite. We hold hands in a circle. Daffodils sing in the wire. 'London Bridge is falling down, falling down, falling down.

53. DISTORTION OF, AND CONTEMPT, FOR FACTS

C&Q for April 1985 focussed on the false picture we are so often presented with — from UK, USA. and USSR. I quoted a vigorous condemnation of this — but without the author's name, which I had mislaid.

> One of the boldest distortions in the western version of deterrence doctrine is the claim that NATO deploys nuclear weapons to counter those of the Soviet Union. So much history is set aside by this tale, such as which states first made, used and began stockpiling atomic bombs, and which first formed a military alliance centred on a nuclear strategy, that one is tempted to regard it as a ritual incantation without even pretence to truth. Contempt for facts is common-place in their explanation of their nuclear weapons put out by both super-powers, as for example when they focus on particular weapons' developments and remain silent on others, so as to be able to denounce the other side as provocative leaders in the arms race. A vital part of the factual distortion aspect of deterrence ideology is the ability to pronounce with utter conviction judgements condemning the enemy which in fact apply in every detail also to one's own side.

But occasionally a little bit of truth leaks out. McGeorge Bundy, the national Security Adviser in the Kennedy and Johnson administrations was reported as saying: 'The SS20 does not give the Soviet Union any nuclear capability against Europe alone that it did not have in overflowing measure before.'

On another side we were able to quote Marshal Ustinov. 'None but completely irresponsible people could maintain that a nuclear war may be made to follow rules adopted beforehand, with nuclear missiles exploding in a gentlemanly manner over strictly designated targets and sparing the population'

Completely out of chronological order in the same issue I gave a particularly nasty quote, said to be from a 'secret memo' of Winston Churchill on 6th July 1944:

'It may be several weeks or even months before I shall ask you to drench Germany with poison gas; and if we do it, let us do it one hundred per cent. In the meanwhile I want the matter to be studied in cold blood by sensible people, and not by that particular set of psalm-singing uniformed defeatists which one runs across now here and there.' I wonder who he had in mind!

54. CENTRAL & EASTERN EUROPE MOVES

We were continually challenged in the western peace movements by those who said there was nothing comparable in east and central Europe. It was true that the latter's groups were quasi-official institutions, endorsed by their own governments and applauded in the official media. But things were by now changing. The European Nuclear Disarmament movement in London had as its basis an Appeal for everyone 'to stop being loyal to East or West, but to one another', and perhaps it was to END that one could credit the changes taking place. Named after the Helsinki Accord of 1977, a new movement was arising called Charter 77 and it issued an Appeal which began: 'It is 40 years now since there was a war on European soil. Notwithstanding, Europe has not been a continent of peace. Far from it, as Europe has been one of the main points of friction between the two power blocs: tension has been a permanent feature throughout the period, thereby posing a threat to the entire world. The reason is the divided state of our continent. Our common hope therefore lies in overcoming this division. This can only be achieved through a conscious decision by all gradually to transform the very political realities which are responsible for the present situation.' The Appeal rightly declared: that 'a democratic and sovereign Europe is inconceivable so long as individual citizens, groups of citizens, or nations are denied the right to take part in decisions affecting not only their everyday lives, but also their very survival.' What Helsinki had sanctioned was 'a framework whereby citizens may not only exercise public oversight of governments but also find imaginative ways of loosening ossified positions.' They continued: 'It should be possible to come forward with different disarmament initiatives and proposals: the creation of nuclear free and neutral zones; the encouragement of relations between individuals, groups and states; support for agreements on non-aggression, as well as the renunciation of the use of force or nuclear weapons.

They were not afraid to look at several taboo subjects like the self-determination of the two Germanies. They went on: 'Another taboo subject has been the withdrawal of foreign troops. Let us therefore propose that NATO and Warsaw Pact enter forthwith into negotiations on the dissolution of their military organisations, on the removal of all nuclear weapons either sited in or aimed at Europe, and on the withdrawal of US and Soviet troops from the territories of their European allies …

We do not seek to turn Europe into a third super-power, but instead to overcome the super-power bloc structure by way of an alliance of free and independent nations within a democratic and self-governing all-European community, living in friendship with nations of the entire world … Perhaps this sounds like a dream. However we are convinced that it expresses the desire of a majority of Europeans. It is therefore an ideal worth striving for; all the more so, in view of the fact that today's world will hardly surmount its crisis unless Europe also takes the path its citizens desire.

At the end of 1984 a remarkable letter had been received from others in G.D.R. and Czechoslovakia to which Bruce Kent of CND had replied:

Thank you for your courageous declaration. There can be no justification for the deployment on your territories of new nuclear weapons subsequent to the siting of Cruise missiles and Pershing rockets in the West. No-one today can increase their security anywhere by increasing the insecurity of other nations... Independent initiatives by medium-sized European nations aimed at removing nuclear weapons from their soil could help to break the escalating spiral of the arms race and to assert national sovereignty, We campaign for these unilateral initiatives at the same time as we support genuine bilateral and multilateral negotiations on arms reductions ... You rightly blame not just the weapons but rather power politics for the terrible situation which we are all in today. But there is also a sense in which the scientific dynamic of the arms race has its own momentum... Real peace depends indeed on an observance of human rights everywhere by everyone. We in the West hear a deafening noise from our official propagandists about the human rights' failures in the socialist states. We knew about them and firmly condemn them. But we also have eyes and ears for the gross violations which take place in many of the areas of western political and economic influence which our official propagandists ignore. We find it hard therefore to separate peace in Europe from peace in the world. There will be no true peace until we all see ourselves as members of one community, sharing one small planet.

55. OTHER VIEWS OF SOVIET COMMUNISM

For the most part we believed that the Soviet leaders thought their system was unchallengeable; and for the greater part of the Stalin regime this was so. But some self-criticism does now emerge, even at an official level. Witness this remark from Brezhnev in 1980 (quoted by Jonathan Steele):

Critical judgements of separate concrete developments in our country are sometimes voiced in some Communist parties. Far be it from us to think that everything we had was ideal. In the USSR socialism was built in incredibly difficult conditions.... Nobody knows better than we do what difficulties and shortcomings occurred along the way, and which of them still have to be overcome.

There had rightly been severe criticism of the Soviet's invasion of Afghanistan. One explanation had been offered (in 1980) by Alexander Bovin, the *Isvestia* political columnist — somewhat unconvincing perhaps: 'We knew the decision to bring in troops would not be popular in the modern world even if it was absolutely legal. But we also knew that we would have ceased to be a great power if we refrained from carrying the burden of taking unpopular but necessary decisions — extraordinary decisions prompted by extraordinary circumstances.' But he also added: 'What kind of evolution is it that has to be supported with the help of Soviet troops ? What kind of new rule is it against which not only landlords but peasants also are rising up in arms? These questions are quite legitimate.' There's a measure of honesty about that. Jonathan Steele interestingly noted about the covert military help being given increasingly by the Reagan administration. 'Its strategy has been to give the rebels enough help to prevent the Russians winning, but not enough to enable the rebels to win. Some officials in the Reagan administration seemed to relish having the Russians tied down for years in Afghanistan.' Since the twin towers tragedy of 2001 and the wars, theoretically against terror, people have recognised that among the rebels helped by the USA, — indeed trained and armed — were Osama Bin Laden and his cohorts.

Most remarkable was the continuing presence in USSR of Roy Medvedev. He wasn't an unqualified critic of Communism. He was still a Marxist, but believed that the Stalinist tradition betrayed the possibilities of Marxist socialism. He believed it was possible to distinguish between 'socialism as a political system and Soviet power, between the governmental structure of socialist society in general and the particular regime that now rules the USSR, which is only one variant, and not the best by far, of state socialism.'

'The Soviet Union hasn't yet achieved advanced socialism, only a complex mixture of socialism and pseudo-socialism... The men in power persist in treating the labourers, the peasants, the white-collar workers and the great mass of non-manual workers like immature children, who must be safeguarded against evil ideological influences. Thus they impoverish the nation's moral consciousness; they fail to educate people and prepare them for real political maturity... The men in the saddle fear rising opposition without realising that in most cases opposition would be most useful to them. It means a healthy society whereas total consensus indicates an ailing society. Pluralism is the natural corollary of a developed socialism; where it doesn't exist you have an immature society... Only a socialism that tolerates legal opposition to the government and the ruling party can avoid slipping into totalitarianism and abuse of power.'

Well, slip into totalitarianism the USSR certainly did; but Roy Medvedev had not given up on 'the search for a theory of a new and more human socialism and its implementation', and in spite of severe publishing and other restriction, he was still strangely not imprisoned. His brother Zhores Medvedev, the geneticist and bio-chemist, was not so lucky. He came to a London conference and was never allowed to return to the Soviet Union; he was formerly incarcerated in a psychiatric hospital for his dissidence. He too was optimistic after describing the ups and downs of Soviet science he said: 'The general forecast which I can provide for the reader is optimistic if considered from the point of view of those who would like to see the USSR as a peaceful member of the international community.' The trouble is that there were plenty of people in the West who didn't want that; or a priori they believed it was impossible.

What came as a surprise to me was when Roy Medvedev said 'Lenin envisioned Soviet power functioning as a pluralistic system allowing for free competition within the soviets among all parties representing the workers.... The ban on parties outside the system of soviets was meant as a temporary measure.' He was convinced 'that the Bolsheviks would come out ahead of all other parties in any free competition (after showing its) political and economic successes.... But all that was lost because of the sharp conflicts that developed, particularly the civil war.' Then 'Stalin took actions that Lenin meant to be only temporary, magnified them and transformed them into permanent procedures.'

On the Western side, George Kennan, as former US ambassador to Moscow, wrote:

> The image of a totally inhuman and totally malevolent adversary ... is reconjured daily, week after week, month after month, year after year, until it takes on every feature of flesh and blood, and becomes the daily companion of those who cultivate it, so that any attempt on anyone's part to deny its reality appears as an act of treason or frivolity ... The planner's dummy of the Soviet political personality (has taken) the place of the real thing, as the image on which a great deal of American policy and military effort came to be based.

It was sad that such remarks were not better known.

Roy Medvedev also said: 'I will say beyond all doubt the vast majority of the (Soviet) population endorses the Soviet Communist party. Naturally the millions of party and state functionaries are anxious to preserve the system; it makes life easier. A more pluralistic order would create too many headaches for them. Then don't forget too that if most people approve of Soviet Communism, at least passively, they've never lived under any other system'.

There were other 'dissidents' of course; some quite different. Solzhenitsyn didn't simply denounce the Soviet system; he was in favour of 'the creation of an authoritarian theocratic state in Russia, in which people would get along with a minimum of necessities, and would perfect themselves morally and spiritually on the basis of the Russian Orthodox religion'. But (Medvedev remarked) 'It is quite obvious that what has happened in Iran could not happen in modern Russia. The Soviet Union is not Iran, and Solzhenitsyn is no Khomeini.'

Sakharov represented another strand of dissidence, described as the 'liberal' or 'legalist' movement, concentrating his attention on basic human rights. He was abominably treated; but somehow his appearing to support NATO Euromissiles on grounds of 'balance' was inconsistent.

Vladimir Bukovski was also treated ferociously by the KGB, and after imprisonment and psychiatric 'treatment' he was expelled in exchange for a Chilean Communist leader. E. P. Thompson wrote of him: 'His experiences have been savage and were endured with stoicism and they entitle him to deploy some verbal savagery in arguments with opponents. Indeed, if he were testifying on matters within his direct experience I could only attend to his testimony with humility.' However, in a famous *Times* piece he attacked the Western peace movements as a gigantic political manoeuvre of the World Peace Council — the Soviet-front organisation. On the misrepresentations and falsities of that article has been based much of the attack of British right-wing opposition to the quarter million supporters of CND

56. BACK AT GREENHAM

The women kept their camps going, and we tried to keep in touch. Somewhere there must be a whole history written up about that phenomenon. We had a special interest in Wrexham since (as I have said already) Janet Tyrell from our group had been one of the original Cardiff to Greenham marchers; but others had paid long and short visits to support the camps. Among them was Myra Hughes of Rhosllanerchrugog; and we printed a long letter she wrote to us in May 1985. Here is one extract:

'In August 1984 a High Court Judge's ruling (that we could not be evicted until the ownership of the land, called Primrose Path, on which we were living, had been settled) was totally ignored, and evictions have taken place every day, sometimes twice a day, in temperatures ten degrees below zero. In September 1984 the bailiffs were under orders to steal our standpipe, despite the fact that we had paid £69 to the water authority for it, and our water rates were paid up to April 1985. The Council and the water authorities denied all knowledge of the theft, so we applied to them for another one only to be told 'the law has changed now; you must apply to Newbury District Council and they will consider your application'. We applied to the Council and were told 'the law has changed now. You are now classified as an evicted camp, so we cannot consider your application.' We bought one elsewhere. Some weeks later we received a hand-delivered a letter informing us that our money would not be accepted after April. When we pointed out that we would open a special water rate account and continue to draw water, we were informed that if we were caught drawing water after the date given, we would be sued. Also it seemed an admission to the theft of the standpipe, that we were offered back our money, which we naturally refused.

On April 1st this year, the new military bye-laws were implemented. This is the government's last desperate attempt to close the camp at Greenham. In the past if we have been caught in the base without bolt cutters, paint etc. the practice has been to throw us out at the farthest gate from which we lived, entailing a nine mile walk back to our own gate. However with the implementation of the new bye-laws, women can now be arrested simply for trespass. On April 1st 67 women were arrested for trespass. Their cases have been split up to prevent an impact on publicity. The dates set are 2nd and 3rd May; then 17th and 28th MAY. This means that 67 women will go to prison in May. There is nothing the government would like better than to get the media to Greenham to show the world that Greenham is not in existence any more. Their plan must not be allowed to succeed, so we are appealing for women to come to Greenham for the month of May, and a continual rota to be set up by peace groups throughout the country.'

Myra ended her letter : 'Due to the miners' strike and the blackout on publicity, donations have been practically nil, with the result that women are suffering from lack of proper food, and go hungry quite a lot; so donations will be gratefully accepted.'

57. REMEMBERING THE END OF THE WAR — BUT NOT OF WAR ITSELF

There were in May 1985 lots of anniversary celebrations for the end of World War II; but within a few hours of these we read of the explosion by France of a huge nuclear weapon in the Pacific at Mururoa Atoll, as if all the warnings of what this nuclear testing has already done to the islanders were unknown or non-existent. New Zealand's Prime Minister, David Lange, voiced his objections: 'All the countries of the South Pacific are absolutely opposed to nuclear testing in their region, and have said so on many occasions'. It seems that it makes not the slightest difference to those with power. Yet there were also signs that people were not going to lie down and accept this madness. The US Congress have offered some refusals to Reagan's military intervention policies in Nicaragua, even though the President now announces severe economic sanctions which displease many Europeans. An American woman's group is reported as saying, 'We believe you, the people of New Zealand, are a beacon of reason and morality. We agree that nuclear weapons do not enhance world security, but rather endanger it. As Americans we are opposed to suggestions of economic or other forms of reprisals by the US government. We respect your right as a sovereign nation freely to determine your domestic and foreign policies.'

Nicaragua was only the latest in a long story of USA. interventions in Central and South America. I had just spent a weekend in conversation with Brian Davies (of CAFOD) and Dr Sheila Cassidy, exploring 'The Church of the Poor' in a residential centre. Sheila's personal story of the Allende government in Chile, and her subsequent torture by General Pinochet's men, spelt out the sinister element of power politics. (It happens also that the date of Allende's assassination by American intervention was another September 11th, in 1973.)

Another quotation was from William George Hayden, the Foreign Minister of Australia; 'The greatest hope for peace lies in ordinary people demanding of their leaders that they commit themselves to the cause of peace with all the intensity that is now devoted to the preparation for war. This will only be done if ordinary people are alerted to the dangers we all face.'

Comments & Quotes for May 1985 took up some important extracts from John Keegan's (the military historian) new book 'The Face of Battle'. Of course modern weapons have increased the scale of the horror of war; but when reading the story of Agincourt, Waterloo and the Somme, I was now inclined to think that it was always vast and abominable. Keegan wrote:

> War in Christian theology is sinful activity, unless carried out within a framework of rules which few commanders are in practice able to obey; in particular those which demand that he shall have a just aim and a reasonable expectation of victory. Any objective study quickly reveals that most wars are begun for reasons which have nothing to do with justice, have results quite different from those proclaimed as their objects, if indeed they have any clear-cut result at all, and visit during their course a great deal of casual suffering on the innocent.

After Waterloo was over, the troops collapsed into sleep and left the casualties without any succour till the next day:

> There is something amounting almost to a universal and specific insistence in the accounts of survivors that nothing was done until daylight, or in many cases for some time afterwards. Heartless as it sounds, it accords with what we know of much human behaviour in disaster situations, where the greater the scale of the devastation and loss of life, the more profound is the survivors' feeling of helplessness and frustration, from which they escape by inactivity … Waterloo was a disaster of a very considerable

magnitude. Within a space of about two square miles of open, waterless, treeless and almost uninhabited countryside, which had been covered at early morning by standing crops, lay by nightfall the bodies of forty thousand human beings, and ten thousand horses, many of them alive and suffering dreadfully.

When John Keegan describes the way in which wars are actually fought, it is obvious that much of the time no-one knows for sure what is happening or where. The sheer noise, smoke and general chaos is so vast. 'What battles have in common is human; the behaviour of men struggling to reconcile their instinct for self-preservation, their sense of honour and the achievement of some aim over which other men are ready to kill them. The study of battle is therefore always a study of fear and usually of courage; always of leadership, usually of obedience; always of compulsion sometimes of insubordination; always of anxiety, sometimes of elation or catharsis; always of uncertainty or doubt, misinformation and misapprehension, usually also of faith and sometimes of vision; always of violence, sometimes also of cruelty, self-sacrifice, compassion; above all it is always a study of solidarity and usually one of disintegration — for it is towards the disintegration of human groups that battle is directed.'

One historical fact Keegan brings out which had simply never occurred to me.

....for all the elaborate explanations used by civilised societies to exculpate the soldier who kills in battle from taint of personal guilt or social disapproval — that he undergoes the same risk of death as his opponent, that he kills in order to overcome a greater evil than killing — it is worthy of note that the one sort of front-line soldier who has some choice over whether he will kill or not, the officer, has throughout … consistently and steadily withdrawn himself from the act itself…

Keegan then gives historical examples.

During the First World War (the officer) often had no lethal weapon at all, just a walking-stick. And this impression of a distancing of the officer from the infliction of death is reinforced by the citations written to endorse high decorations for bravery. Those written for soldiers lay stress on their success at killing: 'Lance Corporal … courageously worked his way round the flank of the machine-guns and then charged it, firing his carbine from the hip, so accounting for six of the enemy.' Those written for officers minimise their direct responsibility for killing and emphasise their powers of inspiration and organisation when all about are losing their heads: 'Captain … quickly rallied his men and without regard for his own safety led them back over the open to the position they had earlier been forced to leave.

At the end of his remarkable book, John Keegan thinks about the future of battle and the inhuman face of war:

What almost all the soldiers of the First World War, and many of the Second, even from the victor armies, testify is to their sense of littleness, almost of nothingness, of their abandonment in a physical wilderness, dominated by vast impersonal forces, from which even such normalities as the passage of time had been eliminated ... It must be counted as one of the particular

cruelties of modern warfare that, by inducing even in the fit and willing soldier a sense of his unimportance, it encouraged his treating the lives of disarmed or demoralised opponents as equally unimportant.

At another level, the fostering and infliction of deliberate cruelty marks a second major divergence between the facts of everyday and battlefield existence in the 20th century. Weapons have never been kind to human flesh, but the directing principle behind their design has usually not been that of maximising the pain and damage they can cause ... It is now a desired effect of many man-killing weapons that they inflict wounds as terrible and terrifying as possible ... Might the modern conscript not well think, at first acquaintance with the weapons the state foists on him, that its humanitarian code is evidence either of a nauseating hypocrisy or of a psychotic inability to connect actions with their results?

As always I peppered these longer extracts from my reading with significant quotes and I rarely noted their origin. The following ones seemed to be apt at this moment:

> Obedience, the keystone of military order, is incompatible with the candid expression of opinion, and the right to question and critically examine courses of action, prerogatives that are inherent in the role of mature citizens in a democracy. Obedience instilled in Basic Training leads effectively to dependence, with a reliance upon and acceptance of the will of others. Responsibility for one's welfare and for the consequences of one's acts is relinquished and remains habitually in the hands of superiors. (Peter Bourne in *From Boot Camp to My Lai* 1971)

> Never think that war, no matter how necessary, nor how justified, is not a crime. Ask the infantry, and ask the dead. (Ernerst Hemingway)

From a new American book SIOP — *Nuclear War From the Inside* by Peter Pringle and William Arkin, I offered:

A Classical Understatement: 'Levelling large cities has a tendency to alienate the affections of the inhabitants, and does not create an atmosphere of good will after he war' (US Rear-Admiral Gallery in 1949)

A Classical Overstatement: 'Senator McMahon liked to be known as 'Mr Atom', and he once told the Senate that he thought the bombing of Hiroshima had been ' the greatest event in the world since the birth of Jesus Christ'.

A Classical Non-Statement: '… the young Air Force officers who would 'turn the key' to send the Minuteman missiles on their way to the Soviet Union gave the chilling reply to our question; 'Don't you ever think about where the missile is going?' 'It makes no difference to us, sir; our job is to launch them.''

Only fractionally less alarming, though from a totally different perspective, is Lord Zuckerman saying: 'During the twenty years or so that I myself was professionally involved in these matters, weapons came first, and rationalisations and policies followed …The weapons had to be fitted into a presumed tactical doctrine, which in turn had to be fitted into an illusory strategy, usually elaborated by arm-chair warriors.'

It was Pringle and Arkin who informed us that the average age of the men with their fingers on the 'buttons' of the 26,000 warheads is only 26 'men in the first flush of their service careers when 'job satisfaction' comes from donning a smart uniform and proudly accepting the heavy responsibilities that the armed forces gives much earlier than in most civilian jobs' After screenings and training and assessments of family, political and military views, up to 10% of the 'successful' men drop out before ever they see a missile command capsule. 'I've thought it over and I could never turn the key' is the oft-heard reason.' Well, that's encouraging!

58. ENEMY IMAGES AND STEREOTYPES

In June 1985 I had a blatant advert for a booklet from Pax Christi called 'Looking at the Russians' in which I had a part. I introduced it by saying that it was a common accusation against those who work actively in the peace and disarmament movements that they are simply naïve about the Soviet Union. Others suggest (as the Daily Mail did after our delegation to Moscow) that we are 'dupes of the Kremlin', or, as stated by the Vatican's Nuncio to Great Britain some years ago about Bruce Kent and others, that we are 'blinkered idealists'. Anyway in our booklet Peggy Attlee, Gerry McFlynn tackled 'Who Are the Russians?', and 'How the Soviet Citizens See Themselves & Their Country', and I had a section on 'The Soviet Union — a Military Threat?' Bishop Guazzelli said about it:

> This is not a whitewash by politically naïve Soviet dupes who are more humanist than Christian. It does not ignore the truth of Soviet repression of human rights or the reality

of its armed strength; but it does try to explain, without condoning, the reasons behind Soviet policy and encourages Western readers to begin to remove the beam from their own eye before working on the splinter in their brother's.

I continued of course to recommend the widening range of real experts' books on the Soviet Union, and quoted them wherever I could find relevant extracts. I wondered what the politicians and diplomats read; and then one day I had a partial answer accidentally. I was sitting as Pax Christi's representative on the Peace Forum of the British Council of Churches. At its meetings, David Summerhayes (formerly Ambassador to UN as I have mentioned earlier) attended as Disarmament Adviser at the Foreign & Commonwealth Office and 'consultant'. One day he was clutching a new book from the Office's library which he recommended, so I found a paper-back version within the hour. It was called 'The Soviet State' with sub-title 'The Domestic Roots of Soviet Foreign Policy'. It turned out to be a co-ordinated set of studies edited by a former British Ambassador to Moscow 1978–82, and had some valuable insights from the scholarly contributors. For instance Hugh Seton-Watson wrote:

> In practice it is rather silly to assert that the Soviet leaders are 'out for world domination'. It is extremely unlikely that any of them consider this a realistic aim in the predictable future. However, ideology and security seem normally to convince them that, whenever any crisis occurs anywhere in the non-communist world, they must do what they can to exploit it and if necessary exacerbate it, mainly in order to harm their American and Chinese adversaries, but also, if circumstance permit, to give a helping a hand to local communists. If they decide they can do nothing, they do nothing. If they can do something to damage a Western interest, but at the cost of accepting the suppression of local communists, they will settle for that. In a nuclear age undue risks must not be taken, and the risk of direct super-power military conflict is an effective constraint.

'There you are', some will have exclaimed, 'that shows that deterrence works!' I doubt if any of us questioned the 'constraint' that is imposed on everyone by the potential of superpower conflict. I remember being assured in our peace delegation to the Kremlin in 1982 that the Soviet Union and the USA would never directly go to war simply because they knew the result; but it was agreed that by accident, by escalation from some lesser conflict than a nuclear one (say in the Middle East) it could still happen. Brinkmanship is a game played however by both sides. There is a thin line between new defence systems and provocative weapons.

Seton Watson continued:

> The study of Soviet history, the record of the behaviour of the Soviet government and the experience of those who have had to deal personally with Soviet officials for

substantial periods, all point to the conclusion that these men are in no sense starry-eyed revolutionary enthusiasts, or indeed any sort of revolutionaries. They are extremely conservative men, resolved above all to preserve the hierarchy of power and privilege which they and their predecessors have painfully constructed, and from which they benefit. One of the principal instruments for its preservation is the revolutionary rhetoric which proceeds from the leadership and which involves the active participation of the population. The abstraction 'the working class' is the object of unending hymns of praise: everything that is done is done in the name of the working class which allegedly holds power; and the flesh and blood workers are engaged in continuous paeans of themselves and their rulers. The real workers are at least as subordinate to their bosses in factory and in government as workers in any capitalist country, and doubtless many of them are aware of this; but still their voices swell the chorus.

It was useful also to read John Lawrence's piece on 'Religion in the USSR'. Lawrence worked for Keston College, an institution which focussed mainly on the persecution of Christians. Yet he was able to tell us

... there may be as many as 50 million firm Orthodox believers, though not all of them can get to church regularly, if only because not enough churches are open. A total community of up to 100 million persons with some degree of adherence to Orthodoxy, as shown by baptisms and religious funerals, is sometimes suggested on the basis of studies by Soviet sociologists. This is speculative but it could be true. If the numbers of Muslims, Catholics, Protestants of various denominations, Jews and indigenous Russian sects such as the Old Believers, are added, it would appear that something like half the total population of 270 million may have some adherence to religion.

It is the truth that neither the Russian Orthodox Church nor any other religious body has yet any influence on policy, but it is clear from official Soviet statements that the Kremlin regards religion in the long run as a serious threat to the Soviet Union's established order. It is possible to understand the fears of the Soviet authorities, but it should be made clear that there is no evidence that Soviet religious believers are opposed to socialism; indeed rather the contrary. But they are opposed to the dogmatic atheism, the untruthfulness, and the cruelty which have accompanied the Soviet form of socialism.

The editor of this book, Curtis Keeble, drew the conclusions to the book in a very balanced way:

Russian history and Marxist-Leninist philosophy coincide to produce an obsession with power, both political and military, internal and external, which may perhaps be called a national instinct. The mantle of Marxism-Leninism has been slipped smoothly over the imperial heritage, shaping itself to the broad shoulders on which it rests. We have to deal today with a power which over the centuries has sought security against the threat and the reality of invasion across open land frontiers. Having done so, it has found the need to secure tranquillity within areas newly brought under control as well as stable, compliant administration in those adjacent to the imperial frontier.

I felt like saying: 'Okay Mr Summerhayes' you can read that!'

59. KEEPING UP THE LOCAL MOMENTUM

It is an important factor which had to be borne in mind that there is a limit to the length of time people can sustain their energies in any 'campaign'. By the end of June 1985, several things were happening to change the scene in Wrexham. We had already lost Richard Andrews to professional studies. Mark Brown had also moved on from residence at the Peace Studies Centre. I had been away in Bruges for Pax Christi's International Council. The local Peace Group's bulletin was behindhand till the end of the month, and expressed regret that the very successful Women's Day in May under the title of 'What Kind of World?' had not received a written report.

All the same there was an on-going programme: e.g. June 21st: Seminar on Star Wars 'Will the Strategic Defence Initiative render Nuclear Weapons Obsolete?'

June 22nd: Showing of two video documentaries on the Philippines *To Sing Our Own Song*, and, on Charter 77, *Nationality Uncertain*. The evening was entitled 'Oppression and Suppression'.

June 26th was for our monthly business and planning meeting but included a video documentary of Ann Thomas *No Place to Hide*.

June 28th featured an important public meeting put together mainly by Fred Starkey of Pax Legalis together with the WEA. The title was 'Citizens Upholding the Law' when Olivier Russbach, a Swiss international lawyer and founder of Droit contre Raison d'Etat, was the main speaker, and a barrister, Geoffrey Kilfoil, led the discussion. We had invited other lawyers, magistrates, councillors personally — though few of them turned up. It was an important part of the campaign to challenge the legality of national and international military and other policies.

The next day, June 29th there was a Clwyd Peace Festival in Mold; and listed were two meetings of Wrexham Christians for Peace.

It is hardly surprising that the activists were getting tired. The July bulletin said: 'There is no lack of personal interest in the nuclear issues. There is far more

knowledge in many people's minds; there is a much greater awareness since we started five years ago; but — like many another peace group — there seems to be a strong dis-inclination to go to meetings; even to our once a month session.' It is certainly not because the meetings are heavy and boring; but we seem to have run out of organisational steam. We agreed to discuss this sensibly.

Meantime the Wrexham Council had decided (under, I think, the influence of Michael and Willow Williams) to make a Peace Garden on The Croft site which was once the Quaker burial ground. Pryderi Llwyd-Jones (still minister at Capel y Groes) and I were asked to devise and conduct a ceremony for its inauguration. It could become a focus for public peace events, and we would mark Hiroshima Day particularly at the start on August 6th.

In the July bulletin I reported a press release from Pax Christi as follows:

> Owen Hardwicke has just been appointed to the post of General Secretary of Pax Christi (UK section). His three year post will probably mean that a large proportion of his time will be based at the London office. His mandate is to re-structure, develop and strengthen the involvement of members in the various aspects of the international work. Some of his work will continue to be in his Wrexham Centre, where he hopes to build a team of helpers to ensure the continuity of this, and the other social welfare work which he undertakes in the charitable Trust of which he is administrator.

I wasn't due to start my new job until October so there was time to revise the Telephone Tree for members to keep in touch, and ensure the Centre would be open for meetings, if I was absent. I began to slow down on the calls I had undertaken during the year so far. In those days schools and colleges (mostly 6th forms) seemed to welcome outsiders with special issues to present and discuss. I was in Denbigh, Manchester, Malpas, Plymouth, Aberystwyth, Bristol, West Kirby, and Lambeth; and to eleven other places for Pax Christi groups. As well as joining some 2000 others for the END Convention in Amsterdam, and the Geneva Freeze Conference, I decided to try to keep producing Comments and Quotes to share with people the findings of scholars and experts. The local group bulletin obviously had to be someone else's task. Alas, my archive file is empty from then on, until three years later when issue No. 100 appears from the hand of Sue Stanford, with Jill McMinn as the contact name for the group. The several Wrexham Groups, and the Clwyd Federation disappeared by then. Those who had been active no doubt continued their concern about national and international affairs, and supported other causes constructively; but it is evident that keeping up the momentum for nuclear disarmament through local groups was more than people could manage as volunteers.

60. GENEVA FOR THE FREEZE

I had the chance of going to Geneva in early September (1985) for the first international conference of the Freeze Movement. This originated in USA, and had gained considerable interest; and the conference was designed to look particularly at the Non-Proliferation Treaty at the same time as the 130 nation-state signatories were having their third review of the Treaty. In this treaty the non-nuclear nations (56 of whom had already signed up) undertook not to obtain or develop nuclear weapons as their side of a bargain with the nuclear states who undertook to stop proliferating vertically themselves. The Treaty is not a long or complicated document; in its preamble it speaks of the 'Parties to the Treaty, declaring their intention to achieve at the earliest possible date the cessation of the nuclear arms race, and to undertake effective measures in the direction of nuclear disarmament …'

This already makes the intention clear. The crucial Article VI states:

> Each of the Parties to the Treaty undertakes to pursue negotiations in good faith on effective measures relating to the cessation of the nuclear arms race at an early date, and to nuclear disarmament, and on a Treaty for general and complete disarmament under strict and effective international control.

It is hard to believe that in the USA/USSR bi-lateral talks which had been going on, that there had been much 'good faith' showing. Both sides tended to make proposals that any ordinary person could see were bound to be rejected by the other side. Anyone who knows anything about the resolution of conflict saw that the diplomats seemed deliberately to flout every known principle for coming to

Frank Cotham, United States

'Before we begin, gentlemen, let's establish a few ground rules. First of all, there will be no *peaceful* solutions."

real agreement. Britain was of course not involved in these bi-lateral talks, so we turned in hope to the other Geneva negotiations, set up by the UN to work out a comprehensive test ban treaty. Without testing no new weapons could be added to the arsenals; and even old ones began to lack credibility. Forty nations had been at work on this since 1978; but in November 1980 the British government followed the USA in refusing to convene the three-power committee which was a pre-requisite for the completion of the treaty. So we concluded that Britain was simply not pursuing negotiations in good faith.

The distinguished Swedish diplomat, Inga Thorsson, was chairing the Review Conference, and gave a withering judgement saying:

> We are painfully aware of the dis-observance by the nuclear weapon states of the preamble paragraph and of Article VI of the Non-Proliferation Treaty, in defiant posture against the non-nuclear world, and world-wide public opinion ....
>
> I share the view of many that in the autumn of 1978 the world was very close to a Comprehensive Test Ban Treaty. There were no technical problems of verification to be solved only a lack of political will to find the solution to some remaining problems.'
> Evidence from the USA showed that they had no intention of signing up to any Test Ban Treaty. Mr Adelman said in Congress that testing was necessary to the US weapons programme. Meantime the USSR has taken a propaganda advantage by promoting a six-months moratorium on nuclear testing, and this, Mrs.Thorsson said, should be taken seriously by any testing state. Mr Adelman had stated explicitly stated 'that the USA will continue underground testing regardless of objections from most parties to the NPT, as this is necessary to the US Defence Programme; regardless, I would add, of binding Treaty obligations.

Mrs Thorsson continued:

> This totally intransigent attitude shows the present US administration to have a very narrow-minded conception of what they consider to be their national interest, disregarding the interests of the world community. In the long run they cannot violate Treaty obligations and defy the world community with impunity, and they will find (although they are obviously incapable of understanding it now) that in the long run they are doing a disservice to their own interests as well.

Dr David Owen was reported as saying 'The reasons put forward by the nuclear weapons states on the inadvisability of a Comprehensive Test Ban Treaty are a combination of misinformation and obfuscation'. I personally found that there was a strange and pleasing accessibility at UN events once you were inside the UNBuildings or the Palais des Nations. I recall wandering aimiably around the UN buildings in New York in 1982 and meeting up with some delegates and ambassadors without any formal appointments. It was the same in Geneva now. Our Freeze Conference had a session with Gregori Berdennekov, a Soviet Adviser to the USSR NPT delegation, and Mary Hoinkes, the senior US adviser. I had a chance in my turn at the microphone to say how disappointed we were to hear the endless feeble excuses being poured out by the USA, as though we were expected to believe them. To the Soviet delegate I said how good it was, after Mr Andropov's much-quoted denigration of 'unilateral measures' that the USSR had made a really significant one with the proposed moratorium on testing. I urged him to press for an extension of this, and to go on making unilateral gestures to prove their credibility, and perhaps shame the West into responding.

The next afternoon I wandered (even without any official lapel badge) through the corridors of the Palais until I found myself at the debating hall of the ambassadors and delegates on the Non-Proliferation Treaty. I was intrigued to find the 'alphabetical' seating of the nation-states: so UK was between USA and USSR, and the Holy See between Haiti and Honduras. I thought I might speak to the Vatican delegate, but perhaps his siesta wasn't over, so I made my way to the New Zealand ambassador and told him how delighted we were at the words and actions of David Lange. A country the size of Wales felt a particular warmth for a similar-sized country refusing to be pushed around by big powers. 'Well, David is a Welsh name already', said the ambassador. I then sat in on the whole of the first meeting of the Main Committee on Article VI and listened to the courageous and perceptive interventions of the Mexican ambassador, in an effort to prevent the superpowers frustrating the production of a final document to the Review Conference. Having made my notes on the pad and with the pencil provided, I replaced the multi-lingual translation ear-phone, picked up my copies of the summary of the proceedings of the conference to date, and slid anonymously out. My later experience in the Palais in 2003 was that outsiders, even recognised NGOS, were much more restricted.

Back at our Freeze Conference it was wonderful to hear a passionate speech by the American Senator, John Kerry of Massachusetts. It is good to be reminded that he belonged at that time to the 'other America'. Might we have hoped that he could have sustained this in challenging Bush for the presidency in 2004?

Yes, we have met at the Conference table on many occasions, and yes, there have been blips of success in an unratified SALT, an increasingly strained ABM Treaty and Limited Test Ban. But the hard fact is that we have not conformed our actions to reality. Instead we have become locked in a pattern of action and reaction, each governed by our perception of the threat the other poses; and in our effort to increase our own security, each unwilling to alter unilaterally that perception with the result that we guarantee yet another cycle of action-reaction. Star Wars and our ASAT programme are grim reminders of this dominant reality of the arms race. Each super-power feeds off the fear that the other is seeking first-strike capability; and these fears, real or imagined, are driving both of us to build a new momentum in the arms race — to pursue a policy founded on the belief that you can fight a nuclear war. Just the other day Dr Edward Teller literally derided those who do not share the view that we can fight with nuclear weapons with little fear of loss of control ... Notwithstanding our lack of clear ability to control, for the first time since the advent of the nuclear age, spokesmen in the government of the USA pronounce the ill-conceived notion that nuclear war is feasible and all-out nuclear war is survivable. We would do better to heed the words of George F.Kennan ... 'the West by its own talk really makes war inevitable by making it seem inevitable.

Today as we meet here we are poised on the brink of the most dangerous and destabilising era of the nuclear arms race. Compared to existing weapon systems, the Strategic Systems being pursued by both super-powers will be more numerous, more difficult to verify and to detect in flight, more prone to drive escalation out of control, and more likely to be placed on a hair-trigger. It is almost as if we are consciously writing the final chapter of the nuclear arms race which will place us squarely on the path to the Armageddon that the world has feared for so long, and all because we do not have the determination or courage, or leadership, to break the perception cycle.

No-one can disagree with President Reagan's goal of rendering nuclear weapons impotent or obsolete. It is the fondest dream of all mankind. But never in human history has the introduction of a defensive system ended the threat of counter offensive systems from an opposing nation of force. Never has it blunted another nation's efforts to better the system. What is worse today is that Star Wars, no matter what assumptions you make about it, cannot and will not accomplish the goals it seeks ... Star Wars send us many signals; but none should make us more wary than to note that it is an idea in search of a rationale. What was announced as a way to end war has been reduced to yet another bargaining pawn and an international high-tech pork barrel. In America contracts are being thrown around universities like candy to children in an effort to create a network of intellectual support. The result may well by that we will simply abdicate strategic decision-making where it is most necessary.

Dr Frank Barnaby reminded us that 90%of the nuclear arsenals could be disposed of without endangering security. He stressed how the new technologies were outpacing diplomacy; and that verification is emphatically not a problem from a technological point of view. What the NPT had not foreseen in 1970 was the move towards a 'plutonium economy' and to the development of fast-breeder reactors. Also it had not foreseen the impossibility of safeguarding reprocessing plants, or that the USA/USSR arms race would go on unabated.

Daniel Ellsberg (of Pentagon papers fame) said that every nuclear test is a rehearsal for a crime. Courage, like that inspired by Greenpeace, is contagious. We must demand that Reagan observes treaties and not change 'cessation' into mere 'reduction' He also suggested that there might be other ways of taking the US to task for violation of existing treaties, maybe via the World Court. As he listened, he said, to those who tried to justify the dropping of the first atomic weapons on Hiroshima and Nagasaki because of the lives that were allegedly saved, he saw that we were allowing a generation to grown up believing that some supreme crimes (of terrorism) could be justified if done in a 'good cause'. He also said that, apart from being courageous we had to be willing to appear ridiculous in the world's eyes if we resisted violence on this scale.

There were other voices at this time, giving solidity to the opposition to the notion of deterrence and the 'balance' of nuclear threats. Dr Evgeni Chazov of the USSR had already received the 1984 Beyond War award. In February 1985 he spoke to Physicians for Social Responsibility and said : 'What we are discussing today is the co-operation to solve the number one problem of our time, that of preventing nuclear war and preserving life on earth. And this is only natural, for when humanity faces the threat of annihilation, the solidarity of those called upon the safeguard life on earth, not only out of their sense of duty but also due to their profession grows stronger. Recently we witnessed such solidarity in action when the idea of peaceful outer space, free from nuclear weapons, united 3,000 Americans in San Francisco and 1,500 Russians in Moscow. The unity of our objectives in the struggle against nuclear catastrophe was at its best when the English and Russian lyrics of a song performed by an international audience resounded through outer space:

> For the world we raise our voices
> For the home that gives us birth,
> In our joy we sing, returning
> Home to our blue green hills of earth.

Perhaps more surprisingly there was an address by Noel Gayler, retired US Admiral, to the Union of Concerned Scientists:

> What should we do? The first thing stop the Star Wars programme. Send it back to the think-tank at the blackboard and computer level. Make a deal with the Soviets to stop anti-satellite testing before space becomes dangerous to our own great disadvantage. Now is the time while we can verify testing and before the situation goes away from us.

Then he outlined moves towards a general nuclear settlement with the Soviet Union, to be joined later by other nuclear powers.

'What would such a settlement look like? Six major ideas:

> Stop this insulting, pointless and childish language used between us, and ineffective attempts to injure each other.
> Give up the nuclear war-fighting doctrines: first use of weapons, counterforce. There is no way nuclear war in any form can be in anyone's interest.
> Provide better communications of every kind between President and Premier, military staffs, government officials, scientists, artists, people in general. Let us know each other.
> We should stay away from threatening deployments, whether they are Soviet tanks unnecessarily far forward, or American anti-satellites.
> By mutual moratorium stop testing and deployment of new classes of nuclear weapons.
> Finally make deep, fast and continuing cuts in nuclear weapons of all kinds until each

power has only a minimum invulnerable deterrent against nuclear attack. These weapons can in fact be beaten into ploughshares in a way that is practical, effective, negotiable, verifiable.

Only in this way can we remove the terrible danger of nuclear war and we can put science to work where it belongs, to the betterment of mankind.

The *Radio Times* published a poem at this time

CLOUDS OF REGRET

Consider the work of the painter
The culinary art of the chef
Or Beethoven dreaming 'the Choral'
And writing it when he was deaf

They stretch on the frame of invention
A canvas, a dish or a score
By mixing ingredients together
In ways never tested before

The scientists, too, had a mission
When chances of failure were high,
But danger from nuclear fission
Increased their temptation to try.

The drive to an act of creation
May merge with an urge to destroy
Like lovers who end a liaison
Or children when smashing a toy

For we are both builders and breakers
Today we are under a threat
Tomorrow, too late, we discover
Is darkened by clouds of regret

61. A DIFFERENT JOURNEY TO THE SOVIET UNION

Though I was about to take up my new job with Pax Christi in London, I was still a member of the International Committee of CND and I was asked to go at the end of September 1985 with four others for eleven days to the Soviet Union. Joan Ruddock (still Chair of CND, now an MP), Jane Mayes and I were to be accompanied by some specially skilled consultants, Dr Paul Rogers of the School of Peace Studies at Bradford University, and Dr Nick Lampert of the Centre for

Russian and East-European Studies at Birmingham University — who is a Russian-speaker. We were able to have some twelve long sessions (sometimes 2/3 hours) with members of some of the most influential think-tanks in Moscow. Our weekend in Leningrad was mainly 'cultural' — and I developed a 36 hour gastric flu there, which made me miss the only significant Orthodox Church visit. I was told that our delegation attended an hour of the Liturgy and then were invited by the clergy to 'take some tea' in the broad sense, which turned out to be a marvellous spread of food and drink.

I received some rich and varied impressions on the visit. There was a notable advance since my 1982 visit in the greater flexibility and openness. I sensed that the Gorbachev phenomenon was symbolic of wider developments. Nothing of course would change in a hurry in a society so vast and so 'controlled' as that of the USSR, but the change of style was already real, and the readiness to discuss differences less defensively was wonderful. Sadly the only context where this change was absent was with the two senior men in the Soviet Peace Committee. They argued about 'balance' of weaponry as conformingly as the Colonel from their Ministry of Defence — or any member of the British cabinet!

By contrast many of the people in the various Institutes of Research and Study — political and strategic study — were willing to listen carefully to the further suggestions we were making for more and more unilateral gestures to break the log-jam in international disarmament. We were made to understand the very natural objections they would have to these ideas, but they did not reject them out of hand. Those with considerable influence assured us that Gorbachev would continue initiatives like the moratorium on nuclear testing over the next months — and sure enough, within a week or two he had offered more items in Paris and in his exchanges with Reagan.

'What would your attitude be', we kept asking, 'if Britain returned a government pledged to non-nuclear defence policies?' They all agreed that the Russian reaction would be notable. One said: 'The response would surpass all your expectations, because we know what a sensational policy this would be.' What impressed me on many occasions was their thorough knowledge of western political thinking, and even the details of movements like CND. Some might have found this sinister. I wondered in how many places in Britain could we find

comparable research being done - Bradford, Sussex and a couple of other institutes perhaps?

In advance we had expressed our intention of making contact with any individual or group which worked for mutual understanding and reduction of tension, whoever they might be. The Soviet Peace Committee (our official hosts) therefore knew that we would surely go to see the Moscow Group of Trust, though their name was not actually specified in the hour-long formal introductory welcome speech. We had two inspiring informal visits to the flat of the Medvekov family and friends; but there was a complete blockage of the meeting called by the group on a third occasion. The first time we went we managed to give the slip to our interpreter/minder. She was a very charming lady, and when we were taken to the ballet one evening, we persuaded her to have the evening off, and we would find our own way home. Then after Act One was over, we made our way to the Medvekov's flat, where we had a lively discussion. They were not a disloyal couple, but anxious to break the distrust between Russian and Western people. Under the present Soviet system independent groups had no right to exist, so they were continually watched. We were due to make our Leningrad visit before we agreed to come again — and were aware that it was likely that this intention had been 'bugged'. So when we set off for this appointment it was perhaps not surprising that some dozen KGB men were waiting for us outside the block of flats.

This was the only act of civil disobedience I had ever indulged in — in Moscow against the KGB! We simply refused to go away, spread out a copy of the Guardian on a bench and sat down to wait a change. The police warned us that we would be taken away in the van that drew up; but on the whole we found them as personally malleable or obstinate as our British police can be. We were firm but courteous with them, and managed to converse (when Nick had to go home) in German. 'Look; I'm sure you're only doing your duty, but you must want to get home; so why don't you let us up to the flat for only five minutes. After all we had been told by the Peace Committee we could meet whoever we wanted' In this we way we kept up a smiling persuasive attitude, even though they only replied by checking in which hotel we were staying, and saying 'Just go home'. They weren't at all rough; in fact their officer in charge advised me to button up my coat as it was a cold night. We kept up our protest for a couple of hours before giving up before midnight, went home by underground, and said goodnight with a smile to the extra security man on duty on our floor (the 25th floor) at Hotel Ukraine.

Of course were a little anxious that this escapade might upset the whole tenor of our visit to the Institutes. We continued to register our dismay on the restriction, which had surely been reported and we sensed a certain sympathy from them. The Peace Committee people were certainly annoyed; but they did not reject us out of hand. They wanted to say that this visit was 'anti-state' and we replied that this notion was absurd; but it illustrated the in-built suspicion of any group working independently of the state mechanisms. One Russian Professor did say to us: 'There are many things in our society which will continue to disappoint you' Couldn't we say the same? In fact later that year in December I was taking a Russian Orthodox priest around on his first visit to London. Apart from the visits to the Houses of Parliament in session, to evensong at Westminster Abbey and to the Festival Hall, I walked him past the dozens of men and women sleeping rough on the pavement at the Embankment. There were certainly restrictions on personal freedom in Moscow but no-one was homeless; and they rightly thought that was a matter of human rights. And they do know how to laugh at themselves, and, contrary to western popular belief, they often do so. 'There is no unemployment in the USSR' said one official to me; 'but then nobody works!'

The Gorbachev anti-alcohol campaign was in evidence. As hosts they could never offer us alcoholic drink; for a life-long teetotaller like me this was no loss. They even jokingly called Gorbachev not the 'General Secretary' but the 'Mineral Secretary'; but this was one of the vigorous efforts being made to halt a grave social evil. The drunks in the street do not get by without police notice now.

Some of the scientists we met made the strongest impression on me. With one, the head of an Institute, we talked of the findings of the scientists about ' the nuclear winter' — which would follow any major use of these weapons. 'What we scientists have realised now', he said, 'is that those who make and deploy these weapons don't really know what they are doing.' As for his attitude to the government's Civil Defence plans, he reacted: ' Civil Defence? That's a retreat for retiring colonels.'

I reckoned there would be many in Britain who would echo that sentiment.

Altogether then I took great hope from what was happening in the USSR as well as in Europe generally. If we could reduce the unnecessary tensions there would surely be a greater willingness to admit the difficulties that the various 'socialisms' have in making a truly more just society. Meantime we could be more honest about the damage done by the 'capitalisms' of the West. I reckoned even then that by far the greater danger to our world came from the hawks of Reaganite America, though thankfully this does not represent all the American people. The rampant nationalism and determined economic hegemony which the USA imposes on so much of the world — and have done not just recently, but from the time of the Monroe Doctrine — cannot be applauded. Central and Latin America, and many other places are riddled with American consumerism, leading to tyrannies, economic slavery and financial debt.

But there is also arising a universal sense that this is no way to run the world. Americans will be among the leaders of the new spirit that is capable of being promoted everywhere. In 2005 as I write this, I feel much the same way.

62. PAX CHRISTI UK AND THE BISHOPS

We had been delighted by the US Bishops wonderful publication of 'The Challenge of Peace' in 1983. We recognised that Pax Christ USA had been a strong influence in its production. We were less sure of the English & Welsh bishops' stance, though proud of the publication of our own chairman's (Brian Wicker) booklet *Nuclear Deterrence: What does the Church teach?* One had the impression that Catholics in general seemed to settle for 'There's a lot to be said on both sides'

The Scottish bishops had a letter read out in all their churches on January 1st 1986 which delighted us. It included this passage:

'Everyone wants peace but often they see different ways to reach their goal. We have to look at these ways in the light of Christ's message and the Church's teaching. Recently the Scottish bishops, in common with all the major churches, called for a freeze on nuclear weapons — a step first urged a year ago. But when a group from our Justice and Peace Commission carried this appeal to NATO HQ in Brussels, they were told that peace was best kept through deterrence, the balance of terror: Britain must keep its nuclear deterrent. No convincing reason is given for Britain maintaining this independent deterrent. Yet Polaris is to be replaced by the much more expensive Trident at a cost of billions of pounds. This when our overseas aid has been cut despite mass hunger abroad and when welfare benefits are being reduced despite massive unemployment at home. That Trident will be based in Scotland is an additional reason for our concern. This is a source of potential danger for our people. It will bring few permanent jobs; but above all, as we said in 1982, if it is immoral to use weapons of mass destruction, it is immoral to threaten their use. Britain has nothing to lose and much to gain by 'freezing' its nuclear weapons, setting a prophetic example and reversing the direction of the arms race. Peace has no frontiers. We are all called to work for peace and to oppose the injustices that threaten it, be they at home or abroad.

John Ryan

'Must be a misprint for "Pax Chrispy" — some sort of cereal ad...'

Further comment came from the group that visited NATO HQ. 'Questions of morality and principle were repeatedly reduced to policy options and matters of expediency. So the scandal of the arms race and the inherent immorality of deterrence as a basis for peace, which underlie the Church's position on Freeze, were turned into questions of how to trust the Warsaw Pact, and how to make a Freeze verifiable. Such an approach smoothes over moral dilemmas and at the same time tends to remove the human dimension from difficult problems. Individuals remain subordinate to organisations or to technology, so nothing is done. Our hope is that the reiteration of our viewpoint by groups of responsible people may begin to erode NATO's present inflexible position.'

63. STAR WARS OR STRATEGIC DEFENCE INITIATIVE (SDI)

While it was being said that scientific researchers did not believe that Star Wars could provide a complete defence of USA, it was still being 'talked up'. E. P. Thompson, and his son Ben, alerted the peace movements to this again in a new book (*Star Wars*) which, with other joint authors, expanded his first booklet on the topic. The phantasies were bad enough; the deceptions were worse; the consequences were obscene. The Star Wars project purports to be the provision of a kind of total defence against ballistic missiles, but takes no account of the weapons that get in under the umbrella. That pretends to be a way to safe disarmament. Accordingly the whole idea was designed to appeal to the mass of people who hate nuclear deterrence. It was shaped to undermine the successful Freeze movement; and also to help Reagan towards his second term in the White House. Glitter, like mud, tends to stick, especially when produced with the glue provided by the Heritage Foundation, a strong right-wing institution which saw in1982 that a 'space defence project would give the US administration to fast-thaw the nuclear Freeze movement.' It was just what the President needed to undercut the Freeze campaign. Thompson gave us a few special quotations: 'We do not want any negotiations for a couple of years or more, in order to get our SDI programmes going full blast' (Presidential Adviser Keyworth) 'There could be serious arms-control negotiations, but only after we have built up our forces, in about ten years' (Arms Talks Ambassador Nitze). As always some US citizens are clearer: Former Deputy Director of the CIA, Herbert Scoville said: 'What SDI is doing is essentially defending missiles and command-and-control centres. It is not a protection of the people.'

Other more sinister facts and figures re-appeared in this book. Behind SDI and motivating it powerfully are (besides NORAD) Boeing, Livermore Laboratory etc. Millions are spent on lobbying. In the past three years 2,300 Pentagon staff have 'retired' straight into jobs with arms contractors. The Director of Rockwell is quoted as saying: 'Rockwell obviously has been spending some time over the years thinking about what the US space programme should be.' Already one in eight of America's scientists and engineers are working on defence retainers. It's not going to be easy to stop that vested interest momentum. Edward Thompson ends with this paragraph:

> There is no technological fix for the fraught and complex political relations between nations. There will never be an impermeable shield against nuclear evil. There is, and there has been for forty years, only one shield against chaos: that pitifully weak and yet somehow indestructible shield, the human conscience. It is as full of holes as a sieve: but it has kept chaos out for forty years. It is time to put it in repair.

Amen to all that!

64. THE MASTER OF BALLIOL ON DETERRENCE

Anthony Kenny had dealt with 'The Logic of Deterrence' in a book of that title. It was an accessible set of arguments, despite coming from a philosopher — if he'll pardon the insult. Among other good things he said:

> 'Better dead than red' may of course be used to express a sentiment which is not a moral judgement at all, but merely a personal preference. If someone tells me he would prefer to be a victim of a nuclear attack than be subject to Russian hegemony, I would not claim the right to disbelieve him. But such a preference can hardly be widely shared. The inhabitants of Warsaw already suffer what we would have to suffer if we surrendered to Russian blackmail. Yet in the worst days of martial law, can anyone really believe that what the Polish people wanted was for the West to put them out of their agony by dropping a nuclear device on the centre of Warsaw?

Then later he wrote:

> If my friend says that deterrence failed, then the only thing to do is to surrender, I know that fundamentally we are morally at one, and can settle to discuss questions of risk, danger and expense. But if he says 'if you are committed to the deterrent you have to stick to what you believe and use it if it comes to the crunch'. If he says that and means it, I can only tell him quite soberly that he is a man with murder in his heart.
>
> We are often told that unilateral disarmament by the West would lead to the Finlandisation of Western Europe. Those who say this don't always realise how impudent is the judgement that we should be prepared to kill millions rather than accept the political arrangements of Finland.

65. 1986 WAS THE YEAR OF CHERNOBYL

I was in Vicenza for the International Council of Pax Christi when the Chernobyl melt-down occurred. It certainly made us think again about the dangers of nuclear power apart from the connection with nuclear weapons. We already wondered how far the pollution would travel; I little thought that it would touch the sheep-farmers of north Wales! Sir Marcus Oliphant, the eminent Australian scientist who had worked on the first atomic bomb had strong views already:

'We have let the genie out of the bottle, and we cannot put it back. I only wish we could. So, after Chernobyl can we live with nuclear power? After Chernobyl can we use bad for good? Can we learn? We have this opportunity. We can do something now. We can remember Chernobyl and use it to prevent this rapid spread of nuclear power stations. We can remember Chernobyl and say to Science, to governments: ' Find other ways'. We can in countries like Australia say 'No' to nuclear power. Countries without it should never acquire it. We can look to the wind, to the sun, to the waves and find there all the power we need.

Of course Chernobyl was not the first nuclear accident. Rosalie Bertell reminded us:

The Soviet Union has never released an estimate of immediate or delayed fatalities attributable to the 1957 accident. The Russian people who survived have never had the human comfort of talking with the survivors of Hiroshima and Nagasaki, Micronesia, French Polynesia, Utah or the other regions of the world victimised by the nuclear age. The voice of these nuclear experts, made so by their personal experiences, are not heard in the Kremlin, the Pentagon, corporate boardrooms or other sterile environments where visions of short-term futures are concocted and long-term tragedies suppressed.

Mary Kaldor (of END) pointed out to us 'Over the next few years the peace movement has to sustain the political pressure through constant vigilance; and that means educating ourselves and extending public awareness of the finer points of security policy as well as spreading a broader vision of a peaceful Europe.'

So while we observed the bombing of Libya by the USA and took serious note of the Chernobyl accident we had to open our eyes to what had been happening to the people in the places where nuclear tests had been carried out. In New Zealand something of a major turning-point in public awareness came with the destruction of the Greenpeace boat. Maori people, feminists, anti-nuclear campaigners, environmentalists and conservationists combined in unity to express their revulsion of nuclear weaponry. There was a strong set of voices favouring the development of nuclear power. In 1983 Lord Walter Marshall said: 'We do not expect big reactor accidents to happen: the chance of their happening is extremely remote.' Then in 1986, that very year, Vitali Skydarov, Ukraine's Minister of Power said: The odds of a meltdown are one in 10,000 years. The plants have safe and reliable controls that are protected from any breakdown with three safety lines'. On 26th April the British Energy Secretary, Peter Walker said: 'The Soviet Union, where I've been last week, is going to double its nuclear energy programme ...In the next century countries with very big nuclear industries are going to have very big advantages. I would like Britain to have these advantages.' On April 28th, two days later, the first reports of the Chernobyl accident began to emerge.

66. IMPERIALISM AND THE USA

Following the second war against Iraq in 2003, many people have awakened to the underlying 'imperialism' of the current Bush administration. Many of us also know that this does not represent the whole of the peoples of the USA; far from it. We also know the dangers of a naïve anti-americanism. Yet not least because of the whole of the history of the British empire, we have to take careful note of the continuing slide into a fearfully risky stance of the only world super-power. There is nothing new about this in US history; there are many items in this that would be recognised in shame by ordinary Americans; but it does no harm to remind ourselves. In a book by Jenny Pearce (*Under the Eagle*) one read that many people were judging President Reagan adversely for his 'imperialism' as though it were something totally new. She gave us some remarkable quotations:

> Fate has written our policy ... The trade of the world must and can be ours: and we shall get it as our mother England has shown us how ... We will cover the ocean with our merchant marine. We will build a navy to the measure of our greatness. Great colonies, governing themselves, flying our flag and trading with us, will grow about our ports of trade. Our institutions will follow: and American law, American order, American civilisation and the American flag will plant themselves on shores hitherto bloody and benighted, by those agents of God henceforth made beautiful and bright.

That, believe it or not, came from the mouth of a senator, Albert Beveridge in 1898!

Then came a list of dates:

> 1898–1902 US troops occupy Cuba
> 1901 US acquires Puerto Rico
> 1905 US troops land in Honduras
> 1906-09 US troops occupy Cuba

169

1908 US troops sent to Panama
1912 US troops occupy Cuba

The day is not far distant when the Stars and Stripes at three equidistant points will mark our territory: one at the North Pole, another at the Panama Canal, and the third at the South Pole. The whole hemisphere will be ours in fact as, by virtue of our superiority of race, it already is morally. (President William Howard Taft in 1912)

1912-25 US troops occupy Nicaragua
1914-34 US marines occupy Haiti
1916-24 US troops occupy Dominican Republic.
1917-23 US troops occupy Cuba
1918 US troops sent to Panama
1919 US marines occupy Honduras' ports
1926-33 US marines occupy Nicaragua
and establish Somosa regime
1924 US marines land in Honduras

Our ministers are credited to the five little republics, stretching from the Mexican border to Panama....have been advisers whose advice has been accepted virtually as law in the capitals where they respectfully reside... We do control the destinies of Central America and we do so for the simple reason that the national interest dictates such a course... Until now Central America has always understood that governments which we recognise and support stay in power, while those we do not recognise and support fail. (Secretary of State Robert Olds in 1927)

1932 US warships stand by during El Salvador matanza
1933 Franklin Roosevelt declares 'good neighbour' policy

I spent 33 years and 4 months in active service as a member of our country's most agile military force — the Marine corps. I served in all commissioned ranks from a 2nd Lieutenant to Major-General. And during that period I spent most of my time being a high-class muscle man for Big Business, for Wall Street and for the bankers. In short I was a racketeer for capitalism ... Thus I helped make Mexico, and especially Tampico safe for American oil interests in 1914. I helped make Haiti and Cuba a decent place for the National City Bank to collect revenues in ... I helped purify Nicaragua for the international banking house of Brown Brothers in 1909–12. I brought light to the Dominican Republic for American sugar interests in 1916. I helped make Honduras 'right' for American fruit companies in 1903. (General Smedley Butler in 1935)

1947 Setting out of Truman Doctrine
1948 Organisation of American states founded

We have about 50% of the world's wealth, but only 6.3% of its population ... In this situation we cannot fail to be the object of envy and resentment. Our real task in the coming period is to devise a pattern of relationships which will permit us to maintain this position of disparity without positive detriment to our national security. To do so we will have to dispense with all sentimentality and day dreaming, and our attention will have to be fixed everywhere on our immediate national objectives. We need not deceive ourselves that we can afford the luxury of altruism and world benefaction.

We should cease to talk about vague and unreal objectives such as human rights, the raising of living standards and democratisation. The day is not far off when we are going to have to deal in straight power concepts. The less we are then hampered by idealistic slogans the better. (State Department Document PPS23 in 1948)

All this is quite sinister, though we do well to note the imitation of British imperialism in its own day. It begins to make sense, of course, of American interventionism, which was fuelled by popular anti-communism, but was really about economic hegemony.

Moving on to the late 70s we find Eugene Rostow former head of the US Arms Control & Disarmament Agency making an interesting comment:

The mission of our nuclear forces goes beyond making it too expensive for the Soviet Union to consider launching a nuclear attack against the USA. They must also provide a nuclear guarantee for out interests in many parts of the world, and make it possible to defend those interests by diplomacy or by the use of theatre military forces whenever such action becomes necessary. The previous sentence needs underlining, for most people do not yet realise the many connections between the strategic nuclear balance on the one hand, and ordinary diplomacy and the use of conventional and other theatre forces in aid of diplomacy on the others. Behind the shield of our second strike capability, we carry on the foreign policy of a nation with global interests, and defend them if necessary by conventional means or theatre forces.

Daniel Ellsberg began to understand the whole of US might in this sense. In 1980 he said:

You wouldn't need all this destructive power to bully a smaller nation if Russia did not exist. But most of the smaller nations that we've been opposed to are allied to Russia. So if we want to be able to say to Russia: 'We may have to batter or even annihilate your small friends here, like North Vietnam, and you had better not get into the fray. You'd better stand back', then we can't have too many weapons in the balance.

Harold Brown, US Secretary for Defense also in 1980 said:

Political, economic and social grievances exist on a world-wide basis, and provide fertile soil for sabotage, subversion, terror and civil war ... (The USA was unable) to provide for the basic needs of people and narrow the explosive disparity between wealth and hunger.

He thought that the Soviet Union exploited these divisions for its own political advantage, 'but the Soviet Union is only part of the problem. (More important by far) are the differences about the proper world distribution of income and natural resources. Military strength by itself can often be productive in dealing with the basic causes of disorder in this tumultuous world … but in some circumstances it may be our only recourse.'

There is something rather sad about this sort of remark; it's as though the USA wants to do the right thing, but it's just impossible if they are to have the advantages of wealth and power.

It is good to contrast all this with the words of other distinguished Americans. Martin Luther King said: 'The ultimate weakness of violence is that it is a descending spiral, begetting the very thing it seeks to destroy. Instead of diminishing evil, it multiplies it. Returning violence for violence multiplies violence, adding deeper darkness to a night already devoid of stars. Darkness cannot drive out darkness; only light can do that. Hate cannot drive out hate; only love can do that.'

And then George Kennan:

> Our main concern must be to see that man, whose own folly once drove him from the Garden of Eden, does not now commit the blasphemous act of destroying, either in fear or in anger or in greed, the great and lovely world in which, even in his fallen state, he has been permitted by the grace of God to live.

67. SIGNS OF HOPE IN THE SOVIET UNION

The times they were a-changing within the other super-power, Mihail Gorbachev, some four months before he became the new Secretary of the Party indicated a new way of doing things within the Union:

> Our contemporaries are well-educated and highly cultured people with a wide range of interests, who have been through a lot; through revolution, collectivisation, and industrialisation, war and the difficult post-war decades. Such people do not accept over-simplified answers to their questions. They easily detect falsity. We must speak to Soviet people only in the language of truth — a language which does not tolerate generalities, insensitivity, cliches, truisms and stilted phrases.

And in a *Time* magazine interview he posed a witty approach to disarmament:

If all that we are doing is indeed viewed as propaganda, why not respond to it according to the principle of ' an eye for an eye, a tooth for a tooth'? We have stopped nuclear explosions. Then you Americans could take revenge by doing likewise. You could deal us another propaganda blow, say, by suspending the development of one of your new strategic missiles. And we would respond with the same kind of 'propaganda'. And so on and so forth. Would anyone be harmed by competition in such 'propaganda'? Of course it could not be a substitute for a comprehensive arms-limitation agreement, but it would be a significant step leading to such an agreement.

Other Soviet figures included Vladimir Petrovski: 'With the USSR and USA's present stockpile of nuclear weapons, it is of no significance whether one side has military superiority over the other, or what degree that superiority might reach.'

Oleg Bykov said: 'There is already so much deadly weaponry in the world that further competition in increasing military potential becomes not only irrational and burdensome, but also more and more dangerous for the participants. With the existing military-strategic equilibrium, there is no possibility of obtaining decisive unilateral superiority.' 'Counter-measures frequently take on the character of over-insurance, which is entirely natural in view of the great number of unpredictable variables, and the many year lead-time for modern weapons. In such cases planning often takes account of the more unfavourable alternatives for the development of the situation in the distant future.'

So there we had it. The absurdity of 'overkill'; the meaninglessness of 'superiority' and the dangers of over-reaction and worst-case-analysis. So much for détente in our century. The gestures were real, and public. Aleksandr Bovin in Isvestia said:

> We have in effect said to the West: We grant that you may be worried by some aspects of our military potential. We too have cause to worry. So instead of increasing our armaments to calm ourselves down, let's start negotiations for reducing them.

It was obviously going to take a long time to remove the western conviction of a wholly evil society in the Soviet Union. It was more than mere anti-communism. So, if self-criticism is really a sign of growing maturity then improvements were on the way. Most of this information I was picking up from the splendid quarterly journal from Birmingham University's Centre for Russian and East European Studies. When it was said that the Soviet people complained a lot, so long as they didn't rock the political boat, we noted our western privilege of complaining as much as we like so long as it didn't make any difference. Boris Yeltsin — soon to become more prominent - spoke at the Party Congress at this time:

Why do we hear at Congress after Congress about exactly the same problems? Why after so many years have we not been able to root out bureaucracy, social injustice, and abuse of power? Why is it that even now the demand for radical change gets bogged down in an inert layer of time-servers with Party cards?

Strong words. More positively were the words in the Literary Gazette of Feodor Burlatski, who was a man with an impish sense of humour:

One way of handling differences in a work collective is the administrative authoritarian one: 'cut out' those opinions (and perhaps their bearers as well) which do not correspond with that of the director. Another method, the rational democratic one, is to integrate various opinions and work out on their basis the most effective solution. That is more complicated but only such an approach justifies itself in practice … We must all accustom ourselves to working in a dynamic, contradictory competitive society. Maybe this is the most difficult problem in reconstructing our consciousness.

This was a real call for pluralism, and something new. He went on:

As experience has shown, State management of one or another sphere of activity, whether in the production of material, or of spiritual values, must be supplemented by a mechanism of real economic and moral competition among enterprises, co-operatives, scientific centres, cinema studios, TV stations, publishing houses, magazines and newspapers. Without the fresh breeze of honest struggle and rivalry, which do not hinder but help co-operation and mutual aid, any sphere of activity may turn into something like a still forest lake — and a marshy one at that!

68. COULD THE COLD WAR HAVE BEEN AVOIDED?

It was interesting to read back to 1945 and to see an alternative view to that which eventually shaped the attitude of the USA to the USSR, and led to the Cold War. The first problem was whether or not to share with the Soviet Union the knowledge won by scientists in the USA about atomic power and its harnessing to the first two bombs on Hiroshima and Nagasaki. On 11th September, only one month after those disastrous events, Henry Stimson, the US Secretary of State wrote a Memorandum for President Truman. It was about how one should deal with a state whose internal system one disapproves of so strongly. His letter and the Memorandum deserve extensive quotation.

> When in Potsdam I talked with you about whether or not we could be safe in sharing the atomic bomb with Russia while she was still in a police state and before she put into effect provisions assuring personal rights of liberty to the individual citizen. I still recognise the difficulty and am still convinced of the ultimate importance of a change in Russian attitude towards individual liberty, but I have come to the conclusion that it would be possible to use our possession of the atomic bomb as a direct lever to produce the change.
>
> I have become convinced that any demand by us for an internal change in Russia as a condition of sharing in the atomic weapon would be so resented that it would make the objective we have in view less probable. I believe that the change in attitude toward the individual in Russia will come slowly and gradually, and I am satisfied that we should not delay our approach to Russia in the matter of the atomic bomb until that process has been completed.

That was Stimson's covering letter The Memorandum was equally suprising.

> Unless the Soviets are voluntarily invited into the partnership upon a basis of co-operation and trust, we are going to maintain the Anglo-Saxon bloc over against the Soviets in the possession of this weapon. Such a condition will almost certainly stimulate feverish activity on the part of the Soviets towards the development of this bomb in what will in effect be a secret armament race of a rather desperate character ... I consider the problem of our satisfactory relations with Russia as not merely connected with as virtually dominated by the problem of the atomic bomb... If we fail to approach them now and merely continue to negotiate with them, having this weapon rather ostentatiously on our hip, their suspicions and their distrust of our purpose and motives will increase ....
>
> The chief lesson I have learned in a long life is that the only way you make can make a man trustworthy is to trust him; and the surest way to make him untrustworthy is to distrust him and show him your distrust ....
>
> We could follow the old custom of secrecy and nationalistic military superiority,

relying on international caution to proscribe the future use of the weapon as we did with gas. But I think the bomb constitutes merely a first step in a new control by man over the forces of nature too revolutionary and dangerous to fit into the old concepts. I think it really caps the climax of the race between man's growing technical power for destructiveness and his psychological power of self-control and group control — it is moral power. If so, our method of approach to the Russians is a question of the most vital importance in the evolution of human progress.

Stimson's advice was not followed. The arms race began. Suspicion and distrust on both sides grew, and we saw the building up of the East–West divided blocs. Yet somehow it is good to know that there were people in high places with the wisdom to think otherwise.

69. SOUTH AFRICA IN 1986

While most of our interest and energy in the peace movements were understandably focussed on the arms race and nuclear deterrence, we recognised that the other urgent issue was the situation in South Africa. Perhaps we felt that we could do even less to make a difference there than we could in the western world. It was however worth pointing out some of the similar or parallel factors. There was certainly a link between the way the white elite wrote off the African National Congress and others, and the way the west tended to reject so much of the world as 'communist'. Then came the insightful Kairos Document; this was a theological comment on the crisis. It spoke of 'State theology' 'which has tried to re-establish the status quo of orderly discrimination, exploitation and oppression by appealing to the consciences of its citizens in the name of law and order. It tries to make those who reject this law and this order feel they are ungodly.

We all know how the South African state makes use of the label 'communist'. Anything that threatens the status quo is labelled 'communist'. Anyone who opposes the state, and especially anyone who rejects its theology is dismissed as a 'communist'. No account is taken of what communism really means. No thought is given to why some people have indeed opted for communism or for some form of socialism. Even people who have not rejected capitalism are called 'communist' in an uncritical and unexamined way as its symbol of evil. State theology must be able to symbolise what it

176

regards as godless behaviour and what ideas must be regarded as atheistic. It must have its own version of hell. And so it has invented, or rather taken over, the myth of communism. All evil is communistic and all communist or socialist ideas are atheistic and godless. Threats about hell-fire are replaced by threats and warnings about the horrors of a tyrannical, totalitarian, atheistic and terrorist communist regime — a kind of hell on earth. This is a very convenient way of frightening some people into accepting any kind of domination and exploitation by a capitalist minority.

The South African state has its own heretical theology and according to that theology millions of Christians in South Africa (not to mention the rest of the world) are to be regarded as 'atheists'. It is significant that in earlier times, when Christians rejected the gods of the Roman empire, they were branded as 'atheists' by the state. As we all know, spirituality has tended to be an other-worldly affair that has very little, if anything at all, to do with the affairs of this world … It is this kind of spirituality that leaves so many Christians and Church leaders in a state of near paralysis. It hardly needs saying that this kind of faith, and this type of spirituality has no biblical foundation. The Bible does not separate the human person from the world in which he or she lives; it does not separate the individual from the social, or one's private life from one's public life. Biblical faith is prophetically relevant to everything that happens in the world.

The fact that the State is tyrannical and an enemy of God is no excuse for hatred. As Christians we are called upon to love our enemies. It is not said that we will not have enemies or that we should not identify tyrannical regimes as our enemies. But once we have identified our enemies, we must endeavour to love them. That is not always easy. But then we must remember that the most loving thing we can do for both the oppressed and for our enemies is to eliminate the oppression, remove the tyrants from power and establish a just government for the common good of all the people.'

Easily said; and hard to apply as we are currently (2005 as I write) seeing in Iraq and Afghanistan. Pre-emptive and internationally unauthorised war, however, can never be a starting-point.

70. COMING TO TERMS WITH GORBACHEV AND CHANGES IN THE USSR

The December Issue of Comments and Quotes focussed again on the Soviet Union. My task, as I saw it, was to help people towards the written sources for understanding events. I found rich quotations from a number of new books:

Christian Schmidt-Hader's *Gorbachev;the Path to Power*; Richard Owen's *Crisis in the Kremlin*: but especially Martin Walker's *The Waking Giant*. Walker was the *Guardian's* correspondent. He was happy to challenge Soviet political absolutism, its territorial expansionism (especially in Afghanistan), its security system and its silence or amnesia about the horrors of the Stalinist era. He would have concurred with a statement by Sir John Lawrence (in *The Hammer and the Cross*).

©1986 HERBLOCK

'So I got up from that table with Gorbachev and walked out. And you can imagine my surprise when I found out what we had been talking about.'

No-one can escape his personal prejudices or the conditioning of his own experience, and no-one knows enough to judge finally.

But we can admit our prejudices and describe our experience ... My aim is to seek the truth in love and to face it squarely when it turns out to be other than I would wish. My method is to start with what I have seen with my own eyes, but to put it into its context after testing it against what I have read and what I have learned from the experience of others.

Walker took a direct quote from a speech by Gorbachev in which he said:

We do not see the diversity of our movement as a synonym for disunity, much as unity has nothing in common with uniformity, hierarchy, interference by some parties in the affairs of others or the striving of any party to have a monopoly over what is right. One of socialism's advantages is its ability to learn: to learn to prevent collisions of the interests of different socialist countries.

We could have wished that this had been said and acted upon at the time of the Czech government under Dubcek. Walker remarks 'Even now it would be unwise to take this at its face value or suggest that it heralds a new era for Eastern Europe. It is too soon to tell. But the rhetoric of Moscow's political supremacy has changed, and this may be reflected in practice.'

The undoubted absolutism of the USSR is a legacy of history. Walker continues:

It began as a pre-requisite of national defence ... The Russians know that the only way they have ever stopped invasions is under the merciless, implacable leadership of a single centralised authority. This centralised absolutism has also been the bulwark against the other age-old Russian fear, of internal anarchy, whether in the form of peasant revolt, pogroms, or the rising of one or other of the minority nations. If fear of anarchy inside their vast territory helps to explain harsh internal controls, so an overlarge military machinery is explained by the Russian experience of war.

Traditionally, for Russia war is something that other people inflict on them. Whereas for Britain and the USA war is something that takes place comfortably overseas, war to the Russians is invasion an enemy advancing into their homes, occupying their cities, behaving with terrible brutality and only being beaten back after heroic and catastrophic national efforts.

The horror of war strikes visitors as unequalled anywhere else in the world. The corollary of this is belief in the need for strong military preparedness. There is virtually no pacifist tradition in the USSR, not even among the Orthodox or Baptist leaders or others who have had a hard time under the communist system.

Then followed a paragraph about Afghanistan and other neighbouring states which has relevance to the developments in our time (2005) over 'terrorism'.

> Afghanistan is perceived in the West as the ultimate proof of Soviet aggression and determination to expand. This is not how it is seen in Moscow, where the invasion was planned as a brief incursion to sort out the chaos of a civil war between two rival factions of the Afghan Communist Party, each of whom was intent on pushing the revolution so far and so fast that they were force-feeding a resistance movement in a still largely illiterate and semi-feudal country. Moscow did not envisage the long and costly guerilla war which followed, nor did it see the Afghan venture as a stepping-stone to the Indian Ocean and the oil of the gulf states.
>
> By the end of the 1970s Moscow was alarmed by the growing wave of Islamic fundamentalism that was lapping its own southern borders and threatening to bring political instability to the area's traditional Muslim population.

Acquiring empires is not only a feature of Russian, let alone Soviet, history. A knowledge of history is necessary to grasp how 'Russia' became so large. Walker makes a useful analogy:

> If the British Empire was acquired in a fit of absent-mindedness, imposed by the need for securely held coaling stations to fuel the fleets and guard the sea-routes to India, the Russian empire was acquired in spite of Moscow rather than on its orders — through the actions of ambitious local generals and zealous governors. Just as the British could never understand why the rest of the world saw them as rampant and greedy imperialists, the Russians were aggrieved when the West accuses them of expansionism. The Russians look at the haphazard way in which the empire was acquired, while the West looks at results on the map. The fact is that the spread of Soviet influence is hugely expensive, a great strain on the economy and highly unpopular with the Russian public, who regularly complain that their own food shortages are caused by the need to send supplies to Cuba, Vietnam and the African client states. This is untrue. Very little food finds itsway abroad, even for example to Ethiopia during the famine. But the financial burden to the SovietUnion of its allies round the globe is enormous.' This is mainly in subsidies to

Cuba's economy, subsidised oil to Eastern Europe and other military and non-military aid to Vietnam

Whatever the expense, the Soviet Union has assumed the responsibilities of a global power. It has done so partly because the West has allowed it to. There is a pattern here. Whenever the West continues to support corrupt and brutal regimes which have no chance of maintaining public sympathy, then a domestic revolutionary movement inevitably develops. The longer the West supports the unpopular government against the revolutionaries, the greater the likelihood the pro-soviet faction will inherit the revolution. After Cuba, Yemen, S.Vietnam, the Portuguese African colonies and Nicaragua, this is nearly a universal rule ... Chile and South Africa wait in the wings.

Stalinism may well have had its day, but many people are still reluctant to agree that anything fundamental has changed in the Soviet Union. There is to be found some nostalgia for those tougher days among Soviet people; but Walker rightly shows that this is because the Soviet people continue to be denied access to their own history. 'There was and remains to this day a hole where the nation's memory ought to be.' But Gorbachev's new policy of openness could just change that. The poet Yevtushenko managed to publish the following recently:

Our socialism is in itself a living text-book, from which we can tear neither the heroic pages of our victories nor the tragic pages of our losses and mistakes. If we do, neither we nor the generations that follow us will ever be able to use this book, nor to learn from it. Now that our state has matured and become strong, there are few grounds to fear our frankness, our own critical expressions of our views. Such an openness is a sign of our maturity as a nation, our strength as a people. And the cover-up is a sign of weakness, public silence is a hidden form of anarchy. Nothing can harm us more than endless, obedient votes, when those dutifully raised hands do not follow the call of our hearts. It is simply inertia, the kind of non-vote that will lead to the sabotage, deliberate or not, of the very decisions we just 'voted' for.

In all kinds of ways I thought it was important to publicise the grounded hopes of real change, at least to those who were so opposed to the 'defence' policies of the UK and USA. We needed mature opinions; and I reckoned Martin Walker provided them. Towards the end of his admirable book he wrote:

The West has to go beyond its archetypes of Soviet commissars and Gulags and try to assess how far the place has changed: to understand the force and scope of the social revolution which has produced the educated Soviet leadership of Gorbachev's time. The Soviet Union remains a country of which we know desperately little; until we know more, we have little right to make judgements, still less to dismiss its proposals as inherently suspect.... A society deserves to be judged by its aspirations as well as by its faults; by its capacity for change as well as by its past misdeeds. We, and they, deserve better.

There was other evidence coming in. The periodical 'Détente' quoted Moscow's *Pravda* with a complaint from a long-standing Party member:

> It is impossible to close one's eyes to the fact that Party, Soviet, Trade Union. Economic and even Komsomol leaders sometimes objectively deepen social inequality, making use of all kinds of special buffets, shops, hospitals and the like. Sure, we have socialism and everyone should be rewarded according to their labour. Let leaders have higher monetary wages without levelling. But there ought not to be the remaining privileges.... But it is doubtful if those who profit by special benefits will themselves renounce their privileges; for this law and a thorough-going purge of the apparatus are necessary.

An earlier article defined 'civilised relations'. He suggested they should include:

- changing the system of the other side must not be a goal of policy
- the use of force must be repudiated
- the illusion of achieving absolute invulnerability must be repudiated. Nuclear arsenals do not raise, but lower, the level of security
- co-operation must be placed higher than monetary political considerations and ideological stereotypes.

Feodor Burlatski, who has advocated action for 'planned peace' for fifteen years, added his own programme:

> I suggest that civilised relations is a synonym for active peaceful co-existence. Negative or passive peaceful coexistence prevailed even during the Cold War. Civilised relations are an advance on détente –towards joint action directed at elimination of the threat of nuclear annihilation. Nuclear weapons are unusable and militarily senseless. They are a means of deterence, but this function can be fulfilled in other ways.

Not all commentators were as optimistic perhaps. Sir John Lawrence was certainly more cautious. 'It should not be concluded that nothing can change, but rather to permit a change in ideology is difficult for the present rulers in USSR precisely because it will undermine the foundation of Leninism which alone legitimates their power. This helps to explain the extraordinary rigidity of Soviet thought.' That was written a couple of years earlier; and he had already noted sudden changes in past Soviet history. For instance in 1963, the year of the fall of Kruschev, 'almost simultaneously vast numbers of people had discovered not only that they themselves did not believe a word of the official propaganda, but that almost nobody else did either.' (This confirmed the truth behind the witty remark I have already quoted in # 8). Lawrence also noted that 'Soviet people have become masters at reading between the lines of anything that is printed, and finding the right interpretation of 'Aesopian' language.'

Keeping up with Gorbachev was becoming a full-time task. He really was saying too much; but complaining about that would make it look as though we would never be satisfied. Some of his speeches had telling sentences. Here were some quotable quotes:

> Every country has its own social and political system with all thinkable tinges, its traditions, achievements and difficulties, its mode of life and its beliefs, convictions and prejudices; its own understanding of spiritual and material values.

> The 'balance of fear' is ceasing to be a deterring factor. This is not only because fear in general is no adviser to reason, and could bring about actions with unpredictable consequences.... It is now clear as clear can be that the old notions of war as a means of attaining political objectives have become outdated. In the nuclear age these obsolete tenets feed the policy that may result in a world-wide conflagration.

> Experts have estimated that the explosion of the smallest nuclear warhead is equal in radio-activity to three Chernobyls. Most likely this is true. If so, the setting off of even a small part of the existing nuclear arsenal will become an irreversible catastrophe. And if someone still dares a first nuclear strike, he will doom himself to agonising death — not from a retaliatory strike, but from the consequences of the explosion of his own warheads. This is neither propaganda, nor political improvisation, nor intensifying of 'fears'. This is reality. It is simply irresponsible to reject it, and criminal to disregard it.

71. OTHER VOICES FROM ELSEWHERE

By this time we had almost come to take for granted the public statements by some dozen ex-NATO generals and admirals who were campaigning against Cruise and Pershing missiles, and Star War plans, and who were also in favour of a Comprehensive Test Ban Treaty. In 1985 a new voice had joined them — Major General Leonard Johnson, till 1983 the Commandant of the National Defence College in Ontario, Canada. He said:

> People will say 'If you knew what I know — but I can't tell you because it's classified — then you would see things as I do.' That's a protective device to enhance their own prestige and to shut off the argument. There's nothing about this that the layman cannot understand; and nothing that some layman doesn't know. I've been very impressed with the level of technical knowledge people in the peace movement have or have access to. It's just as sophisticated as anything in the defence establishment. I don't believe the American system protects Canada. It's a very inept metaphor to say that we're sheltered under the nuclear umbrella, because the nuclear umbrella is the very thing that threatens

us. We need to reduce these great arsenals and get back to some more reasonable interpretation of nuclear deterrence for the time being at least, until we can do away with nuclear weapons altogether. Verification is often used as an excuse for continuing to do some thing that you want to do for other reasons. If you don't really want to have an agreement, you can always use verification to prevent agreement. I've learned a lot from people in the peace movement and I've gained hope from them ... I haven't finished thinking about it by any means, but the time comes when you really have a moral obligation to stand up and be counted; when you need to stand in front of the train. Probably the best deterrent to the invasion of Nicaragua is the prospect of meeting a whole lot of Americans down there waving flags.

There's a book by Robert Malcolmson, a historian at Queens, called *Nuclear Fallacies: How We Have Been Misled Since Hiroshima*. He supports the view that it was deliberate American policy to use their monopoly on atomic weapons as a threat in pursuit of their global interests ... Despite the warnings of the scientists that the secret was no secret, the Americans expected to keep an atomic monopoly for at least ten to fifteen years, and that they expected to stay ahead permanently in science and technology. This confidence prevailed till 1957 when Sputnik started the race into space ... In that perspective, Star Wars can be seen as an attempt to regain that superiority and to break the stalemate of mutual vulnerability that the Americans have found so intolerable since the 1960s.

An extra-ordinarily hopeful remark came also from Robert McNamara — who later turned out to be a champion against nuclear deterrence. He was a former US Secretary of Defence who commented after the apparent failure of the Rejkavik talks. 'Reagan's final proposal at Rejkavik was a gigantic step forward philosophically and strategically. What the President proposed in principle was to move as far as practical back towards a non-nuclear world. It is a totally different strategic concept from what the administration had enunciated in the past. He is saying that the US and its NATO allies can be secure against Soviet and Warsaw Pact conventional aggression without a nuclear deterrent. He has made the discussion of a basic change in strategy respectable — a debate some of us have been participating in for years. The intellectual foundation of NATO and Warsaw Pact strategy has been broken open completely for examination and debate. I understand the difficulty in agreeing on a new strategy, and an arms control regime to support it. I guarantee you that five years from now we will be well on our way to achieving that objective.'

Now let me see; that was 1986; so 1991 should have seen us there. America is backing off from the Comprehensive Test Ban Treaty, from the Anti-Ballistic Missile Treaty, and continues deep research into nuclear weapons in space.

A helpful observation was also being made by West Germany's Foreign Minister Genscher. 'I have always said we shouldn't let the idea of Central Europe be overtaken by a primitive division of Europe into East and West — as though Europe didn't have a centre. We Germans are central Europeans, of course, and so are the Poles, the Czechs, the Hungarians. It depresses me to see East Germans, Poles, Czechs and Hungarians ranged among East Europeans. It is unhistorical, politically wrong and leads to mistaken assessments. Respect for the cultural achievements of other peoples is the best form of immunity against hatred. Throughout history hatred against other people always started by saying they were inferior.'

72. PATRIOTISM — THE FALKLANDS —DIEGO GARCIA

A quite brilliant book by Keith Clements of Bristol Baptist College came to my notice at this time, so I presented extended quotations for people's consideration. Its title was *Patriotism for Today* with the important sub-title 'Love of country in dialogue with the witness of Dietrich Bonhoeffer'. Bonhoeffer identified himself with the Germany that had produced Hitler. He wasn't going to renounce his love of country because it had gone the wrong way; nor yet was he going to keep silent and fail to challenge the evil. That was true patriotism. Love of country is thoroughly justified; we do but love ourselves in this way; but it has to be in proper proportion.

In the 20th century one factor has contributed towards the apotheosis of patriotism to a virtually sacred status — war. The relationship between patriotism and war is not simply, as is commonly assumed, one of cause and effect respectively. War unleashes patriotic feelings and eventually consolidates them. It can generate a sense of national unity and identity in face of a threat from without … And provoking even the blandest citizens to discover just what their country means to them.

The sacrifices involved bind people together and solidify national sentiment afterwards.

When blood has been shed for the country, the rightful claim of the country to that blood must be asserted, or else the unbearable, unmentionable and horrific thought might emerge; their lives were wasted. No, the sacrifice had to be made; they did not 'die in vain'. The sacrifices even take on a justifying power of their own. 'If they're worth dying for, they're worth keeping' was a widely quoted remark of a colour sergeant returning from the Falklands. A soldier who has been involved in the peril cannot be blamed for feeling that way. Whether a whole nation can base its policies on such a feeling is another matter.

One suspects that it is this factor that allowed Britain to stand almost alone in the United Nations in the vote for negotiations on the 'sovereignty' of the Falklands.

If there is to be love of one's country, it must be clear-eyed recognition of the reality of the country, not a wishful indulgent admiration of what might once have been, but no longer exists, or of what one would like to be there but quite simply is not there and can never be. It is the real country we must love.

Bonhoeffer has shown us that there is a loyalty to country which includes recognition and acceptance of one's country's guilt, and intercession and action for its expiation. Denial or excusal of the country's guilt is in the end not true love nor true loyalty by Christian standards. That means they will look honestly and unflinchingly at Britain's record of behaviour as a colonial and imperial power. They need not subscribe to the childishly simplistic view that the whole story was a carefully planned capitalist conspiracy to subdue and exploit the rest of mankind. They will know that the colonial expansion of the 18th and 19th centuries was for much of the time a haphazard and incoherent affair, and not until the late 19th century did it ever achieve widespread and popular approval. They will know that a great deal of personal idealism and sacrifice was channelled into the enterprise, in the sincere conviction that the spreading of British-born justice, education and health care would make a better world. But they will also underline those episodes which show that British people have been as capable as any other of the most brutal acts of inhumanity. They will speak of the opium wars against China as a thoroughly sordid instance of fire-power for nakedly mercenary ends and deliberately introducing a source of misery on a native population. They will not forget the deception of the Maories in the seizure of their lands; nor the persecution of the Australian aborigines, still less the actual extermination of the Tasmanians (genocide did not begin with the Nazis). When South Africa is mentioned, they will remember the horrors of the Boer War, especially the concentration camps (yes; concentration camps) in which during just fourteen months over twenty thousand men, women and children died. Such episodes and much else belong to the story.

Looking at the Second World War Clements reminds us how slow the allies were to respond even when Auschwitz was a known fact.

And still there are people in Britain who refuse to believe that their political or military leaders could ever actually order the deliberate massacre of helpless civilians, despite the implications of the stated aim of the strategic bombing offensive which was to destroy the morale of the working population of Germany. Nothing, but nothing, has yet been produced which even remotely justifies militarily, let alone morally, the holocaust released by the RAF and the USAF on Dresden; an undefended city, known to be crowded with refugees from the East became the funeral pyre of possibly as many as 135,000 people. The heinousness of Nazi crimes in no way mitigates the barbarism of this one, probably the most appaling incident in the whole history of British arms.

Those who love Britain will not try to pretend that such things did not happen, or excuse them … If they draw upon Christian perspectives, they will not be affronted by the suggestion that British humanity shares in the total fallenness of mankind, and that what happened in the past may recur at any time. Whatever else the imperial dream produced of good or ill, it certainly engendered racism, the assumption that certain peoples are usable and, if occasion demands, disposable. We should not be offended by the claim that it is virtually impossible to be British and to be free from racism.

Nowhere was the racist assumption more evident than in the contrast between the heroism and sacrifice expended on behalf of the Falkland islanders in liberating them from Argentine aggression, and the shameful treatment of the inhabitants of Diego Garcia in the Indian Ocean. The latter island was until 1966 associated with Mauritius under British rule. Independence was granted to Mauritius on condition that the Chagos Archipelago, including Diego Garcia, was kept under British authority. The reason for this condition presently became evident when Britain agreed to the USA using the island for a military communications facility — which in effect means its transformation into a full-scale military base. The islanders, numbering about 2,000 (about the same number as the Falklanders) were British subjects — but black. Hitherto they had lived an exemplary peaceful life, but their continued presence on the island was deemed incompatible with American military activities and interests. By a combination of deception, cajolery, economic pressure and sometimes sheer force, the population was compelled to transfer to Mauritius where they effectively became refugees, many living in extreme poverty and squalor. Few in Britain noticed or took up their cause, and not until the spring of 1982 did the British finally agree to anything approaching financial compensation to the Diego Garcians. Both Labour and Conservative governments were involved in this affair which displays only too well how selective British concern for 'freedom' can be.

Britain today badly needs a public education in the realities of the world in which it is living. The empire may have gone, the maps in the atlases may have been re-coloured and re-named, but it is still an imperialist picture which dominates public attitudes: a world which exists for Britain's benefit, or if it cannot be made to work that way, ignored ... In such a world what does national greatness mean? To say it means despatching a fleet to the far end of the globe at the cost of several hundred lives and £700 million to rescue 2,000 islanders from alien occupation, while being blind to the colossal misery already abounding in the southern hemisphere, is, to say the least, unreal. One day, we may hope, national greatness might be conceived in terms of making a determined contribution to an onslaught on the threats to the survival of the human race itself.

I ended these long extracts from Keith Clements' book with one of his quotations from Bonhoeffer himself:

The followers of Jesus have been called to peace. When he called them they found their peace. But now they are told that they must not only have peace, but make it. And to that end they renounce all violence and tumult. In the cause of Christ nothing is to be gained by such methods. His disciples keep the peace by choosing to endure suffering themselves rather than inflict it on others.

The right of war can be derived from the right of struggle as little as the use of torture may be derived from the necessity of legal procedures in human society. War in our day no longer falls under the concept of struggle because it is the certain self-annihilation of both combatants. War today destroys both soul and body ... War today, and therefore the next war, must be utterly rejected by the Church.

73. WEIGHING THINGS UP IN MID-1987

Events had taken place by now which fuelled both hope and despair. It certainly seemed that Gorbachev was the front runner for providing interesting, not to say provocative, ideas in moves towards disarmament. Ronald Reagan under the pressure of the Irangate and connected scandals, had gone beyond his strange dream of a world without nuclear weapons, through a Star Wars programme (which fitted badly with the continuing build-up of other missiles) to a certain readiness to make a reality of zero-zero options on certain classes of weapons which he long ago proposed but clearly never meant. Gorbachev seemed to leap ahead to take these seriously, and some European leaders scuttled for cover, with all kinds of excuses, obstacles or plain disbelief that the Soviet Union was not really anxious to march all over the rest of Europe.

It would have been easy enough for us in Britain, with an imperialist past of our own behind us, to swing to blaming the USA for many of the world's ills. However as I had noted in earlier issues of Comments and Quotes, a closer look at American history reminded us that it wasn't Reaganism alone that has muddied the American story. The peace movements generally were not afraid to call for doubts about the America of the British alliance. One British historian, Arnold Toynbee, gave a harsh judgement when he wrote:

> America today is the leader of a world-wide anti-revolutionary movement in defence of vested interests. She now stands for what Rome stood for. Rome consistently supported the rich against the poor in all foreign communities that fell under her sway: and since the poor have always and everywhere been far more numerous than the rich, Rome's policy made for inequality, for injustice and the least happiness of the greatest number. America's decision to adopt Rome's role has been deliberate, if I have gauged it right.

Here I quoted the words of a US President at the time of the Spanish/American war.

> Whether we like it or not, we must go on slaughtering the natives in English fashion (note that, 'English') and taking what muddy glory lies in the wholesale killing till they have learned to respect our arm. The more difficult task of getting them to respect our intentions will follow.

That may be hard to credit as a rational policy but we read the words of a US embassy political officer commenting on the war against civilians in El Salvador in our time:

> A couple of years down the road, it'll all be seen as the costs of war. It's better for military to do whatever it has to do to retake the region. Then we'll come in with food

and a lot of aid — they'll eat and forget.

It is another American who better represents the human conscience when he said:

Disarmament times

"Sorry. No money left!"

The real victims of American agony are the millions of suffering and tormented people throughout much of the Third World. Our highly refined ideological institutions protect us from seeing their plight and our role in maintaining it, except sporadically. If we had the honesty and the moral courage we would not let a day pass without hearing the cries of the victims … We successfully insulate ourselves from the grim reality. By so doing we sink to a level of moral depravity that has few counterparts in the modern world, and we may be laying the basis for our eventual destruction as well.

For some unknown reason I didn't ascribe that honest remark to anyone; but it would serve as a warning which helps paint the background for the terrorist attacks on the USA in 2001 onwards. I have already described the criminal policies of the UK over Diego Garcia; no-one is squeaky clean. Yet when ordinary people, British or American, really know and understand what is going on in the political world, they are indignant and ashamed.

Much of the bitter evidence comes from the pens of US citizens. A fairly recent book of Professor Noam Chomsky at that time spoke of 'the Fifth Freedom'. There is freedom of speech, of worship, freedom from want and fear; but the fifth is apparently the freedom to rob and exploit, which he suggests marks American history very gravely. He declared that the Monroe Doctrine of 1823 was a policy of the USA, not a fixed principle of international law. Yet President Taft is quoted as saying; 'The day is not far distant when the whole hemisphere will be ours in fact, as by virtue of our superiority of race, it already is ours morally'.

Slightly less arrogantly in 1927 Under-Secretary Roberts Olds said: 'The Central American area, down to and including the isthmus of Panama constitutes a legitimate sphere of influence for the USA., if we are to have due regard for our own safety and protection … Until now Central America has always understood that governments which we recognise and support stay in power, while those we do not recognise and support fall. Nicaragua has become a test case. It is difficult to see how we can afford to be defeated.' That was in 1927, so, as Chomsky comments: 'It is important to recognise that little that is happening today is new. The US has been tormenting Central America and the Caribbean for well over a century, generally in alleged defence against 'outside threats'.'

With quite extraordinary openness Americans quite often spill the beans. For instance, Admiral Turner, Director of the CIA under President Carter said:

> The overthrow of the Nicaraguan government is what we've been trying to do all along. It has been persiflage that they're trying to stop the flow of arms … I'm not a peacenik who's opposed to interfering in the affairs of other countries. These are legitimate activities from my point of view for our government to take. Such actions must be important to national security, achievable and capable of being kept secret.

And he reckoned the current attack on Nicaragua had failed in all three respects.

Chomsky's harshest comment of all probably: 'The truth of the matter is that the US is one of the leading world centres of international terrorism, perhaps the leading centre; but this fact, and the evidence that demonstrates it, are under a strict ban and can never be permitted expression to a mass audience.'

He then quotes a quite hideous remark of Winston Churchill from the year 1919 that surfaces from time to time: 'I do not understand the squeamishness about the use of gas … I am strongly in favour of using poisoned gas against uncivilised tribes.' He was referring to Mesopotamia, Afghanistan and the Bolsheviks in Russia.

At this time labelled war criminals had been in the news; so it was interesting to read Chomsky referring to the 'recruitment and protection of Nazi war criminals in the war against the anti-fascist resistance and the Soviet bloc.' No doubt history, when we are all dead and gone, will reveal the full extent of this procedure. But Chomsky was able to state:

> The most important of the networks funded by the Nazi-US alliance was the Gebler organisation constructed under US auspices by General Gebler, who had headed Nazi military intelligence on the Eastern front. In 1949 Gebler's team became the official espionage and counter-espionage service of the new West German state under close CIA inspection. This post-war project of crushing anti-fascist resistance with Nazi assistance establishes a direct link between Nazi Germany and the killing-fields in Central America.

Chomsky's alarming and rather depressing book did have some items for hope and encouragement, when he spoke of the US anti-war movements. 'This was the product of dedicated and committed efforts over many years by innumerable people, the most important of them unknown outside of the small circles in which they worked. The same is true of every social struggle.' And one of his final comments was this:

> There are no magic answers, no miraculous methods to overcome the problems we
> face; just the familiar ones: honest search for understanding, education, organisations,
> action that raises the cost of state violence for its perpetrators or that lays the basis for
> institutional change — and the kind of commitment that will persist despite the
> temptation of disillusionment, despite many failures and only limited successes, inspired
> by the hope of a brighter future.

Another American of distinction — whom I have already quoted several times
— was George Kennan, writing in the *New York Times* in January (1987). As a
historian and former US ambassador to Moscow his words should surely be
attended to. This time it was about the twelve hour television presentation called
Amerika, where the USA was depicted as groaning under the yoke of a supposed
Soviet military occupation, the enforcement of which had been entrusted to the
armed forces of the United Nations, this latter organisation having now come
under total Soviet control.

> The scenario is devoid of reality. An occupation of this country lies neither in the
> intentions or the desires nor the capabilities of the Soviet leadership. To suggest
> otherwise would be confusing for American opinion and undeservedly offensive to the
> Soviet Union, and this at a moment of extreme sensitivity in relations between that
> country and our own.
> What good purpose could be served by feeding this unreal nightmare hour by hour into
> the minds and imaginations of a considerable portion of the viewing public, with the
> implication that the dangers portrayed are sufficiently real to deserve its prolonged
> attention?
> One may hope that the good sense of the American people will deprive this
> undertaking of much of its intended sting, but it is useless to suppose that twelve hours
> of such suggestions will not leave their marks. With every one of those marks the
> prospects for a better Soviet-American relationship will have been needlessly
> diminished.

74. FORGIVENESS AND NON-VIOLENT ACTION

Forgiving enemies — surely a clear requirement for those who profess to be
disciples of Jesus — is certainly not an easy matter. Sometimes the most heinous
crimes go unpunished for decades; does that make it any easier to forgive? Can
we ever stop hating when the cruellest things have happened not to us, but to
those who are near and dear to us? The father of Martin Luther King saw his son

gunned down on the hotel balcony in 1968. His own wife had been shot as she was playing the organ in church in 1974. Grounds enough for bitterness? But he said: 'I speak to my people about what it means to love. We have to rid ourselves of every ounce of hate. I cannot afford to hate. I know what it leads to.'

Not surprisingly I found that item in the journal of the International Fellowship of Reconciliation. It was followed by the now famous quotation from Solzhenitsyn's Gulag Archipelago:

> If only it were all so simple. If only there were evil people somewhere insidiously committing evil deeds and it were necessary only to separate them from the rest of us and destroy them. But the dividing line between good and evil cuts through the heart of every human being — and who is willing to destroy a piece of his own heart?

Then came a remarkable testimony from Kenneth Kaunda:

> I have come to the conclusion that the willingness to forgive our enemies is not only a religious or moral matter; our very sanity may depend on it. For how at the end of the day can the guilty party make reparation for crimes so horrible that any compensation would be pathetically inadequate? What have those who master-minded or executed the plan to murder six million Jews put in the scales of justice to balance their crime? And what is the minimum the survivors of that horror might be prepared to accept as a just reparation? The whole world does not contain enough treasure to pay that bill. So unless we are able to forgive the enemies who cannot possibly make up to us for what they have done, we go stark raving mad with bitterness and hatred.

So what do you do when confronting aggressive opposition? Is there really any mileage in non-violence? Well, if it were merely a 'non-doing' it is about as empty as the pacifism of mere refusal of military service? That is why its practitioners speak of 'non-violent direct action'; and many people are still uneasy about it. Civil disobedience — the refusal to obey an unjust or immoral law — is something readily understandable. Most of the historic Christian martyrs must have been guilty of this; refusing, for instance, to pay worship to some false god. But taking deliberate action to flout the law is something that goes against the grain for law-abiding people. However there is a time and a place for this, particularly when its 'illegality' is determined in defiance of a greater illegality to which it is designed to draw attention. Breaking into a house is certainly illegal; but smashing down the door when you have reason to believe the place is on fire inside, and people are in danger, over-rides that illegality, and becomes a worthy action. If indeed it is done to prevent an arsonist from setting the place on fire, it is to be recommended, as long as one is sure of the facts.

The 'Snowball' campaign invited people to snip a strand of wire at some nuclear base with the intention of alerting people to the danger, and sometimes to direct illegality of what was going on inside the fences. It was done in obedience to a higher law. Let one non-violent activist give his testimony. Vern Rissman, an American Quaker explained:

> The actions of the 'Plowshares' campaign are characterised by the symbolic and the actual beating of swords into plowshares. We believe that disarmament can begin by converting at least one weapon or part of a weapon. We splash these genocidal monstrosities with our own blood to label them, to expose them for what they are. Ours was an action in which we had elaborately and at length examined and prepared our consciences. We held daily Bible study, prayer and liturgy. We spent several days questioning one another exactly as a Quaker 'clearness committee' does. We compared our beliefs and practice of non-violence and found we fully agreed that none of us would do anything to endanger or even threaten harm to another human being. Moreover we agreed that we would never raise our voices in anger but would speak softly and try our best to show only love to security police, prosecution, judges and jailers. We put to the test the religious foundations of our beliefs, our personal maturity and our willingness to bear the consequences of our actions, including its impact on family members. By the time the retreats were completed we had been welded into a powerful spiritual unity; we had become true conspirators in the original meaning of 'breathing together.

Daniel Berrigan, Jesuit priest, was experienced in action of this kind and said:

> We have never taken actions such as these, perilous, crucial, difficult as they are, without the most careful preparation of our hearts, our motivation, our common sense, our sense of one another. We have never admitted to our group any person whom we could not trust to be non-violent under pressure od crises. This is simply the rule of our lives. we don't go from the streets to this action: we go from prayer, from reflection, from worship always. I talked openly with Jesuit friends and superiors. They respected my conscience and said: 'Do what you are called to do'.

I was touched by a short poem from the pen of Janet Morley, after she had attended the annual Ash Wednesday action of daubing the Ministry of Defence, which she had supported by prayer and worship at the vigil.

KYRIE ELEISON

Police were there before us, robed and ready
and they took away our witnesses at once,
but not before the building had been marked
with ashes of repentance and violent death
and all the hope we've got.
And we who were left tried hard to concentrate,
and sing somehow at that blank defended place,
now smudged with sudden crosses.
But all the other ash had been arrested
and so we touched each other's foreheads

> just with our cold fingers,
> then stood there watching in complicity,
> waiting to hear the charges;
> And when police signified the ritual complete,
> we went in peace.

Somewhat nearer home there was a growing list of people, unknown to the general public, because their action was rarely seen as newsworthy in the national press, who took some symbolic action — like snipping a piece of wire at a nuclear base — are then arrested and charged with criminal damage, or perhaps doing something 'without lawful excuse'. They are duly fined or given some other sentence after they have made personal statements which really ought to be more widely heard.

Here is part of a statement from Elizabeth Rowlands Hughes of Llangollen, made at Chester Magistrates Court in 1986.

It seems that all the ethical, legal and pragmatic reasons have been given over and over again. And yet the great stumbling block for police, magistrates and 'snowballers' alike is the interpretation of the law; what constitutes or does not constitute breaking it; and what is meant by the words 'without lawful excuse'. Who decides? In an effort to present this dilemma in some sort of fable form, the following is the best I can do …

I have imagined that a few miles from where we live, there is a large old country house. The family, whose property it has been for many years, have been obliged to sell up and leave. Its subsequent history has been a bit chequered, and now local people have little idea of what actually goes on there. One day I decide to take a cycle ride in that direction, and after a bit I turn off the good second class road on to a very minor, neglected road running along the park boundary. Here I have the misfortune to ride over some broken glass and into a pot-hole which results in a bad puncture and a twisted ankle. I leave the bike, limp to a small side entrance to the park and set out for the house to try to get help; but when I reach the house I find it deserted and even the bell doesn't work. On my way round to the back door I hear a vehicle coming along the drive. Something tells me to keep out of the way and see what happens next. A van draws up under cover and the occupants proceed to unload a number of objects — TV sets, tape and video recorders etc. The whole operation is done in a hurried and rather furtive manner. I then remember there have been a series of break-ins and thefts of just this type of thing locally a few days ago.

What am I to do? I can't walk far; I can't use the bike. There is a telephone kiosk on the B road a few hundred yards away; but when I reach it, it is out of order. But there's a ramshackle shed in the field across the road, with a small amount of straw, pea-sticks and a collection of light timber, and I have some matches. So I set them alight and make sure there is plenty of smoke. There are no trees to catch fire, no crops to spoil and the field has a fence, not a hedge. The surrounding ground is damp. The smoke signal alerts people in the nearby village and before long two police arrive in a car. They ask me what I am doing and why. I explain that I took this rather drastic but not very damaging action as a last resort, because I was quite sure that a crime had been committed and that stolen goods would be found in the house. But I am told this is no excuse for damaging private property. I am taken into custody and charged with criminal damage, and duly fined. The country house remains undisturbed, only now it has guard dogs and a notice: 'Private Property: Keep Out'.

Well, I hope the magistrates enjoyed the fable, even if they didn't see the point!

A distinguished American, Archbishop Hunthausen of Seattle, decided at this time to be a witness for some of the American non-violent protestors and said: 'I wish to voice my admiration and support for those who at great personal cost continue to remind us of our moral responsibility for the presence of these horrifying weapons in our midst. I see the protestors as acting on their world citizenship. In the light of the scope and breadth of the issues they address, I see it as altogether appropriate that they stand on this ground…. We Catholics have long cultivated a decent respect for the law and the appropriate exercise of authority. It has been a difficult process for me to come to the position that a person has a right to ignore a legitimately established law. I can only take this position because I believe their acts and mine will serve to uphold the law, the divine law first, but just as certainly international law and its recognition in the US constitution.'

Underlying the difficulties that many law-abiding citizens have about taking action of this kind is the much-quoted idea that we mustn't confuse politics with religion. Yet it is increasingly obvious that the political stance of governments which affect the lives of countless people across the world needs to be questioned on moral grounds first, before devising political and economic conclusions. Bit by bit the inner workings of the International Monetary Fund, the World Bank and other structures are being examined in this way. A document from the Catholic Institute for International Relations stated: 'Much Catholic concern for justice and peace is translated into individual or group forms of charity, rather than effective action for social change and the transformation of institutions. This, largely because the task of changing society and institutions is immense, is daunting, but also because such goals impinge on areas clearly defined as political. The fear of politics stems from a fear of taking sides, thereby revealing differences within the Catholic community. At root this is a fear of applying the Gospel and preaching it in and out of season.'

75. MILITARY BALANCING ACTS

In November 1987 I noted again that there was a certain weariness among peace activists about keeping up the momentum. We had reason to hope that some progress was being made between the Soviet Union and USA. with the new INF treaty, reducing the role of intermediate nuclear weapons. Yet people still needed to be watchful over the political manoeuvring of the european powers. At a meeting in Brussels in October I had attended (on behalf of Pax Christi International) of the International Peace Communication and Co-ordination Centre there was general agreement among all the representatives from Western European countries that the revival and new growth of the Western European Union was a dangerous factor. The political excuse or explanation for this was the possible, even probable, withdrawal of US troops as well as some of their weapons. Western Europe, so far from wanting to encourage, applaud and support new détente and actual disarmament, was almost panicking in its efforts to restore deterrence at another level. It continued to read the military capability of the USSR and the Warsaw Treaty states as evidence of political and military intention, and seemed set on creating a new West European super-power. The basic assumption that there was a 'Soviet threat' was sustained in spite of all the possibilities arising from the new thinking in the Soviet Union and elsewhere.

Of course the basis was to be that of conventional, not nuclear weapons; and it was a dogma of faith that the Soviet Union was massively superior in this area. The 'numbers game' demonstrated the overwhelming superiority of the Warsaw Pact states; but a research paper from the School of Peace Studies puts this in fuller context. Quoting B. R. Rosen in an article in an International Security periodical, Andrew Kelly (the *Bradford Researcher*) said: 'there is no need for the military to lie; all they have to do is to select. The first technique of selection is very simple: draw attention to weapons improvements on the other side, and make no mention of your own. The second method is simply to cite those systems where the other side has superiority and to omit the rest.' But the comparisons also ignore the non-military factors, like geography and economics. Harold Brown, President Carter's one-time Defense Secretary wrote: 'The USA and USSR have different political and military objectives. The impact of geography on their needs and goals is bound to be quite asymmetrical; their respective allies differ greatly in wealth, motivations and loyalty. For all those reasons the simple comparisons you hear so much about rarely illuminate more than the idiosyncracies of their authors.'

Now and again a bit of honesty creeps through. For instance the British Statement on Defence Estimates in 1985 had caveats to mitigate their insistence that the USSR was dangerously ahead in the field of conventional weapons. It read: 'In the illustrations we make every effort to compare like with like, and to apply the same criteria rigorously to both sides. It is nonetheless necessary to avoid placing too much reliance on the figures used; they should be regarded only as illustrating the general scale of the opposing forces and not necessarily as showing how effective one side would be against the other.' The statement went on to show the multitude of other factors — training, leadership, morale, sustainability, supply lines for fuel etc. — which need to offset any plain numerical superiority. Unfortunately that kind of small print statement never reaches the popular press.

76. CONFLICTING IDEOLOGIES AND COMMON SECURITY

This was the title of a document that came out of a fascinating meeting between leaders of the Central Committee of the German Democratic Republic's Socialist Unity Party and the Basic Values Commission of West Germany's Social Democratic Party. The maturity with which they faced their differences was wonderfully encouraging. They were really trying to listen to, and to understand one another. On peace and security they said:

> In East and West there is a growing number of people who realise that peace and security cannot be achieved in the nuclear age through ever greater arsenals and more perfect military arms, but only through political action, if it is to last. It is not the quality of the weapons but the quality of the policies which is decisive for security and stability in the world. The active involvement of all the people is required to help this insight to win through and to translate it into practical policies … Common and equal security for all must be organised, and this requires either side to take into account and respect the other's legitimate security interests. Either side must concede the other the same measure of security it claims for itself … An effective and enduring system of international security must include also the political, economic and humanitarian spheres. For disarmament, dialogue and confidence-building, the establishment of a just world economic order and a common approach to global problems and international co-operation to overcome hunger are mutually promotive.
>
> The co-existence of, and controversy between, qualitatively differing and opposed socio-economic and political systems are fundamental characteristics of international relations. But the argument about which is the better social system can only be conducted if peace has been secured and history continues. Therefore the controversy can only take one form — the form of peaceful competition without the use of force. Each system can show the advantages it claims to have only by example, and one which convinces people inside and outside its boundaries. The objective of the competition should be to prove which of the two systems makes the most effective contribution towards solving the

over-arching questions facing mankind: which provides the more favourable social conditions for the full development of human values; which offers better opportunities for the people to turn their interests and rights to account and to attain their values and ideals.

Social Democrats and Communists both feel pledged to the humanist heritage of Europe. Both claim that they are perpetuating this heritage, that they are committed to the interests of the working people and that they translate democracy and human rights into reality. But for seven decades they have argued fiercely about the manner in which this should be done. This argument is aggravated by the fact that both often assign different meanings to one and the same term. The Social Democrats see themselves as part and parcel of Western democracy. They consider a democracy organised on the principles of pluralism, with its multiple forms of the separation and control of powers to be the binding framework which they are prepared to defend at all costs if necessary, and within which they want to put their notion of democratic socialism into effect. The Marxist-Leninists see democracy as a form of the exercise of power, characterised by the ownership of the decisive means of production and the resultant political power. Therefore they consider the transfer of the most important items of production into public ownership and the political power wielded by the working class in alliance with other working people to be the foundation of comprehensive democratic rights. They understand democracy above all as the genuine involvement of the working people in the management and shaping of the economy and society, and the control thereof.

Social Democrats believe human rights as such have an absolute value and are able to be protected and implemented in an ever new way against all the forms of economic and governmental power. In the form of basic rights they constitute the yardstick and objective for governmental action. They base their policy of security in society and equal opportunities in life and education on these fundamental rights and on the basic values of democratic socialism Marxist-Leninists claim that they have established the socio-economic foundations for the free development of the individual through public ownership and the resulting relations of political power. They regard social security, full employment, social justice and real educational opportunities for each and everyone as the inalienable foundations for democracy and the full implementation of human rights. They insist that the implementation of human rights is linked to the further development of their socio-economic system.

There was, and still is the fear in both systems that the other system, given its structure of interests and the prevailing ideology, is intrinsically bent on expanding its sphere of influence and power. In the West there is the fear that the Marxist-Leninist thesis of the world revolutionary process amounts to an export of revolution and serves to justify Soviet power claims. Marxist-Leninists base their respective fear on Marx's analysis of the nature of capitalist commodity production, on works by Lenin on the nature of the monopoly and on their perception and interpretation of the dominant anti-communist strategies and policies of the present day. For this reason such fears will have to be scaled down in the process leading to common security. Both sides must try to do so even if they feel that such fears are based on misunderstanding.

It must become a normal thing to trade, negotiate and work with each other, while at the same time expressing frank and clear criticism whenever, as we se it, the desire for peace and understanding, human rights, and democracy is not complied with on the other side. Co-operation, competition and conflict must become equally accepted forms of our dealings with each other. Common security cannot be achieved if ideological differences are fought out in ways that jeopardise or poison relations between states or even make power conflicts appear as irreconcilable and unavoidable struggle between good and evil.

This was a brave effort for political common sense, and, while there was no sign that those with political power took any notice, it was good to be reminded that some people really were thinking beyond prejudices and slogans. It reminded me of the informal conversations we had in the Kremlin in 1982, when distinguished Russians were ready to concede the lack of many personal rights in their system, but argued forcefully for their provision of social rights (employment, housing) where the capitalist world often failed. Even so, perhaps the German debate did not sufficiently recognise that what we mean by 'security' should not start with military security. That already de-personalises the issue of human relations.

77. THE LAW AND NUCLEAR WEAPONS

An excellent book was published about this time by George Delf, called *Humanising Hell.* We were directed towards considering the issues of legality partly because Fred Starkey of Mold was a founder member of Pax Legalis — a group dedicated to the examination of national and international legality of weapons of mass destruction. So here was a new challenge from other writers. Peace activists were legitimately criticised: 'By insisting on the moral and political objections to nuclear weapons without reference to their criminal status, the peace movements have obscured rather then exposed the core of the problem'.

Then came a quotation from the American Law Professor Falk: 'Everyone has a right and duty to say No to illegal state policy. And it is very important that it is understood not as disobeying the law — on the contrary it is the enforcement of law to refuse to be an accomplice to preparation for nuclear war.'

More tellingly perhaps, because he was Attorney General, Shawcross wrote:

> It is true that the lawyers and statesmen who at the Hague and elsewhere in days gone by, built up the code 'of rules and established customs by which the world has sought to mitigate the brutality of war and to protect from its extreme harshness those who were passive non-combatants, never dreamed of such wholesale and widespread slaughter. But murder does not cease to be murder merely because the victims are multiplied tenfold. Crimes do not cease to be crimes because they have a political motive.

Another American lawyer, Meyrowitz, wrote:

> When the essential foundation for our security rests upon a logic that has the potential for destroying our population, democracy no longer exists. The discretion to launch a nuclear war gives our political leaders a control over human destiny that no tyrant, however despotic, has ever claimed. In short, the very nature of nuclear war destroys all the values that the law obliges us to preserve.

Delf pointed out that:

> ... the same four states which accepted and enforced the Nuremberg judgement now seek to evade its plain logic. Far from warning their nuclear operatives to carry out 'international duties which transcend the national obligation of obedience imposed by the individual state' they are ordered to do the opposite ... Their behaviour recalls the loyalties of the SS concentration camp guard who considers the law to be relevant to everything except his victims. Our judges have proved no more willing to draw attention to this calculated evasion of the law than were their Nazi counterparts, who administered German law with meticulous care within the criminal context of Nazi rule.

Delf drew on a number of personal stories of World War II experiences to point out the way in which there was a descent into intolerable immorality, even prior to the use of nuclear weapons. Freeman Dyson's story was very moving:

> The last spring of the war was the most desolate. Even after Dresden the bombing of cities continued ... I began to look backward and to ask myself how it has happened that I let myself become involved in this crazy game of murder. Since the beginning of the war I had been retreating step by step from one moral position to another, until at the end I had no moral position at all. At the beginning of the war I believed fiercely in the brotherhood of man, and was morally opposed to all violence. After a year of war I retreated and said unfortunately non-violent resistance to Hitler is impractical, but I am still morally opposed to bombing. A couple of years later it seemed that bombing is necessary in order to win the war; but I am still morally opposed to bombing cities indiscriminately. After I arrived at Bomber Command I said unfortunately it turns out that we are, after all, bombing cities, but this is morally justified as it is helping to win the war. A year later I said unfortunately it seems that our bombing is not really helping to win the war, but at least I am morally justified in working to save the lives of the bomber crews. In the last spring of the war I could no longer find any excuses. I had surrendered one moral principle after another and in the end it was all for nothing.

Now I realise that Dyson's sentiments would not be shared universally, but they do raise the questions about legality at several stages. Our position today is that nuclear weapons are necessarily indiscriminate (*pace* the Bishop of Oxford) and we have to make decisions before ever they are used. So people take action against them, and are arrested for 'breach of the peace'. Delf remarked: 'If

Auschwitz had been sited outside London, the first local citizens to protest would have been arrested for 'breach of the peace' or 'obstructing the highway'. Criminal nuclear bases have been protected by such means.'

People will no doubt argue, especially in the immediately more optimistic days, that the politicians see this and will soon agree to ban them. 'What credibility has a drug addict who claims that heroin has kept him in peace of mind since childhood, and adds that he wants to sign a comprehensive Drug Ban Treaty?'

In this same book, some of the fiercest criticisms are kept for religious people, and Delf singles out Cardinal Hume. Quoting the Times article of 1983, Delf says:

> ... the Cardinal offers comfort to servicemen who manage the deterrent 'since the purpose and intention of deterrence is to avoid war and keep the peace, service personnel can be rightly commended as custodians of the security and freedom for their fellow countrymen and as contributors to the maintenance of peace ... Nonetheless they too face grave moral issues which they themselves do not ignore ... Deterrence has to be seen clearly as a means of preventing war and not waging it. If it fails and the missiles are launched, then we shall have moved into a new situation. And those concerned will have to bear a heavy responsibility.

That rather sounds like the end justifying the means — 'unless it is a dead end, in which case we will be with the Cardinal in a 'new situation' All that differentiates this rationalisation of deterrence from that of governments is its tortuous solemnity, as if the sheer weight of sorrow adds up to religious insight. The Cardinal had a blessing for all concerned in the nuclear apocalypse: the priest who wrestles mightily, the government leader who does his best, and the missile operator who wants peace. But he has nothing to say about the hard, simple fact that existing laws prohibit any form of mass destruction, blessed or unblessed, and that all who collude with violating these laws commit a crime.'

After reference to the Chief Rabbi's condemnation of unilateral nuclear disarmament, Delf felt obliged to comment: 'To follow church advice is to wander deeper into the labyrinth of suspended annihilation. A search through the cathedrals and synagogues for inspiration leaves us where we were.'

I recognised, when presenting this in Comments and Quotes, that it might give offence to some readers, but that is because we think of those who commit atrocities and mass murders, or who authorise them to be done by others, as totally different from ourselves. It is salutary, but shocking, to discover that this is not so.

> Fritz Stangl was arrested in Brazil and tried in Germany for contributing to a million murders while commandant of two extermination camps in Poland, Treblinka and Sobihor. He was sentenced to life imprisonment in 1970 and died six months later of a heart attack. He was always a devout Catholic and went to Mass every day while on leave from Treblinka. He had no interest in ideology and thought the Jews were being killed for their money. Far from being as monstrous as his deeds, Stangl has been described as utterly commonplace and boring. He was not a sadist or fanatic or criminal, but a dreary, mindless blinkered official, obedient and conventional. He did what he was told and imagined his orders were legitimate.

Meantime we had to note that some of the most unquestioning supporters of current deterrence policies were devout Catholics: Casey, Haigh, North, Kirkpatrick. In close alliance with them were the born-again fundamentalists with their passionate crusading against Communism, and their pious hope for Armageddon. In our time, it took a Chomsky or Gore Vidal to reveal them for what they were. Yet at the same time thousands of good Evangelicals and Catholics were witnessing for peace also. Those being arrested in the USA's Nevada Testing site included some bishops.

Our alliances in the peace movements are found with people of good will and deep commitment from across the religious and humanist frontiers.

An interesting flashback to the fifties I uncovered at this time was from Commander Stephen King-Hall:

> It is not because of a repudiation of my past beliefs that I am one hundred percent against the use in our defence plans of nuclear energy for military purposes. I object to our present strategy because it is useless; it is stupid; it is absurd; and the cost is beyond our means. Also it is part of a world-wide development which may, and unless checked probably will, destroy humanity. In the campaign to abandon the present ridiculous defence policy, I welcome the support of the moralists and they should welcome co-operation from those who, like myself wish for military reasons to attain the same ends. Morality can join hands with expediency in this vital problem without becoming less moral and it is comforting to those of us who are thinking in terms of expediency to feel that we are also being moral.

78. THE SIGNIFICANCE OF GORBACHEV

It was still surprising to find the changed political perspective that came with the rise to power of Gorbachev in the Soviet Union. He was still a Communist, of course, and came as a reformer; for that reason he was not really a popular figure on his home scene, but even in externals he heralded a real change; his manner, his younger age than most of his predecessors, his appearing with Raissa, his wife. I thought it important to give some quotations from his speeches and writings, and peppered them in little 'little boxes' through the main items of my 'broadsheet'. Here are some of them.

The Soviet Union and the Soviet people consider themselves part of an international community. The worries of mankind are our worries, its pain our pain, and its hopes our hopes. With all the differences between us, we must all learn to preserve our one big family of humanity.

The stockpiling and sophistication of nuclear armaments mean the human race has lost its immortality. It can be regained only by destroying nuclear weapons. We reject any right for leaders of a country, be it the USSR, the USA or any other, to pass a death sentence on mankind. We are not judges and the billions of people are not criminals to be punished… The nuclear powers must overstep their nuclear shadow and enter a nuclear-free world, thus ending the alienation of politics from the general norms of human ethics. A nuclear tornado will sweep away socialists and capitalists, the just and the sinners alike.

Trust is making ground very slowly; and I think this is why more and more people are realising that the fate of the major cause of our time should not be left to politicians alone. This cause concerns not only politicians. We are witnessing the emergence and rise of a world-wide mass movement which embraces scientists, intellectuals of different professions, clergymen, women, young people, children, more and more, and even former military men and generals, who know full well what modern weapons are.

There would be no second Noah's Ark for a nuclear deluge. Everyone seems to understand this. So it is time to realise that we can no longer expect things to take care of themselves. The question stands like this: either political mentality is geared to the requirements of the times, or civilisation and life itself on earth may perish.

The development and subsequent stockpiling of nuclear weapons and of their delivery vehicles beyond all reasonable bounds have made man technically capable of terminating his own existence… The militarisation of mentality and of the way of life weakens and even removes any moral inhibitions altogether with regard to nuclear suicide. The imagination is powerless to envision the hell, the negation of the idea of man, if any part, however small, of the present nuclear arsenal is used.

Confidence needs to be built up through experience in co-operation, through knowing each other better, through solving common problems. It is wrong in principle to say that first comes confidence and then all the rest — disarmament, co-operation and joint projects. Confidence, its creation, consolidation and development comes from common endeavour. This is the rational way.

A notable feature of recent decades has been that for the first time in history mankind as a whole, and not only individual representatives, has begun to feel that it is one entity, to see the global relationships between man, society and nature and to assess the consequences of material activities.

Before my people and before the whole world I state with full responsibility that our international policy is more than ever determined by domestic policy, by our interest in concentrating on constructive endeavours to improve our country. That is why we need lasting peace, predictability and constructiveness in international relations. 'We want to be understood and we hope that the world community will at last acknowledge that our desire to make our country better will hurt no-one, with the world only gaining from this.

79. JUST TESTING!

A useful (though somewhat unevenly so) collection of essays turned up under the title of *On The Brink*. In the Preface Kofi Buenor pointed out:

> The nuclear 'haves', including the USSR and China, have tried to argue that nuclear weapons are essential for the defence of their countries and the preservation of world peace. Were other countries to get them, on the other hand, this would be a very different thing: it would constitute a most dangerous process known as 'proliferation'. Their own development of the Bomb is never called that. Angered by this double standard, Third World elites have argued that they too have the right to exterminate other peoples by the most modern means available and to defend their peoples to death.

The argument is, of course, that these devastating weapons would then be in 'the wrong hands'; but the image of the rational, sober western nuclear strategist is just as fictitious as the unbalanced, trigger-happy Third World leader.

The book then went on to examine the necessity of drawing Third World issues into the campaigns against nuclear weapons. Fred Halliday lists four major connections between concern about the arms race and about militarism in the Third World:

> a) political objection to military spending, the consequent waste of resources, and the use

of force applies to the Third World as much as it does to developed countries.
b) the build-up in strategic nuclear weapons is itself designed for use in Third World crisis situations.
c) for all the focus on nuclear weapons, the current arms race and arms build-up is one primarily involving conventional weapons for use in the Third World.
d) if there is going to be a Third World war it is most likely that it will be brought about by a Great Power confrontation over A Third World crisis spot.

The logic of that seems undeniable; and the peace movements are increasingly recognising the necessity of this added dimension to their work. Then, in a piece by Glenn Alcalay, the book related the almost total unconcern about Third World consequences from the time of the experimental hydrogen bomb explosion at Bikini in 1954 — a thousand times the size of the Hiroshima bomb. Apart from the Japanese fishermen caught in the fall-out, the people of Rongelap Atoll were hit downwind by the fall-out. One woman wrote:

> One of my babies was born in 1955, a year after the explosion, and it did not have any bones in its body. My oldest son was a year old at the time, and he was playing outside. Now he does not grow and is one of the boys the US scientists use to test their new drugs to make children grow.

There is reason to think that this risk was no 'accident' at all. The inhabitants had been evacuated earlier before much lesser explosions. By now it has become well-known in some quarters what Darlene Keju-Johnson said before the World Council of Churches in Vancouver in 1983.

> The list of health problems resulting from this exposure is virtually endless, and includes many cases of thyroid cancer, leukemia, cataracts, miscarriages and still-births. The Marshalese describe these babies as 'jellyfish'. The baby is born on the labour table, and it breathes and moves up and down, but it is not shaped like a human being. It looks like a bag of jelly. These babies live for a few hours. Sometimes babies are born with growths like horns on their heads, while others have six fingers or toes.

French involvement in the Pacific, even in 1987 was no less horrific. Since the independence of Algeria, the French moved their testing sites to Mururoa in Polynesia. Jean Chesneaux wrote: 'We have a bomb. It is nobody else's problem but ours where to test it'. Such was the message of President Mitterand's visit to Mururoa in October 1985. It is sad but interesting to note what a younger Mitterand said in August 1967:

> The left Opposition solemnly warns French public opinion against the policy of developing atomic weapons upon which General de Gaulle has launched our country by embarking upon the development of a national strike force. There is no greater danger to

the survival of the human species. What France wants for itself today, Israel and Egypt, India and Pakistan will want for themselves tomorrow — and Germany and every other state in earth. Let us be clear: the proliferation of nuclear weapons means the extension of conflict.

Johan Galtung contributed an essay in the same collection, where he tries to see peace movements as part of liberation movements. Fundamentally he thinks they are an expression of lack of faith in governments, against 'experts' who are prisoners of their own basic ideas. To begin with there is a relatively symmetric perception of the two super-powers in our present predicament. Then he goes on:

> Which super-power has by and large been ahead in the arms race? Which has made almost all the qualitative changes, introducing new systems designed to be ever more destructive, to penetrate defences on the other side even more effectively? Which is involved in conflicts over almost the whole world, trying to maintain impossible, repressive regimes, mainly in order to secure markets for their own products and raw materials for their own industrial processes? Which develops rapid deployment forces in order to come to the rescue of client regimes all over the world? Which goes far beyond any kind of historically justifiable tradition to secure its own borders, by trying not to have any challenge in the 'backyard' — four countries away (Nicaragua) or even ten countries away (Chile), which even develops a strategy that, regardless of intentions, looks increasingly like a first-strike strategy?The answer is clear enough. It reflects something that Washington seems never able to understand: that people in Latin America, in Asia, or in Europe, particularly western Europe, seem to be more afraid of what a reckless US could start doing, and are consequently more afraid of nuclear war as such than of the much touted Soviet attack. And that leads one of course to a less symmetric view of the two super-powers. The distribution of responsibility for our predicament is no longer 50%-50%. But that does not mean that it should be 100% for the US and 0 % for t he USSR. Certainly not; only the ideologically very biased and the politically very naïve will accept such a distribution. The European peace movement has to become a liberation movement … For it is fighting the same system that liberation movements around the world are fighting — in Latin America, Africa, Asia and Eastern Europe: against expansionist, exploitative, repressive systems of all kinds, whether they are referred to as capitalist or socialist imperialism.

So many of these insights and remarks have been validated again and again to our day.

80. THE SHADOW SIDE OF THE USA

In March 1988 I was noting the start of Central America Week. It seemed to me that the huge quantity of support given by the USA. (not only under the Reagan administration) to dictators, tyrants and those who exploit the poor so mercilessly, was so alarming that one wondered how Britain and many other European countries could continue to be proud of any alliance. Fortunately the US also has its own vigorous and well-informed critics at home, and I was happy to refer at once to a booklet from the American Friends Service Committee called *What Are We Afraid Of?* with the sub-title 'Facts and Fears about the Communist threat in Central America'. In a section entitled 'Obstacles to clear thinking' it said:

> The US government, like many others, works to shape the way its citizens understand world events. During the Vietnam era the phrase 'credibility gap' became commonplace referring to misleading or false government statements. Many US administrations have lied to the public about the 1954 CIA-organised overthrow of the elected government of Guatemala. President Kennedy about the Bay of Pigs invasion of Cuba, another CIA operation: Lyndon Johnson about intervening in the Dominican Republic in 1965: Richard Nixon about destabilising the elected government of Chile in the early 1970s. In addition government agencies, including the CIA, practice deception. One technique is planting false stories in foreign news media, which are picked up and reported in the United States with no hint of their true origin. In an August 1986 government memorandum, the White House National Security Adviser, John Poindexter, advocated a technique that 'combines real and illusory events through a dis-information programme' as part of a US campaign against Libya.

The great wonder was that the US intervention in Central America deepens in spite of the wishes of the majority of US citizens. 'Polls in 1986 continued to show a clear majority of US citizens opposing US backed Contra war against Nicaragua. The administration's determination to step up the war therefore calls into question its dedication to democracy at home as well as abroad.'

Somewhere I found a quotation from J. Michael Kelly in 1984. He was the Deputy Assistant Secretary of the US Air Force, and said: 'I think the most critical special operations mission we have today is to persuade the American people that the communists are out to get us.' Over and again that turns out to be the means of gaining support for aggressive political behaviour. Tell the people they are under threat. Was that not part of the preparation for the war against Iraq? What was particularly sad in 1985 was the judgement of the World Court in the Hague where, by a large majority, the US was declared guilty of breaching international law in its covert activities in Nicaragua; for it made no difference to American leaders. Incidentally, of the fifteen judges at the World Court, the American judge refused to accept the judgement.

It was the US State Department which defined 'terrorism' as 'premeditated, politically motivated violence perpetuated against non-combatant targets by sub-national groups or clandestine state agents.' International terrorism is 'terrorism involving citizens or territory of more than one country.' September 11th 2001 certainly is covered by those definitions; but the AFSC Report of 1987 concluded also: 'The US campaign against Nicaragua by means of the Contra forces and other CIA 'assets' is precisely 'international terrorism'. 'It is hard to see how anyone could conclude otherwise; and these are Americans who made the judgement. Some parallel statements from Britain make interesting reading: Margaret Thatcher in 1985 said: 'Britain's attitude to Nicaragua will depend on the extent to which the country is prepared to reduce the level of its armaments, to put an end to its interference in the affairs of its neighbours, and to establish genuine pluralist democracy'Neil Kinnock in a speech to the 1986 Labour Conference said: 'The people of Nicaragua are struggling to keep their infant democracy alive against the attacks of terrorists armed and funded by the United States. How can a President who is rightly the enemy of terrorism sponsor the terrorism of the Contras in Central America?'Alan Beith, Alliance Foreign Affairs Spokesman in February 1987 said: 'The Liberal/SDP Alliance is totally opposed to President Reagan's policy of supporting the Contras. The Alliance will continue to support the territorial integrity of Nicaragua and its peoples' right to self-determination'

It was in August 1987 that the Central American Presidents signed a peace agreement in Guatemala city which could have had enormously valuable effects in the whole region, where violence and suffering had plagued these long-term US dependencies. Noam Chomsky — the extraordinarily outspoken American Professor — wrote an article in November which gave evidence for serious doubts as to whether the US administration would ever really let peace break out. The agreement said that 'an indispensable element in achieving a stable and lasting peace in the region was the termination of any form of aid to irregular forces or insurgent movements on the part of regional or extra-regional governments' Chomsky pointed out that this central feature was really redundant since such actions were already forbidden by international law and treaty, and thus also by the US, constitution.'This fact, Chomsky continued, was underscored by the World Court in June 1986 as it condemned the US for its 'unlawful use of force' against Nicaragua, and called upon it to desist from these crimes. Congress responded by voting 100 million dollars of aid, and freeing the CIA to direct the attack and to use its own funds on an unknown scale. The US vetoed a United Nations Security Council resolution, calling on all states to observe international law, and voted against a General Assembly resolution to the same effect, joined by Israel and El Salvador. On November 12th 1987 the General Assembly again called for 'full and immediate compliance' with the World Court decision. This time only Israel joined with the US in opposing adherence to international law — another blow to the Central American accords, and unreported by the national press as usual.'

'The media dismissed the World Court as a 'hostile forum' whose decisions are irrelevant, while liberal advocates of world order explained that the US must disregard the World Court decision. With this reaction, US elites clearly articulate their self-image: the United States is a lawless terrorist

state, which stands above the law and is entitled to undertake violence as it chooses in support of its objectives.

'To ensure that the accord would be undermined, the US at once directed its proxy forces to escalate military actions, also increasing the regular supply flights that are required to keep them in the field. The proxy army followed Washington orders to attack 'soft targets' such as farm co-operatives and health clinics instead of trying to fight it out with the Sandinistas directly — as explained by General John Galvin, commander of the US Southern Command, who added that with these tactics aimed at civilians lacking the means of defence against armed terrorist bands, prospects for the Contras should improve. The State Department officially authorised such attacks. There are other terrorist states, but to my knowledge the US is alone in officially endorsing terrorism.'

Chomsky also reported that shortly after the accords were signed, the CIA offered three thousand dollars a month to fourteen Miskito Indian leaders to induce them to maintain the military conflict. The spokesman for the Indian opposition said this was a last-ditch US attempt to undercut their plan to pursue a negotiated settlement with the Sandinistas. The US officials had stressed what they call the strategic importance of retaining Indian participation in the war to help gain international support — the usual cynical exploitation of indigenous peoples. He continued:

> US government officials quoted in the Mexico press report that the CIA salaries come from a secret account 'for political projects' unrelated to the 100 million dollars in congressional funding. Under-secretary of State Elliott Abrams conducted a news conference by radio in the Central American capitals on October 22nd (unreported in the national press) at which he announced that the US 'will never accept a Soviet satellite in Central America' — meaning a country that is not loyal as a US satellite.

And then suddenly in March 1988 we heard of an astonishing agreement for a three-month cease-fire. There had been pictures of the Contra leaders apparently accepting a new agreement direct with the Sandinista government, and we hoped and prayed that this would remain effective. Yet we couldn't help wondering how it was that people in Europe could give any credibility to the Contra rebels, and we were greatly helped by a piece by Liduine Zumpollo, a Pax Christi worker in Managua, in the END journal for this same month.

> The CIA has organised and financed a political campaign in Europe to alter the political climate which had been sympathetic to the Sandinistas. There were frequent visitors, high American officials to their European colleagues to 'inform' them about the Nicaraguan problem. This began in Madrid with a meeting of the United Nicaraguan Opposition. Visits of Contra leaders to Europe were planned and the involvement of Nicaraguans already living here. A Spanish paper got hold of the plans: a scandal followed, and that ended the Opposition's career in Spain. In West Germany and England Contra representatives were invited by Conservative and Christian Democratic parties: they spoke at political fora, and human rights symposia. They were cited in approval in the press. Their goals were promoted by the World Anti-communist League, the Unification Church, Opus Dei and Resistance International, and the well-funded Heritage Foundation in the US. Thanks to Iran-Contragate and other factors, they are not respected guests in Europe any more. But the CIA and the Contras have been successful with the aim of the campaign: isolating the Sandinistas from West European governments ... It is the task of the peace movements which favour non-intervention and self-determination to identify the forces that are responsible for this.

It is of course thoroughly heartening to read of a different set of US citizens. Drawing on an issue of the Liverpool Diocesan Just and Peace broadsheet, there was a report from Sojourners: 'On November 25th in Washington, fifteen former intelligence operatives announced the formation of ARDIS — Association for Responsible Dissent. The men and women, who had taken part in covert actions, are now out to stop them. ARDIS President, Marine Colonel Philip C. Roettinger, said:

> The founders of this organisation have all taken part in covert actions of one sort or another. We know from personal experience how bad covert actions are ...These have included assassination, drug trafficking, funding and training of notoriously brutal police and paramilitary forces, drug and disease experimentation on unwitting US citizens, and a massive illegal propaganda apparatus directed at the people'. The alleged covert operations have resulted in the death of more than six million people. 'Such activities are inappropriate for this great nation. The US political process is being profoundly altered to accommodate the national security apparatus at the expense of democracy, human rights and individual liberty.

In November 1987 International Affairs reported an opinion poll taken in the USA. in 1985, when 44% of those questioned did not know that the Soviet Union and the USA. were allies in World War II. 28% felt sure they had fought each other. 58% believed that the US lost more lives than the USSR. When asked which of the two powers had pledged itself not to be the first to use nuclear weapons, 80% said 'USA'.(After the terrorist attacks of Nine Eleven there were thousands in the USA who apparently believed that the Iraqis were responsible for the terrorist act on September 11th. There really is a curious innocence or ignorance in the USA about anything outside its own shores!)

81. THE NEED FOR WATCHFULNESS

The rising importance of the Oxford Research Group, led by Scilla McLean (now Elworthy) was being shown by their exposition that Mrs Thatcher and her ministers had been insisting in Parliament that the NATO meeting in 1983 at Montebello made no decision about modernising shorter-range nuclear weapons in Europe. Yet now it seemed that George Younger was speaking of 'the decision taken four years ago at Montebello for the modernisation and bringing up to date of the existing nuclear weapons that are part of the West's armoury against attack. That process is only partly completed.'.

Scilla pointed out that this meant that the work had been decided upon, initiated and in part completed while Parliament had been told that nothing has even been decided. What is more, he refers to 'stand-off weapons' which were not part of the existing armoury. Aldermaston had already begun to design an entirely new warhead for it. She quoted Fred Ikle (until recently US Under-Secretary for Defence) as saying 'These highly accurate small warheads nuclear weapons add up to the most important military development since World War II'. Scilla asked 'Why has Parliament been refused information, which is available to other parliaments? Why have no costings been disclosed? Why has the truth not been told when a crucially important new weapon is under way, a weapon which will begin a new escalation in the arms race?'

Meantime many of us were still anxious about the failure of the US ratification of the INF agreement. This was, after all, the first actual dis-armament treaty; and Gorbachev had actually started to remove some of these weapons from East Germany possibly an act of one-upmanship, but surely a sign of real intent. Apart from the new stand-off missiles already mentioned, there were now in the West (and quite possibly mirrored in the East) the development of other sea and air-launched varieties when the ground-launched Cruise, Pershing and SS20s went. There would be an attempt to transfer some of the US Navy's growing arsenal of sea-borne Cruise missiles to NATO; and these would be carried on submarines and surface ships. Another option would be to bring more US F-111 planes to the United Kingdom. We already had 156 of them at Upper Heyford and Lakenheath, and many of us have tramped round those bases and had seen the monsters. The

US had another 292 which might be moved to Europe. And all this was to 'compensate' for the removal of the intermediate weapons which everyone was said to be happy to see departing. General Galvin had been speaking of the need to buttress NATO's defences; so we began to wonder if any of the military really wanted to disarm from nuclear weapons. We knew Mrs Thatcher did not, so it is hardly surprising that the evasions were on the cards.

Ash Wednesday was the day for another symbolic act at the Ministry of Defence in Whitehall, and something similar happened in Liverpool. Several hundred Christians enacted a liturgy of repentance, and signed the buildings with the ashes. Now it is not everyone's cup of tea to participate in such acts, but the care and prayer that had always been associated with this annual event made of it a religious act. One parish priest, Fr David Standley, explained it all to his people the Sunday beforehand. Quite simply: 'The use of any weapons of mass destruction is condemned by all the churches. The intention to use them is equally condemned; an intention is father to the act. Our current policy of nuclear deterrence is not bluff. We declare ourselves willing to use nuclear weapons in certain circumstances for reasons of national security; and we mean it. We are prepared to annihilate vast numbers of innocent people.'

Another priest, Fr Enzio, a missionary who had met witnesses for justice and peace putting their lives at risk couldn't cut off from those memories. He said:

> The arms race and the nuclear shrines spread across the country appeared to me as a symbol of arrogance and delirium of power. I tried to relate the hunger and disaster of the Third World with the £4,000 million earned last year by Britain selling arms, most of them to poor and repressed countries. I tried to relate the future holocaust with the present plunder of resources of the Third World. The Ministry of Defence cannot claim innocence with regard to the plight of these orphans, widows and strangers I met along my Latin American journey. So the demonstration outside the Ministry of Defence appeared to me as an act of courage, and risky imagination versus the logic and despair of the raison d'Etat.

Meanwhile we read of nineteen recruits in the Federal Republic of Germany who, when they were being sworn into the Bundeswehr, added a reservation that they only 'felt bound by this oath if the Federal Republic and its allies refrain from the use of atomic, biological and chemical weapons' They were charged with violation of orders which was later confirmed in March by the Federal Administrative Court. Although the use of such weapons has been declared to be a crime against God and man in official declarations by the Christian churches, they had made no comment so far.

Conscientious objection of this kind is still not respected anywhere. More than 2,000 Israeli soldiers have refused to serve in the Occupied Territories, many of them suffering imprisonment as a result. A British Iraqi soldier refused to serve in the invasion of Iraq. We need to hear more about such cases and give them support.

The International Physicians for the Prevention of Nuclear War had 2,000 medical people attending within their West German section, and pointed out that even a conventional war would be hardly less disastrous than a nuclear war, because of the great number of nuclear power stations, and hazardous industrial plants. Professor Lohs, a leading German toxicologist, described the result of conventional bombing of the chemical industry in East and West Europe where 'it would turn hundreds of square kilometres into outright gas chambers of a gigantic Auschwitz.'

82. McNAMARA, BURLATSKI AND KENNAN

Among the valuable and interesting reports in the Guardian from Martin Walker was a dramatic piece about Robert McNamara, the former US Defence Secretary, sitting in a conference room in Moscow.

It was October 27th 1962, a beautiful fall evening, the height of the crisis' McNamara began, 'and I went up into the open air to look and to smell it, because I thought it was the last Saturday I would ever see'. This was the man who ran the Pentagon in those fraught days of the Cuban missile crisis. He had been talking with Feodor Burlatski, one of Kruschev's advisers during the crisis; and when McNamara said this, Burlatski went pale. 'That Saturday evening in Washington, he said, that would have been early Sunday morning Moscow time. That was when I went and telephoned my wife and told her to drop everything and get out of Moscow. I thought your bombers were on the way.' My mouth went dry. I had always blithely assumed that however far brinkmanship went, the men in the war rooms under the White House and the Kremlin knew what they were doing, that cold and professional calculation went into policy and decision-making, even on the knife edge. We could almost watch the same awful realisation dawning in each other's minds, that nuclear war had been that close back in 1962. I looked at the faces of the journalist students; they were looking pole-axed, and it was their expressions which sparked off in me a sudden irrepressible burst of optimism. This was, after all, something only détente could do; bringing together so many influential Russians of the future with a former custodian of the US military-industrial establishment a man uniquely placed to explain exactly what is at stake when super-powers fall out.

I admit to having found that passage especially moving, as I had spent some time, as an unimportant 'peace activist' with Burlatski over a shared dinner when I was in Moscow in 1985. I was so glad that his humanity could be shared through this report.

McNamara then went on to expose the 'numbers game' about weapons for its absurdity. 'At the time of the Cuban missile crisis, we had 5,100 nuclear weapons that we could deliver on to the Soviet Union: and they only had 300 that they could deliver on to the USA. We knew that; and we knew our knowledge was reliable; and that was strategic parity. We were prevented from using our 5,100 nuclear weapons because we knew that whatever damage we did to you, you would have enough left to inflict unacceptable damage on the US So that was parity.'

By this time, (continued Martin Walker) my eyes were fixed on the reactions of the audience. Scales were dropping from Russians so hard and fast, you could hear them clatter to the ground. This sort of thing is not normally on the curriculum of the Moscow University journalism faculty. That faculty has asked me to give some lectures and I think the first one will be about the pitfalls of communication, taking as my text something else that McNamara said:

> After the Cuban crisis we set up the hot line in the understandable belief that this would help in future crises. The first time the hot line was ever used was in the Middle East war of 1967; and the first message we got down the line was not helpful. 'If you want war, you can have one' Moscow said'.

Another quotation from George Kennan, (the historian and former US Ambassador to Moscow), serves to bring us down to earth:

> Whoever does not understand that when it comes to nuclear weapons the whole concept of relative advantage is illusory: whoever does not understand that when you are talking about absurd, preposterous quantities of overkill, the relative size of arsenals has no serious meaning; whoever does not understand that the danger lies, not in the possibility that someone else might have more missiles and warheads than we do, but in the very existence of these unconscionable quantities of highly poisonous explosives; and their existence above all in the hands as weak and shaky as those of ourselves or our adversaries or any other mere human beings; whoever does not understand theses things is never going to guide us out of this increasingly dark and menacing forest of bewilderments into which we have all wandered.

83. THE TIMES, THEY WERE A-CHANGING

Looking back from the new century to the end of the '80s, it now seems to me that, without any universal co-ordination of thinking, more public voices were being raised not merely against the dangers of nuclear proliferation, but the sheer waste of creation's resources, and the failure to address poverty, hunger and disease across the world. At the beginning of the third term of Thatcherite politics in Britain, it was good to read a vigorous piece by Canon David Partridge.

For so long has the Church — established, Roman and Free — seen itself in the role of servant to the nation, the change of stance and style now required of it finds us all pathetically inadequate and wrong-footed. So powerful have been the spire and squire, priestly and policing connections, with the parish system covering every part of the nation's body from head to toe, cradle to grave, in the Anglican case; so hard is it to disentangle the Church's obsequious attendance on the nation's every beck and call, to prize genuine pastoral concern away from all its less acceptable political presuppositions.

So where and what for the Church as the start of a third-term government unashamedly dedicated to the philosophy of the market-place, the enshrined trinitarian doctrines of growth, prosperity and castle ownership, a Victorian private sector morality which keeps the table-legs of its public ethics covered in secrecy lest they cause offence, and, by no means last, an aggressive defence posture against the blatantly unexamined cardboard enemies without? Because of our give-away, tell-tale clothing, we are simply not believed when we come running into society proclaiming what the fire of the Spirit is saying to us concerning the increasing numbers of those with their backs to the inner and outer city walls, or about the ever widening credibility gap between the nightly media tale of peace talks' progress and the relentlessly escalating research, production and marketing of the world's weaponry.

If then it was the case that the 'sleeping giant' of the churches was being aroused more noticeably, the more remarkable was the turn-around of the leadership of the USSR. There are many other rich quotations from Gorbachev's book on perestroika to add to those already given. Here are two more:

The time is ripe for abandoning ideas on foreign policy which are influenced by an imperial standpoint. Neither the Soviet Union nor the United States is able to force its will on others. It is possible to suppress, compel, bribe, break or blast; but only for a certain period.

It was the political function of war that has always been a justification for war — a 'rational' explanation. Nuclear war is senseless: it is irrational. There would be neither winners nor losers in a global nuclear conflict: world civilisation would inevitably perish. It is suicide rather than a war in the conventional sense of the word. But military technology has developed to such an extent that even a non-nuclear war would now be comparable with a nuclear war in its destructive effect ... Security can no longer be assured by military means — neither by the use of arms nor deterrence ... Attempts to achieve military superiority are preposterous. From the security point of view the arms race has become an absurdity because its very logic leads to the destabilisation of international relations and eventually to a nuclear conflict.

Freeman Dyson in his excellent book *Weapons and Hope* made some valuable comments about militarism, and ended with a hopeful forecast.

The traditional respect which nations pay to the military cannot be denied. As every country has a right to self-defence, every country has the right to give honour to its military leaders. But the honouring of military leaders brings deadly danger to mankind unless the moral authority granted to them, and the technical means at their disposal are strictly limited. Military power should never be confused with moral virtue, and military leaders should never be entrusted with weapons of unlimited destruction.

The cult of military obedience and the cult of weapons of mass destruction are the two great fallacies of the modern age. The cult of obedience brought Germany to moral degradation and dismemberment. The cult of weapons of mass destruction threatens to bring us all to annihilation… It was, regrettably the armies of England who led the world into the cult of destruction. The Italian Douhet first preached the gospel of strategic bombing in the 1920s but the British Sir Hugh Trenchard was the first to put Douhet's gospel into practice.

We may already be approaching a time when further increases in offensive nuclear armament are no longer politically acceptable. A longer time must elapse before public opinion can be expected to turn against nuclear weaponry altogether. But shifts of public opinion are unpredictable, and sometimes happen more quickly than anyone expects.

Most surprisingly to some, who had not heard of this initiative, was a little report of the fifth meeting of the organisation founded for retired generals and admirals from NATO and Warsaw Treaty countries, which had taken place in April (1987) This time they were Generals from Canada, Bulgaria, Greece, Czechoslovakia, Italy, Hungary, East Germany, Norway, Portugal, Poland, USSR and Britain — nineteen top brass in all. Their Final Statement from Vienna stated that the problem for European security 'is to ensure that real disarmament continues and accelerates (after the INF Treaty) The greatest advantage of the post-INF era is that it opens up a longer vista of hope for the future of peace-building. And while even long-term prospects are clouded by the US threat of perpetuation of the flawed theory of deterrence, and particularly by its newest variation, labelled 'discriminate deterrence', the Generals believe that a quite different future trend discredits old-fashioned military thinking of that kind. It is the emerging realisation that neither alliance any longer has any conceivable reason for attacking the other, and that, in any event, neither has sufficient resources to win. From this follows that the two great military machines are in their present form devoid of purpose.'

This initiative of experienced military men should surely have been applauded all round. But why do we have to wait till they are retired before they talk sense?

84. THE PRETENDED JUSTIFICATION FOR HIROSHIMA AND NAGASAKI

The commemoration of the first use of atomic weapons was an opportunity again to challenge the standard fallacies that have allowed good people to 'justify' the monstrous crime of indiscriminate destruction. An interview with Norman Cousins (now in the Medical Faculty of UCLA) was a year old when I included this in the broadsheet. He had carried out special missions for Eisenhower and Kennedy, and helped towards the signing of the Partial test Ban Treaty. The interview followed the publication of his book 'The Pathology of Power', when he spoke of this first atomic bombing:

The evidence is definitive that the government lied to the American people about the decision to drop the bomb. It was made to appear that the President believed that the bomb was necessary to avoid a mainland invasion that would cost hundreds and thousands of lives. But when you study the actual documents in the Pentagon and the State Department, and Truman's own diaries, you see that the President knew an invasion was not necessary to bring about the defeat of Japan, that the outer defences of Japan were down by early summer of 1945 and that Japan was ready to capitulate if we would agree to the retention of the emperor. Truman was opposed to the latter, though ultimately he had to agree to it. In the meantime hundreds of thousands of lives were lost.

The War Department had prepared a report which showed an invasion was not necessary and which alerted the field commanders to prepare for the possibility of an early Japanese surrender. We also know that Admiral Leahy, the military adviser to the President, was opposed to the dropping of the bomb, which he thought would be a barbarous act, and certainly not necessary to bring about an end to the war. We also have the testimony of Eisenhower, who was appalled at the notion of even entertaining the possibility of using the atomic bomb, all the more so because he knew that Japan was on the verge of surrender. Finally we have Truman's own diary. He was at Potsdam… working out a timetable with Stalin for the entry of the Soviet Union into the war with Japan. This had been scheduled for August 8th; at Potsdam it was changed to August 15th. In his diary Truman wrote that the entry of the Russians in the Far East would bring about an immediate Japanese surrender.

When you study the documents (especially the interview with Secretary of State Byrnes) you get the impression that the decision to drop the bomb was based not on the need to avoid an

invasion, but to make the Soviet Union more manageable in the post-war world. We wanted to demonstrate the power of the bomb. Of course this was not what the American people were told at the time. They were told the bomb made an invasion unnecessary. We've been on a trail of deception, and we haven't reversed our direction.

85. STAR WARS AND WORLD DISARMAMENT

Norman Cousins then went on to expose the continuing deceptions in American policy about Star Wars, the developing ideas about the use of space.

> The President (Reagan) asked Congress to approve additional appropriations for SDI … He said we needed it as a bargaining chip for arms control and reductions with the Russians. That was his own statement. But the moment he got to Iceland he said he had no intention of using Star Wars as a bargaining chip. Now by his own admission, and Schultz's own statement, if he'd been willing to do so, they could have had far-reaching agreements. This is a matter of record.

Then there is another turn-about, 'The President said that Star Wars is a defensive weapon. Yet one of the recent arguments used by the administration to get the appropriations was that the Russians had perceived the offensive capabilities of SDI, and we wanted to get there before the Russians. Another contradiction. I think we have the obligation to push as hard as we can to reveal the trail of government deception, as we have seen the public can be powerfully effective once it is fully informed.'

Michio Kaku, Professor of Nuclear Physics in New York, went so far as to say: 'In spite of staggering odds against them, the people, the community of peace activists world-wide, have influenced and shaped US defence policy.' His surprising view turns on the existence of a 1950 top-secret document NSC-68, written by Paul Nitze for President Truman, which guided Cold War policies. 'It stated that the USA could ring the Soviet Union with a massive belt of nuclear bases. At the same time the American government should engage in peace talks with the Soviet government. This was to attempt to satisfy public opinion. But the document recommended that American peace proposals should be carefully worded to sound reasonable to the people but to include terms that were unacceptable to the Soviet Union. In this way there could be a propaganda gain when the Soviets rejected the proposals. For almost four decades this strategy worked brilliantly because the Soviets were clumsy and inflexible. It was not until Gorbachev accepted the Zero Option that the tables were suddenly turned on Nitze and NSC-68.'

Michio Kaku explained how SDI was not a defensive system; it was not 100% effective against a Soviet first strike; but effective enough to back up a first strike by the USA. 'The true purpose of Star Wars is to make the world safe for nuclear weapons.' The documents which were used for his researches 'paint a depressing picture of a nation on the brink of nuclear disaster. But hidden in all the militaristic jargon and dogma is a surprising and uplifting fact. However close we have come, nuclear war has not been waged because of the power of the American people.' Nitze had to admit in NSC-68 that:

> A surprise attack on the Soviet Union would be repugnant to many Americans. The shock of responsibility for a surprise attack would be morally corrosive. The message of history is clear; the peace movement has played a significant role in preventing nuclear war What the Pentagon fears more than the Soviet Union or a Soviet SS 18 missile, is an educated American public.

Meantime, the United Nations had held its Third Special Session on Disarmament, and, compared to the efforts we made for the Second Special Session in 1982, this one was all over and done with between May 31st and June 25th. The press was, as usual, virtually silent over the whole proceedings The Guardian of June 26th (1987) simply informed us:

> The rifts between the US and most other countries in the 159-member General Assembly dashed the high hopes for a forward-looking document on disarmament following the US-Soviet Summit. At the session the Soviet Union called for the elimination of all nuclear weapons by the end of the century: troop reductions of 500,000 soldiers each by Warsaw Pact and NATO, and invited the US to join a mutual nuclear Test Ban. US delegates ignored the Soviet proposals which were lauded by most other delegates, and concentrated on making sure that the Final Document would not rule out the space-based missiles defence system, Star Wars. The Americans opposed any sweeping calls for world disarmament, a nuclear test ban, naval disarmament and an expanded UN role in monitoring disarmament treaties.

All this was bad but perhaps not quite as bad as was rumoured at the 2003 meeting in Geneva of the NPT Preparatory Committee which I attended in preparation for the 2005 Special Session. There we had been told that the US, backed possibly by the UK, planned to renege on major items of the 1978 &1982 Final Documents ; but it was all depressingly negative just the same.

86. POP GO THE MISSILES — WELL, SOME OF THEM

I never thought I would enjoy watching an explosion but on August 3rd 1988 I was one of twenty-eight peace movement people invited to be present high in the hills above Taldy-Kurgan on the Chinese border, north of Alma-Ata, the capital city of the Soviet Republic of Kazakhstan, to have this unusual thrill. (Incidentally my knowledge of real geography advanced considerably when we spent two hours with the Prime Minister of this second largest republic of the Soviet Union. Kazakhstan is a well organised industrial as well as agricultural republic after the Soviet pattern, with seventeen million people of eighty nationalities and four language TV/Radio channels etc.) This was the first public disarmament action to implement the INF Treaty between Reagan and Gorbachev — an agreement to eliminate one whole range of nuclear missiles, those which are land-based and of intermediate range. We had been invited as guests by the Soviet Peace Committee with the warm agreement of the Soviet Defence Ministry, to join the military observers who were required by the Treaty to monitor such events. In Soviet opinion — no doubt disputed in western government circles — the activities and agitation of world-wide peace movements had contributed to the work of diplomats and politicians in bringing about this Treaty. For myself I was sure we had at least helped towards an increase in human trust, and our hope now was that the start of weapon demolition would enable further trust to develop in an ever rising spiral. Of course we knew there was a long way to go. Realistically the Treaty only referred to a tiny fraction of the existing nuclear arsenal. The Soviets spoke of this as a four per cent demolition; the American scientists of two and a half per cent. Yet as a symbol of what might now happen, the event was well worth the fatigue of a 7,500 miles journey in six days

The Soviet Peace Committee delegation which attended was under its new very approachable Vice-President, Mr Oryol; others present included a retired Soviet General, as well as the usual group of distinguished academicians, scientists, engineers, journalists, and a twelve-year-old girl ('Olga' of course) who had mastered English and had recently travelled across the USA, taking part in the politically ecumenical musical called 'Peace-Child'. The twenty-eight peace movement guests included myself as representative of Pax Christi International, one from CND, Mary Kaldor from END; others from India, Egypt, Nicaragua, Australia, New Zealand, Canada, Scandinavia, and most western countries. The USA was represented by a member of the Freeze Movement, and by Captain James Bush, a former nuclear submarine commander from the Centre for Defence

Information in Washington , which I had visited on my second USA journey to find distinguished ex-military officers working hard in diffusing some of the real facts about the failures in disarmament.

We were well briefed and sited for the explosion, and I was able to take some memorable photos, and I still have with me five small pieces of the burnt-out missiles as a trophy, picked up from the crater after the site had been declared 'safe' again an hour or two after the explosions. I shall always enjoy the memory of the little queue going through airport security in Alma-Ata on our way back to Moscow. Obviously all of us had a little explaining to do as our baggage indicated pieces of metal inside. By the time it was my turn, and my brief-case showed its sinister shadows, the guard was used to it: 'What's that?' he asked, 'a nuclear missile?' 'Indeed it is', I replied. 'OK, pass on through' — all as though it were the most natural thing in the world!

There remained a lot of curious questions to ask, which people were not slow to raise when I was telling groups about the historic event on my return. 'Wasn't it dangerous to be only one and a half kilometres from such an explosion?' Not really, since the nuclear warhead had of course been removed. Colonel Petrenko, the demolition officer in charge, said it wasn't exactly his field of competence, but he understood the fissile material would be processed in a nuclear reactor. I wasn't sure we would get a similar assurance in the west, where there were signs of an increase in the deployment of air-borne and sea-borne intermediate missiles not covered by the INF Treaty. There were other signs on both sides of 'modernising' plans which, unless checked by new trust and further pressure from peace movements, could lead to there being more rather than less nuclear weapons around. He said that the 'guidance systems' had also been legitimately removed; so in a way all that they had been exploding was a pile of scrap metal, and two tons of TNT certainly reduced it all to a crumpled mess. As for the exact nature of the weapons they were blowing up, they were not any SS20s as we had been given to expect. Petrenko and his staff had been in charge of SS12s and SS23s in east Germany or Czechoslovakia. These had been the first to be withdrawn under the Treaty — indeed even before it was ratified; and incidentally they had been the only Soviet nuclear weapons ever to be deployed outside the territory of the USSR. They had been placed there after the bringing of Cruise and Pershing IIs to western Europe in the old arms race game. We asked what the soldiers thought about their destruction and they said that after looking after these missiles for so long, with their sinister conditional intent to target western Europe, they thought it might have been more suitable for western troops to demolish them, leaving themselves to deal with the US weapons. But the Colonel was glad to see them go; he said he wished they had started on this earlier, before they had been piled up

In the light of this event, and the news that the USA had also started to demolish its own land-based intermediate missiles (and a few had been taken from Molesworth in Britain), it was disappointing in the extreme that none of the political parties showed any sign of seriously revising their thoughts about the 'Soviet threat' with a view to more fundamental disarmament. The Trident system was still being manufactured because of Mrs Thatcher's determination for Britain to remain a nuclear power. But even among Americans there were voices to challenge the Trident system.

In particular the Catholic Bishop of Alaska, Michael Kenny, had spoken up again:

> It is my deep conviction that those who protest the production and commissioning of Trident submarines and demonstrate against them in a non-violent manner, are truly the conscience of our nation... To say that Trident is a weapon that should never be used is to say that it is a weapon that should never have been made. To claim that we only built it to keep the peace, and that we possess it only to deter war is also claiming that we have the ultimate will to use it. And never, never could we justify the massive and indiscriminate slaughter that would follow.
>
> Each time an additional nuclear weapon is produced, the peril in which the human race lives is multiplied. Such instruments of death and destruction do not advance any true peace; they simply add to the reign of terror.

87. THE MORAL ARGUMENTS ALL OVER AGAIN

Those of us who felt compelled to argue like this for the moral case against weapons of mass destruction insisted, at least in the Christian tradition, there were only two possibilities. The way of non –violence or the so-called 'Just War Theory'

The latter often sounds like a justification of war, whereas it is meant to be a re-affirmation of the presumption against war, which may be over-ridden in certain very limited circumstances, and it then goes on to give the extremely strict criteria for what is morally legitimate within a war that is deemed to be 'just'. Many find these criteria so limiting in modern times that they suggest that the whole theory needs re-shaping to deal with the new technological developments. That often seems to some of us as a means of 'chickening out' of the clear conclusions from the tradition.

I was then shown an interesting and entertaining cautionary tale, drawn from an appraisal of Just War Theory by Richard Mouw, an evangelical theologian in the USA. 'Suppose that a German Christian male had the opportunity during Hitler's reign to form an adulterous relationship with Eva Braun, Hitler's mistress, and thereby gain important information which might lead to the downfall of the Third Reich. It is at least conceivable, I believe, that this might constitute a case of Just Adultery. But suppose — and it is very interesting that we have often been much stricter with the adultery commandment than we have with the killing commandment — that having recognised the legitimacy of such a rare undertaking, Christians went on to formulae a Just Adultery doctrine....

Such a doctrine on my hypothesis might very well be legitimate and proper. But suppose that this doctrine created a tendency towards unjustified adultery — merely by acknowledging the fact that under certain circumstances adultery might be morally justified. Suppose then that people were trained to commit adultery in the event that their services might become necessary. Suppose also that special medals of honour were awarded to outstanding adulterers....

Some doctrines, however true and appropriate they might be in application to rare cases, become dangerous when they are propagated and institutionalised. They can themselves become a lure to sin.'

It was a reviewer of this tale who remarked: 'The pitfalls of political theology in a fallen world have seldom been so succinctly stated.'

It was John Harriott, writing in the *Tablet* several years ago, who said the following:

> How much are we under the spell of a war won by treating moral scruples as a luxury? How much are we seized by the habit of violence and unconsciously transmitting it to others? I wonder this whenever discussion of nuclear deterrence excludes the morality of nuclear warfare as an academic debate irrelevant to practical-minded politicians and generals. Or when our Prime Minister behaves like a commercial traveller for the arms trade, waxing lyrical over the merits of British warplanes and guns to potential Arab buyers.Or when a state dinner is used like a piece of cheese in a mousetrap to tempt African Presidents into buying British weapons systems. Are we seen anywhere in the world as clearly committed to the disciplines of peace, or merely as another set of pragmatists readily discarding, should our own advantage so dictate, even the disciplines of war? Are we subtly fostering, even while we condemn it, the spirit of violence?

88. WINDING UP

It is now 2005 as I write and we are still in a muddle over the US initiated, and UK supported, war against Iraq. All the 'Just war' arguments have been trotted out again to validate Tony Blair's passionate belief in its legitimacy, in spite of some clear failures to warrant this — not least the 'Last resort' and 'Legitimate authority' items. More significant as time goes on is the realisation of the gap between peoples and their governments. Certainly democratic structures will rarely satisfy all the requirements of the common good; there is no way of establishing total consensus on political policies; but increasingly there is a conviction that organised terror and violence — which is what war entails — is not the way people want to see problems solved. Somehow we have to increase governments' accountability and transparency before thousands of people are ordered into murderous combat, when they personally have no quarrel with those they are required to savage with impersonal bombing and blasting. It was not enough to say 'We had no quarrel with the Iraqi people' when they were the immediate victims of sanctions and warfare. Somehow we have to devise ways of facilitating people to meet people and to look first at their humanity; and to do this without the background threat of violence. Disarmament is a necessity, and an urgent one; even though it will surely involve graded steps, starting with limitation to methods of 'defensive defence', and getting rid of all those weapons and machinery that only have aggressive use. Behind all this must be a foreign policy that does not have a distorted ideology, such as that underpinning the current US administration, a blatant imperial vision of an American century with 'full spectrum dominance'. The British Empire has been down that road, as have other empires; but the great modern hope has to be in the United Nations Organisation which, for all its failings, needs to be the focus of international respect. It is time to review its structures and procedures, because the kind of power that the nuclear-weapon states have as permanent members of the Security Council demonstrates a fundamental disrespect for the 180 other member states. Maybe here too there could develop a parallel structure of non-governmental people, so that the UNO reflects its starting point as 'We, the Peoples ...' rather than 'We, the current governments of the nation-states ...'

By now a whole new generation of peace activists has emerged, and all kinds of groups and coalitions have been formed. It was good to see the Wrexham Against War group, linking with the Stop The War Coalition, making its mark up to the outbreak of the Iraq war. Since then it has developed into the Wrexham Peace and Justice Forum, with a small 'steering group' meeting monthly, open to anyone to attend. Its Newsletter is a shining example of what modern technology can make available at modest cost, and it reaches a couple of hundred people for each issue, and keeps alive the interest of many more than those who can get to planning meetings. Links have been made, of course, with CND Cymru, (whose broadsheet, *Heddwch*, is another good example); and membership of Cynefin y Werin (Common Ground) unites a coalition of many other Peace and Justice organisations in Wales.

There is no shortage of deep commitment and responsible awareness. Perhaps this collection of quotations, diary items and anecdotes, could be a helpful source of ideas for those who desperately search for the things that bring us true peace and justice, and always in pursuit of alternatives to war.

FOR ALL THOSE
— who have died or are dying in wars.
— who have died or are dying because resources that could have fed or housed them have gone to war preparations instead.
— who will die until we learn to live in peace.

WHEN SHALL WE EVER LEARN?

Books Referred to or Quoted

(I trust that by listing them here, it will increase their likelihood of purchase and not offend any copyright rules)

Aronson, Ronald, *The Dialectics of Disaster*, Verso, 1983.

Burro, Kofi, *On the Brink.*

Bourne, *From Boot Camp to My Lai*, 1971.

Carr, E. H., *The Twenty Years Crisis*, Macmillan, 1978.

Carver, Lord, *A Policy for Peace.*

Chomsky, Noam, *Hegemony or Survival*, Pluto Press.

Clements, Keith, *A Patriotism for Today*, Collins, 1986.

Coates, Ken, *The Most dangerous Decade,* Spokesman, 1984.

Cousins, Norman, *The Pathology of Power.*

Delf, George, *Humanising Hell*, Hamish Hamilton, 1985.

Dyson, Freeman, *Weapons and Hope*, Colophan, 1985.

Generals for Peace and Disarmament, *The Arms Race to Armageddon*, Berg, 1984.

Gaddis, John L., *The US and the Origins of the Cold War*, Columbia University Press, 1972.

Gorbachev, Mikhail, *Perestroika*, Collins, 1987.

Holloway, David, *The Soviet Union and the Arms Race,* Yale University Press, 1983.
    The Choice.

Jungk, Robert, *Brighter than a Thousand Suns*, Penguin, 1947.

Keegan, John, *The Face of Battle*, Penguin, 1983.

Keenan, George, *The Nuclear Delusion*, Hamish Hamilton, 1973.
    Russia and the West, Mentor, 1961.

Kenny, Anthony, *The Logic of Deterrence*, Firethon, 1985.

Lawrence, John, *The Hammer and the Cross*, BBC, 1986.

May, Brian, *Russia, America and the Fall of Western Europe*, Routledge & Keegan Paul, 1984.

Monro, Richard, *Just War Theory.*

Noel-Baker, Philip, *The First World Disarmament Conference*, Pergamon Press, 1979.

Owen, Richard, *Crisis in the Kremlin*, Gollancz, 1986.

Pearce, Jenny, *Under the Eagle*, Latin American Bureau, 1981.

Pringle, Peter & W. Arkin, *SIOP Nuclear War from the Inside*, Sphere, 1983.

Schell, Jonathan, *The Abolition*, Picador, 1984.
    The Limits of Soviet Power.

Schmidt-Hauer, Christian, *Gorbachev, the Path to Power*, Pan Books, 1986.

Smith, Hendryk, *The Russians*, Sphere, 1983.

Tawney, R. H., *The Acquisitive Society,* G. Bell & Sons, 1945.

Thompson, E. P., *Star Wars,* Penguin, 1985.

Thubron, Colin, *Among the Russians,* Heineman, 1983.

Walker, Martin, *The Waking Giant*, Michael Joseph, 1986.

White, Andrew, *The Terror of Balance.*